Lines of Narrative

Social scientists are increasingly invoking 'narrative' in their theory and research. This book explores the wide range of work in sociology, psychology and cultural studies where narrative approaches have been used to study meaning, subjectivity, politics and power in concrete contexts.

The book presents a range of case studies, including:

- Princess Diana's *Panorama* interview
- media coverage of the LA uprising
- memoirs of the wives of scientists who made the first atomic bomb
- popular images of gay marriage
- the effect of the 'velvet revolution' on writing autobiography.

The book brings together contributions from European, Australian and North American researchers, indicating the diversity and potential of narrative approaches. The editors adopt a distinctive and unique psychosocial approach to narrative, and set the individual chapters in the context of three broad themes: culture, life histories and discourse. This book complicates, challenges and stimulates – it will be of vital interest to sociologists, psychologists, social theorists, students of cultural studies and others who are interested in the relationships between meaning, self and society.

Molly Andrews, Shelley Day Sclater and **Corinne Squire** are Co-Directors of the Centre for Narrative Research in the Social Sciences, University of East London. **Amal Treacher** is Co-Director of the Centre for Adoption and Identity Studies, University of East London.

Routledge studies in memory and narrative

Series editors: Mary Chamberlain, Paul Thompson, Timothy Ashplant, Richard Candida-Smith and Selma Leydesdorff

Lines of Narrative

Psychosocial perspectives

Edited by
**Molly Andrews, Shelley Day Sclater,
Corinne Squire and Amal Treacher**

London and New York

First published 2000
by Routledge
11 New Fetter Lane, London EC4P 4EE

Simultaneously published in the USA and Canada
by Routledge
29 West 35th Street, New York, NY 10001

Routledge is an imprint of the Taylor & Francis Group

Typeset in Garamond by
The Running Head Limited, Cambridge
Printed and bound in Great Britain by
University Press, Cambridge

British Library Cataloguing in Publication Data
A catalogue record for this book is available from the British Library

Library of Congress Cataloging in Publication Data
Lines of Narrative: psychosocial perspectives / [edited by] Molly
Andrews [et al.].
p.   cm.
Includes bibliographical references and index.
1. Social psychology–Methodology. 2. Sociology–Biographical
methods. I. Andrews, Molly
HM1011.L56   2000
302′.01–dc21   00–042472

ISBN 0–415–24233–9

Contents

Contributors

Jackie Abell is a Research Associate at Lancaster University. Her current research interests include the study of national identity in the context of constitutional change in Britain, and the discursive analytic investigation of nationalism in the political and media debates surrounding the BSE crisis.

Molly Andrews is Senior Lecturer in Psychosocial Studies at the University of East London. Her research interests include the psychological basis of political commitment, psychological challenges posed by societies in political transition, and gender and ageing. She is the author of *Lifetimes of Commitment: Aging, Politics, Psychology* (Cambridge University Press, 1991).

Michael Billig is Professor of Social Sciences at Loughborough University. He has been awarded the Erik Erikson Prize for distinguished contribution to Political Psychology. His books include *Fascists: A Social Psychological Analysis of the National Front* (Harcourt Brace Jovanovich, 1978), *Ideology and Social Psychology* (Blackwell, 1982), *Arguing and Thinking: A Rhetorical Approach to Social Psychology* (Cambridge University Press, 1987), *Ideological Dilemmas* (Sage, 1988), *Ideology and Opinions: Studies in Rhetorical Psychology*, *Talking of the Royal Family* (Routledge, 1992), and *Banal Nationalism* (Sage, 1995).

Phil Bradbury is a Principal Lecturer at the University of East London, where he is Course Tutor for the Psychosocial Studies Honours degree. He teaches research methods, and provides training in the use of life history methods of research. He has used narrative methods in curriculum evaluation, in educational research and, latterly, in research into the governance of schools. His recent research appears in *Education Today* and *Rising East: The Journal of East London Studies*.

Ian Craib is Professor of Sociology at the University of Essex and a group analytic psychotherapist. His books include *The Importance of Disappointment* (Routledge, 1994).

Shelley Day Sclater is Reader in Psychosocial Studies at the University of East London. Formerly a family lawyer, she has recently completed an

ESRC-funded study of divorce, using a narrative approach. She is the author of *Divorce: A Psycho-social Study* (Ashgate, 1999) and *Access to Sociology: Families* (Hodder and Stoughton, 2000), and co-editor of *Undercurrents of Divorce* (with Christine Piper; Dartmouth, 1999) and *What Is a Parent? A Socio-legal Perspective* (with Andrew Bainham and Martin Richards; Hart, 1999).

Norman K. Denzin is a Distinguished Professor of Communications, a College of Communications scholar and Research Professor of Communications, Sociology and Humanities at the University of Illinois, Urbana-Champaign. He is the author of numerous books including *The Alcoholic Self* (Sage, 1987), which won the Charles Cooley Award from the Society for the Study of Symbolic Interaction in 1988, *The Recovering Alcoholic* (Sage, 1987), *Interpretive Interactionism* (Sage, 1989), *The Research Act: A Theoretical Introduction to to Sociological Methods* (Prentice Hall, 1989), *Hollywood Shot by Shot: Alcoholism in American Cinema* (A. de Gruyter, 1991), *Images of Postmodern Society: Social Theory and Contemporary Cinema* (Sage, 1991), *The Cinematic Society: The Voyeur's Gaze* (Sage, 1995) and *Interpretive Ethnography: Ethnographic Practices for the 21st Century* (Sage, 1997). In 1997 he was awarded the George Herbert Mead award from the Society for the Study of Symbolic Interaction. He is the editor of *The Sociological Quarterly*, co-editor of *Qualitative Inquiry*, and series editor of *Cultural Studies: A Research Annual* and *Studies in Symbolic Interactionism*.

Mark Freeman is Professor of Psychology at the College of the Holy Cross in Worcester, Massachusetts. He is the author of *Finding the Muse: A Sociopsychological Inquiry into the Conditions of Artistic Creativity* (Cambridge University Press, 1993), *Rewriting the Self: History, Memory, Narrative* (Routledge, 1993) and numerous articles on the self, autobiographical narrative and the psychology of art.

Wendy Hollway is Professor of Psychology at the Open University. She has researched and published on questions of subjectivity, gender, sexuality, parenting, anxiety and the history of work psychology and gender relations in organisations. Her published works include *Subjectivity and Method in Psychology* (Sage, 1989), *Work Psychology and Organizational Behaviour* (Sage, 1991), *Mothering and Ambivalence* (co-edited with B. Featherstone; Routledge, 1997) and *Changing the Subject* (with J. Henriques, C. Urwin, C. Venn and V. Walkerdine; Routledge, 1998 [1984]).

Ronald N. Jacobs is Assistant Professor of Sociology at the State University of New York at Albany. His work, which has appeared in the *American Journal of Sociology*, *Sociological Theory* and *Media, Culture and Society*, focuses on the relationship between civil society and the media. His most recent publication is *Race, Media and the Crisis of Civil Society: From Watts to Rodney King* (Cambridge University Press, 2000).

Tony Jefferson is a Professor of Criminology in the Department of Criminology, University of Keele. He has researched and published widely on questions of youth subcultures, the media, policing, race and crime, masculinity, and the fear of crime. His published works include *Resistance Through Rituals* (edited with Stuart Hall; Hutchinson, 1976), *Policing the Crisis* (with Stuart Hall, Chas Critcher, John Clarke and Brian Roberts; Macmillan, 1978), *The Case against Paramilitary Policing* (The Open University Press, 1990) and *Masculinities, Social Relations and Crime* (edited with Pat Carlen; *British Journal of Criminology* 36, 3, 1996, Special Issue). With Wendy Hollway, he has written on methodology, sexuality, and anxiety and fear of crime. Their joint book is entitled *Doing Qualitative Research Differently: Free Association, Narrative and the Interview Method* (Sage, 2000).

Zdenek Konopasek is Senior Lecturer in Sociology at the Charles University in Prague. His scholarship is in the areas of auto/biographical research, and science, technology and society. He is co-ordinator of the life history project, 'Ourselves Selves' and the editor of *Opening the Past: Autobiographical Sociology of State Socialism* (Charles University Press, forthcoming) and of the Czech journal *Biograf*.

Helen Malson is the author of *The Thin Woman: Feminism, Post-structuralism and the Social Psychology of Anorexia Nervosa* (Routledge, 1998) and is currently lecturing at the Centre for Critical Psychology at the University of Western Sydney.

Michael Rustin is Professor of Sociology and Dean of the Faculty of Social Sciences at the University of East London. He was associate director of 'Social Strategies in Risk Societies', a seven-nation, EU-funded research project on social exclusion, 1996–9. Recent publications include *Welfare and Culture in Europe* (with P. Chamberlayne, A. Cooper and R. Freeman; Jessica Kingsley, 1999). He is co-editor of *Soundings* magazine.

Clive Seale is Reader in Medical Sociology at the Department of Sociology, Goldsmiths' College, University of London. His books include *Researching Society and Culture* (Sage, 1998), *Constructing Death: The Sociology of Dying and Bereavement* (Cambridge University Press, 1998) and *The Quality of Qualitative Research* (Sage, 1999). He is currently engaged in a study of media representations of health and illness.

Marion V. Smith is Research Fellow at Keele University. She is co-holder of an ESRC award for the project 'Moral Education and the Cultures of Punishment: A Study of Children's Discourse'. Her previous work has been on the communicative value of words used to describe pain and suffering, and the role of language in experiences involving pain.

Corinne Squire is Senior Lecturer in Psychosocial Studies at the University of East London. Her books include *Women and AIDS* (Sage, 1993), *Morality*

USA (with Ellen Friedman; Minnesota University Press, 1998) and *Culture in Psychology* (Routledge, 2000). She is currently researching and writing about HIV and citizenship.

Elizabeth H. Stokoe is a Senior Lecturer in Psychology at University College Worcester. She completed her PhD in 1997, entitled 'Exploring gender and discourse in higher education'. Since then, she has been looking at a variety of texts from a discursive and/or conversation analytic perspective, including the political interview.

Amal Treacher is Co-Director of the Centre for Adoption and Identity Studies, and Senior Lecturer in Psychosocial Studies at the University of East London. She is currently engaged with theorising children's autobiographies, specifically focusing on their phantasies and narratives of family life. She also undertakes work on adoption and on ethnicity, especially mixed-parentage identity.

Suzanna Danuta Walters is Associate Professor of Sociology and Director of Women's Studies at Georgetown University. She is the author of *Lives Together/Worlds Apart: Mothers and Daughters in Popular Culture* (University of California Press, 1992), *Material Girls: Making Sense of Feminist Cultural Theory* (University of California Press, 1995) and numerous articles on popular culture, feminist theory, and lesbian and gay studies. Her current research focuses on gay identity and politics in an era of increasing visibility and commodification.

Tom Wengraf is Senior Lecturer in Sociology at Middlesex University. Co-editor (with Prue Chamberlayne and Joanna Bornat) of *The Turn to Biographical Method in Social Science* (Routledge, 2000), he is currently completing a textbook on semi-structured depth interviewing, *Qualitative Research Interviewing: Biographic Narrative and Semi-structured Method* (Sage, 2001). He has researched agrarian reform in Algeria and British students' experience of higher education, and he is a participant in the EC-funded Social Strategies in Risk Society (SOSTRIS) Project.

Carol Wolkowitz is a Lecturer in Sociology at the University of Warwick. She is co-author of the recent *Glossary of Feminist Theory* (with Sonya Andermahr and Terry Lovell; Arnold, 2000) and co-author of two books on homeworking. She is currently writing a book on gender, embodiment and the labour process.

Foreword

Narrative's moment

Norman K. Denzin

We live in narrative's moment (Maines 1993: 17). The narrative turn in the social sciences has been taken. The linguistic and textual basis of knowledge about society is now privileged. Culture is seen as a performance. Everything we study is contained within a storied, or narrative, representation. Indeed, as scholars we are storytellers, telling stories about other people's stories. We call our stories theories.

The essays and editorial commentary in this volume brilliantly advance our understandings of the implications of the narrative turn. The editors and their co-contributors are clear on these points: persons are constructed by the stories they tell. The self is a psychosocial, narrative production. There is no dualism between self and society. Material social conditions, discourses and narrative practices interweave to shape the self and its many identities. Narrative's double duty, as the editors note, is complex; self and society are storied productions. This is why narrative is a prime concern of social science today.

Narrative is a telling, a performance event, the process of making or telling a story. A story is an account involving the narration of a series of events in a plotted sequence which unfolds in time. A story and a narrative are nearly equivalent terms. A story has a beginning, a middle and an ending. Stories have certain basic structural features, including narrators, plots, settings, characters, crises and resolutions. Experience, if it is to be remembered, and represented, must be contained in a story which is narrated. We have no direct access to experience as such. We can only study experience through its representations, through the ways stories are told.

The editors wisely inform us that what we take narrative and story to be determines how it will be collected and studied. (Ian Craib notes that narrative, or story, can be defined so broadly that the term applies to any and everything a sociologist or psychologist might want to study.) If stories are defined as a form of narrative, then stories can be obtained through structured, semi-structured and unstructured interviews, free association methods and collectively produced autobiographies. Methodologically, narratives-as-stories can be subjected to content, discourse, cultural, literary, psychoanalytic, formal, structural, semiotic and feminist analyses. Of course pre-existing narratives can also be examined, for example the Princess Diana interview analysed by Abell, Stokoe and Billig in Chapter 12. On the other hand, stories can be connected to larger narrative structures. Examples of this form of inquiry can be found in Wolkowitz's analysis of the memoirs of the wives of US nuclear weapons scientists (Chapter 7), and Walters' study (Chapter 3) of heterosexual and gay wedding and family narratives.

Jean-Paul Sartre (1963) and Holstein and Gubrium (2000: 103) remind us that as social constructions, stories always have a larger cultural and historical locus. Individuals universalise, in their singularity, the unique features of their historical moment. Narratives of the self, as temporal constructions, are anchored in local institutional cultures and their interpretive practices. These practices shape how self-narratives are fashioned. Various contributors in this volume examine the realities shaped by such specific cultural narrative forms as the official death certification procedure (Seale, Chapter 2), print news journalism (Jacobs, Chapter 1; Freeman, Chapter 5; Wolkowitz, Chapter 7; Konopasek with Andrews, Chapter 6), children talking with adults (Smith, Chapter 11), and autobiographical speech (Wengraf, Chapter 8; Malson, Chapter 10; Hollway and Jefferson, Chapter 9).

Storytellers have agency and self-reflexivity. Their stories are temporal constructions which create the realities they describe. Stories and lives connect and define one another. However, narratives come in many different forms: contradictory, fragmented, grand, local, institutional. The editors note that narratives can reveal forms of repression that operate in the social world. At the same time, narratives can function as forms of bad faith, concealing these self-same processes of repression and injustice. Many of the contributors to this volume elaborate these connections and concerns.

The three major sections of this volume trace the interconnections between narrative, culture, life history, and different forms of discourse. In Part I, Jacobs, Seale, Walters and Craib treat culture and civil society as complex productions, stitched together through interconnected semiotic, emotional, linguistic, and narrative acts. In Part II, Freeman, Konopasek with Andrews, Wolkowitz and Wengraf trace the relationship between life histories and narratives, showing how critical life events are given meaning within various narrative schemes. Influenced by Foucault, the chapters in Part III by Hollway and Jefferson, Malson, and Smith, Abell, Stokoe and Billig show how humans with agency actively negotiate the meanings that are brought to their life situations.

In their concluding chapter Bradbury and Day Sclater emphasise how the essays in this volume see narratives as cultural productions, as manifestations of life histories, as sites where agency is played out. Indeed, subjects inhabit narrative, even as the self, in its private, public, and gendered versions is constituted in narrative. And in their narratives people push against prevailing systems of discourse, including those connected to sexuality, family, work, labour, race, intimacy, politics, ageing, unemployment, death. Of course narratives do not establish the truth of such events, nor does narrative reflect the truth of experience. Narratives create the very events they reflect upon. In this sense, narratives are reflections *on* – not *of* – the world as it is known.

And so at the end of this valuable and most timely collection we see how the narrative turn forces the social sciences to develop new theories, new methods and new ways of talking about self and society. This new language will reveal how the individual and the social are opposite sides of the same coin, to use Charles Horton Cooley's metaphor (1902: 110).

It remains to reflect on where narrative might go next. Borrowing from Peter Brooks, William Kittridge reminds us that our lives are 'ceaselessly intertwined with narrative, with the stories we tell or hear told, those that we dream or imagine or would like to tell . . . We live immersed in narrative' (1996: 157). The stories we tell help us wrestle with the chaos around us, helping us make sense of the world when things go wrong.

Selves, narratives and sacred places

We live in stories, and do things because of the characters we become in our tales of self. This narrated self which is who I am, is a map. It gives me something to hang on to, a way to get from point A to point B in my daily life. But we need larger narratives, stories that connect us to others, to community, to morality and the moral self. At the dawn of a new century we need new stories.

Speaking of Montana and the West, Kittridge says we need new narratives based on new and different ways of performing Montana. Kittridge is asking for narratives that embed the self in storied histories of sacred spaces and local places. We need to invent new stories for ourselves 'in which we live in a society that understands killing the natural world as a way of killing each other . . . We need a story in which the processes of communality and mutual respect are fundamental' (1996: 142). We need stories that encourage us to 'understand that the living world cannot be replicated . . . We need stories that will drive us to care for one another and the world. We need stories that will drive us to action' (1996: 164–5).

This is where narrative must go next. And thus do the contributors to *Lines of Narrative* chart the future for all of us.

References

Cooley, C. (1902) *Human Nature and Social Order*, New York: Scribner's.
Holstein, J. and Gubrium, J. (2000) *The Self that We Live By: Narrative Identity in the Postmodern World*, New York: Oxford University Press.
Kittridge, W. (1996) *Who Owns the West?*, San Francisco: Mercury House.
Maines, D. (1993) 'Narrative's moment and sociology's phenomena: toward a narrative sociology', *Sociological Quarterly* 34: 17–38.
Sartre, J.-P. (1963) *Search for a Method*, New York: Knopf.

Introduction

Molly Andrews, Shelley Day Sclater, Michael Rustin,
Corinne Squire and Amal Treacher

Narrative intersections

This book aims to provide a contemporary profile of sociologists' and psychologists' work on narrative. It clarifies the views they share and the issues that divide them, and points to the value such work has for generating new ways of conceptualising and investigating the social world. Adopting a distinctively 'psychosocial' approach, the book draws together examples of narrative theory, methods and research from North America, Western and Central Europe and Australia, to provide the reader with an overview of this increasingly popular field. Narrative's double meanings, at once modern and postmodern, seem to allow research in this field to avoid many of the limitations of more traditional sociological and psychological approaches, and in particular to challenge the conventional dualism between individual and society. Using narrative, the 'self' can be located as a psychosocial phenomenon, and subjectivities seen as discursively constructed yet still as active and effective. Material social conditions, discourses and practices interweave with subjectively experienced desires and identities and people make choices, reconstruct pasts and imagine futures within the range of possibilities open to them. This is the realm where sociology overlaps with psychology and neither the 'social', the subject matter of traditional psychology, nor the 'individual', the subject matter of conventional psychology, is privileged. Rather both are constructed in relation to each other, not in the 'outer' realm of society and culture, or the 'inner' realm of personality characteristics, but in a distinct, 'psychosocial' zone.

If we are constructed by stories, or are storytellers by nature, or perhaps both, then narrative must, surely, be a prime concern of social science. Yet the 'story' of narrative in the social sciences is long and complicated. Since the 1970s, the study of narrative has been a point of intersection, even crossover, between the social sciences and the humanities. In the social sciences, narrative is one element in a broader cultural and linguistic 'turn' through which recognition has been given both to the shaping effects of cultural environments, and to subjective experience. The growing status of qualitative methods in sociology and psychology is a compelling indication of this 'turn'. Today, ethnography, biographical case studies, discourse and conversation analysis, semiotics and social constructionism, as well as more narrowly focused narrative studies, are all commonplace, even mainstream parts of these disciplines.

In the humanities, especially in literary and cultural studies, studies of narrative have, in contrast, served to objectify or formalise research. Literary and cultural critics had previously relied on implicit and intuitive procedures, whose affinities with 'creative' forms of writing and art they valued. During the 1960s, this intuitive approach began to seem insufficient. One factor was the greater international exposure of cultures to one another – an early consequence of 'globalisation'. Another was the emergence of 'new' voices within national societies, as social change movements such as civil rights, feminism and gay rights achieved some measure of cultural democratisation. The literary and cultural-critical mainstream was attacked for its anglocentrism, for being middle-class, for its uncritical humanism and individualism and for a 'high-cultural' bias against the plethora of new cultural forms – film, radio, television, journalism, popular fiction. In place of trained sensibility, literary and cultural studies now became dominated by theories and analytic procedures which it was hoped would bring some conceptual order to the expanding cultural field. These theories and procedures were trawled for in many different places – in the interpretive ethnographies of US sociology, in several varieties of Marxism, in structural linguistics, in discourse theory, in hermeneutics – and in the idea of 'narrative'.

So, just as the social sciences were discovering the importance of 'subjectivity', the humanities were starting to celebrate the advantages of 'objectivity' – the application of formal concepts and methods to cultural artefacts of all kinds. One can see this process as a kind of reintegration of the sciences and the humanities, after a long post-Enlightenment period in which they were sharply counterposed. To the horror of many traditional humanist scholars, the humanities came to be approached in a quasi-scientific way while, to the equal horror of many partisans of 'science', cultural and social perspectives were increasingly deemed integral to sociology and psychology. At the same time, the social sciences became affected, in a kind of reverse transmission, by the formalist enthusiasms of the humanities, and the humanities themselves were subject to a barrage of 'backlash' scholarship reinstating the authority of intuition.

The study of 'narrative' is on the rise at a late and complex stage in this intersection of the disparate disciplinary approaches. Narrative researchers attempt to produce formal theories of culture and society. But because stories also seem to have intimate and important connections with the nature of human experience, narrative research incorporates other dimensions – notably those of historical time and subjectivity – that were in danger of being left out of other language- or discourse-based research. As this portmanteau account of narrative research suggests, the field is a wide one. Part of this book's concern is to explore the field's extent, and the parameters that define it.

Defining narrative

Contemporary social-scientific definitions of narrative are extremely variable. In general, narrative is taken to mean a sequence of events in time (Berger 1997). Thus defined, 'narrative' includes much more than what we think of as the usual materials of social-scientific narrative research: spoken, often personal stories, like those explored in many of the chapters in Parts II and III of this book. 'Narrative' must take in writing – fiction and documentary writing, which have clear time sequences, but also explanatory writing, where narrative sequence lies in the causal succession that a text proposes, as in Wolkowitz's and Jacobs' chapters. Narrative includes image sequences too, as well as still images which imply event sequences while only showing a moment of them, as Abell *et al.* and Walters' chapters demonstrate. In addition, 'narratives' are now often taken to include sequences of actions: the living out of story structures in everyday life described by Seale.

The term 'narrative' now also extends to cover phenomena beyond verbal, visual or acted 'texts'. Sociologists and psychologists working with both personal and media narratives tend to assume that these narratives bear a strong resemblance to the structure and content of the lived, social world, as in the chapers by Freeman, Wengraf, and Konopasek with Andrews in this volume. Some contributors, like Malson, also claim that individual 'stories' contain elements of cultural meta-narratives, stories that are much more significant than the apparent narrative totalities in which their elements appear. Moving in the reverse direction, from the personal narrative towards the intrapsychic rather than towards cultural formations, Hollway and Jefferson argue that some autobiographical narratives express, to an interpretive researcher, a 'story' of unconscious affect, spelled out in the associations, gaps and idiosyncrasies of language rather than in its overt narrative content and structure. This book, by paying attention to the variety of narrative forms at stake in the social sciences, aims to disestablish conventions that make stories of human lives, or – in the psychological, literary and cultural-studies tradition – narratives with idealised linguistic, fiction or filmic forms, the canonical centre of narrative analysis.

Narratives and methods

What we take to be 'narrative' determines how narrative will be studied. From the definitional differences discussed above flow considerable differences in narrative methodology, which manifest themselves across the chapters. The first way in which narrative is commonly studied is by obtaining stories through individual interviews. Even here, though, anomalies arise. The stories produced by Smith's group interviews with children, who are rather rare participants in narrative interview research, raise questions about the power relations of 'narrative' interviews, who usually get to tell their stories, and the place of the researcher. Hollway and Jefferson, seeking to theorise the psychosocial subject, found traditional interview procedures wanting and developed their own Free Association Narrative Interviewing method. Konopasek's collectively produced autobiographies, generated by a kind of written 'interview' with self and others, may lead us to ask about the textual and collaborative nature of other, apparently simpler autobiographies, where individuals seem to be sole authors of their own life stories and as such accountable only to themselves. Seale's parallel investigations of the 'narratives' derived from semi-structured interviews and from ethnographic observations render permeable the boundaries between these methods, so that actions become stories to be 'listened' to, and stories 'acts' to be observed.

If, moreover, we examine how even the more traditional interview material is analysed, we see an instructive span of categories. For Wengraf, the narrative method *is* the analysis: stories told within a life history interview tell their own significance to a sensitive reader who can hear the 'told story' as opposed to the facts of the 'lived life'. Other contributors venture away from interview data more explicitly, Hollway and Jefferson perhaps most controversially when, drawing from psychoanalysis in their analytic procedures, they uncover 'narratives' of unconscious affect. In so doing they challenge some conventional but rather fragile distinctions between social-scientific and psychoanalytic interpretation. Moving in the other direction, Freeman and Malson deploy larger understandings of cultural narratives within which they situate individuals' stories. To do this, Malson works explicitly from a discourse-analytic perspective that allows her to set up in advance analytic categories based on previous research as well as on what she finds in the data. Freeman relies rather on comparisons with literary models. For both, stories 'mean' more than they say. Contributors to the book have well-formulated modes of analysis to demonstrate this richness of meaning, and use concepts of triangulation and reflexivity as checks on their interpretive range.

The second way in which social scientists commonly study narrative is by analysing pre-existing written, visual or spoken stories. In a sense, such studies have a 'partial' method, because they work with found texts. In Wolkowitz's case, even selection is obviated because the texts in the category that interests her, memoirs of the wives of US nuclear weapons scientists, are small in number. However, these are not methodologically unproblematic narratives; Wolkowitz has to contend with the possibility that they are 'ventriloquised' rather than authentically authored. Other contributors must develop principles of selection, as in Jacobs' careful empirical assessment of all news coverage of the Los Angeles uprisings, or Abell *et al.*'s choice of what they argue is a single but iconic and culturally defining televisual moment – Princess Diana's *Panorama* television interview. As with the interview studies, these text-based contributions deploy analytic methods drawn from a range of fields, with varying explicitness; given their objects of study, it is not surprising that they borrow more from the methods and theories of literary and cultural studies. Jacobs makes explicit use of categories of literary form and Abell *et al.* deploy a functionalist discourse and conversation analysis, also influenced by cultural-studies precedents for the analysis of broadcast narratives. Wolkowitz makes implicit reference to conventions of written stories, memoirs specifically, and Walters conducts a wide-ranging address to the cultural dynamics of Othering and assimilation as played out in popular media stories of lesbian and gay relationships and parenting, which again draws creatively on emergent traditions of cultural-studies analysis.

Narrative methodologies exemplify the uneasy yet productive fusion between increasing formalism in the humanities – as in Jacobs' deployment of literary-critical categories to understand popular media – and increasing subjectivism in the social sciences, as with Wengraf's interpretive reading of life stories. Yet the methods also indicate the blurred nature of this distinction, in for example Walters' reliance on an entirely implicit methodology for her cultural analysis, or Smith's use of the rhetorical structure of drama to understand her interviews with boys. Such disciplinary crossovers seem one of the most helpful and hopeful aspects of the narrative research showcased here. For where social-science and cultural studies collide in the study of narrative, as they inevitably will, researchers have to make difficult choices between methods that do not need to be justified or even explicated – which are still, in the main, used within cultural studies – and methods obliged to justify themselves rigorously, if not scientifically, as social-scientific methods still in general must. The resulting confrontations between different approaches to method have considerable value in developing ideas of what narrative analysis means, while acting, again, to destabilise conventional concepts of what social-scientific research on 'narrative' entails.

Narrative, construction and culture

How has the 'discovery' of narrative influenced the social sciences, and what fields of investigation does it open up? To answer this question, we need to distinguish between understandings that are products of the 'cultural turn' in general, and those that are specific to the study of narrative. What has followed from the 'cultural turn' is a recognition that the forms in which experience is encoded, accounted for and represented help constitute that experience. This recognition displaces the idea that there are realities of nature, society and individuals wholly independent of the languages and cultural patterns through which they are represented. It makes problematic what was formerly taken for granted and thus invisible, namely the way in which representations construct and form part of realities.

The contributors to this book are clear that stories always have a 'cultural locus' (Denzin 1989: 73) without reference to which they cannot be understood. The chapters consistently concern themselves with this 'top-down' (Berger 1993) perspective on narratives' significance: how narratives derive from specific cultural loci, how they can be described with reference to these cultural locations, how culturally particular forms of narrative are routed through individual narratives and narrating subjects, and how apparently 'personal' stories impact back on the culture (Plummer, 1995). While the chapters in Part I are especially preoccupied with the confluence of narrative and popular culture, similar concerns appear in Part III, where contributors address the discourses, the structures of power and knowledge, within which stories are told, and the discursive effects those stories themselves have.

What is narrative research's specific contribution to the 'culturalist' or 'constructionist' perspective? Such research seems both to constrain and enable it. Narrative work does not examine the constructing effects of individual, symptomatic words, or silences, or cross-textual 'discourses': these all have to be placed in the context of a 'story'. However, a narrative is itself an accumulating construction. As you follow it, you hear meanings and realities accrue. In this sense, narrative research offers object lessons in the construction of the social world. A principal resource of the constructionist perspective has been its investigation of the patterns of representation which emerge in each field of study and through which different 'realities' are constituted, and such patterns are often dramatically obvious in the field of narrative. In this volume, contributors examine, for instance, the representations and realities effected by the specific narrative forms of official death-certification procedures (Seale), television celebrity interviews and sitcoms (Abell *et al.*, Walters), print news journalism (Jacobs), literary genres of fiction and autobiography (Jacobs, Freeman, Wolkowitz, Konopasek), children talking with adults (Smith), and autobiographical speech (Wengraf, Malson, Hollway and Jefferson, Freeman). From these investigations emerge valuable understandings of how particular narrative patterns interact with individual and social representations of the world.

Narrative, history and subjectivity

Narrative theorists have accepted and have even been able to exploit the systemic concepts and procedures which followed the linguistic 'turn'. Their more unique contribution has been to draw attention to some specific dimensions of the process of cultural construction, those of history and human subjectivity. These dimensions have been an important corrective to the objectifying effects of formalist studies of cultural forms, which sometimes merely substituted a kind of 'culturalist' determinism for previously materialist ones.

Narrative is most generally defined as temporal sequencing of events. Paul Ricoeur (1984, 1985, 1988), one of the most widely cited writers on narrative research, argues that human experience too is arranged and bound in time. Human actors cannot but engage with time, and therefore narrative, in their formation of desires, intentions, expectations and memories. As a consequence, the histories that human beings write are not the 'objective' accounts of events occurring across time that they seem to be; rather they are, like fictions, creative means of exploring and describing realities. They follow narrative principles of 'emplotment'; they describe sequences of events with beginnings, middles and ends, and generate intelligibility by organising past, present and future in a coherent way. For Ricoeur, and for many other narrative theorists – Wengraf, and Hollway and Jefferson, in this volume, among them – this narrativity affects the speaking and writing of individual 'histories' too. Our time-inflected phenomenology places creating and maintaining meaning at the centre of all human activity. The 'first-order' activity of lives as they are lived is mirrored in 'second-order' activities of reflection, representation, accounting and storytelling. For Anthony Giddens (1984: xii–xxxvi), these second-order activities provide the resources for the 'first-order' world-making of each next generation – as, indeed, many contributors to this volume, such as Walters, Jacobs, Smith and Konopasek, would argue. For Zygmunt Bauman (1992), moreover, resistance to our narratives' unavoidable end, the inevitable fact of mortality, explains much in human work and culture, as Seale, Freeman and Craib might themselves say.

What, though, of subjectivity, agency and intention? Intentions give shape to our perceptions and accounts of what we and others do – for example, in the various forms of rationalisation and false consciousness named by Nietzsche, Marx and Freud. The narrative perspective makes possible the acknowledgement of this dimension of 'agency', both as reality and as belief, in the ways in which accounts of experience are framed. Narrative trajectories are, like agency, purposive; they move towards endings, they aim for closure. In writings throughout this book, people are helped to or barred from agency in narrative.

The contributors to this volume differ over the extent to which they believe stories and lives mirror one another. Is subjectivity contained within narratives, spoken through the cultural and social languages available, or is there more to subjectivity than the storied self? For Seale, there is almost nothing which is *not* narrative – but narrative is still not, for him, a sufficient description of every phenomenon. For Freeman and Wengraf, spoken narratives and life paths run in inexact, approximate parallel. Malson and Walters take it for granted that cultural and life narratives both reflect and resist each other, but they use the term 'narrative' broadly enough to take in non-linear metastructures like 'patriarchy' that would not be susceptible to conventional narrative analyses. Hollway and Jefferson propose a parallelism between spoken and unconscious narratives, but this latter notion again departs from conventional, verifiable notions of what a narrative is. Smith, Wolkowitz, and Abell and her co-writers register implicit reservations about the scope of narrative analysis by concentrating on theorising the narrative structures of particular spoken and written texts, with some cautious suggestions about their meanings and effects. Konopasek and Jacobs are interested in how individual and cultural narratives both derive from and feed into specific sociopolitical situations, but they avoid describing these conditions as 'narratives'. At the far end of the continuum, Craib suggests that concepts of narrative in the social sciences have become so encompassing that they now include, homogenise and simplify every psychological and sociological phenomenon. He wants to reserve a place outside narrative for some of subjectivity's contents – unconscious fantasy and emotions, whose psychic dynamics are linked with but partly independent of cultural and social domains.

It is now taken for granted in much contemporary work on subjectivity that a narrative is drawn from social, cultural and, perhaps, unconscious imperatives, which it at the same time reveals. These imperatives, however, do not entirely constrain the production or understanding of narratives. Narratives come in many kinds; they are contradictory and fragmented; there is no such thing as a coherent story. There is also, in the aftermath of grand 'narratives' of the social and political order, and in a time of identifications rather than identities, no entirely firm sociocultural ground from which to tell stories. Moreover, human subjectivity itself is diverse and fragmented, and carries within it the pushes and pulls of various available narratives, which are contingent upon social and cultural positioning.

Narrative futures

Within this book, there are two contrasting views of the future of narrative research. The more optimistic poses narrative as a means to recuperate individual and social agency in the social sciences. It argues that narratives provide solace, a means of keeping on with life, even resistance – as in Seale's notion of narrative as resurrective practice. Stories may be crucial in helping you to survive or even to live in new and progressive ways. They may also reveal lies, vulnerabilities and fracture lines within the dominant culture. This viewpoint is perhaps most obviously associated with the life history, oral history and biographical-interpretive methods work presented in Part II of the book, but it appears in other chapters too.

The other, more negative viewpoint has come to be as important a part of narrative studies as the first. It centres on the assertion that narratives can lie, may foreclose more imaginative ways of living, and often hide the operation of power relations. Some narratives are defensive, concealing difficult aspects of subjective life, or subjects' 'true' feelings of, for example, guilt, shame or envy. Ian Craib tellingly characterises these as 'bad faith' narratives, showing how they can be observed even in a psychotherapeutic situation whose conventions were devised for precisely the opposite purpose. Other narratives mask powerful hidden relations of subjection and coercion. More subtly, narratives drawn from acceptable social and cultural sources can operate sub-textually as stories of exclusion or assimilation. Subjects find themselves subsumed in conventional stories that impose on them a particular definition of the normal and the possible. At the moment when a life seems most individual and particular in its telling, the narrative forms within which it is encoded, and by which it is made to seem recognisably ordinary, simply reproduce and reinforce social norms. The chapters by Walters and Wolkowitz show, for instance, how established cultural narratives of family displace all other aspects of the lives of those they aim to describe, neutralising their differences.

This contradiction, that narratives both reveal and conceal, enable and constrain, is in many of the contributions to this volume, and looks to be one that will powerfully inflect narrative research for the foreseeable future. From both sides of the contradiction, however, contributors would perhaps agree that the way narratives are spoken and negotiated bears witness to the patterns of lived experience (Bollas 1995). The construction of meaning through narratives seems to be a fundamental aspect of both individual and social experience. For this reason, the narrative 'turn' has refocused attention on agency and subjectivity, as well as enriching the structural possibilities available for thinking about texts and the construction of subjects. Once the centrality of narrative temporality is recognised, it becomes impossible to ignore individual and collective active subjects. But the discursive resources through which narratives are made are themselves cultural products, and these constrain and construct individuals at the same times as they provide them with means of autonomous thought and expression. The 'discovery' of narrative has, then, as its main benefit, the possibility of opening up new spaces for investigating relations between subjects and structures. The study of narrative is not of cultures of individual subjects, but of their relations. Individuals and collectivities can be seen to be making their own history, but not, as Marx (quoted in Giddens 1984: xxi) pointed out, in conditions of their own choosing.

The first part of this book focuses on how cultural narratives relate to everyday narrative talk, writing and practices. The chapters examine the place of narrative as a cultural resource for understanding, and even for living, many aspects of our lives, from the most intimate to those determined at the furthest distance from us. They look at the opportunities and constraints offered by cultural narratives for challenging social and individual circumstances. Finally, they examine how some ways of telling cultural stories may themselves help change the shape of the world the stories and their tellers inhabit.

Part II explores different approaches to narrative theory and method in biographical work. How do individuals construct the stories they tell about their lives? What is the relationship between living and telling: between our day-to-day experiences and the way in which we internally organise these experiences and subsequently represent them to ourselves and others? Through the recounting of stories, people reveal what they perceive as the dominant influences which have shaped the course of their lives. These chapters examine the possibilities and limitations of narrative work for representing individual meaning-making systems which take account of the larger social context in which lives are enacted.

The chapters in Part III highlight the dynamic relations between discourse and narrative, problematising the autonomy of discourse as well as the completeness of narrative. Attention to intertextual discourses also has implications for how we 'do' narrative work. It becomes necessary to hold in mind both the narrative 'parts' and the discursive 'whole' as we explore the dynamic relations between them. Moreover, discourse analysis depends heavily on the analyst's own familiarity with dominant cultural discourses if discourses are to be identified from the fragments that populate narrative accounts. The researcher's constructive role is therefore highly visible, challenging the traditional 'invisibility' of the researcher and raising issues of reflexivity and research ethics as well as questions about the 'truth' and 'validity' of narrative work. The analysis of narrative and discourse together is, then, a microcosm of narrative research and its problems. It is beset with methodological uncertainties and theoretical complexities, but it also affords powerful possibilities for addressing both the sociocultural dimensions of human lives and all that is most 'subjective' about subjectivity.

Acknowledgement

The authors would like to thank Phil Bradbury for his ideas on narrative methods, and his careful reading of the work.

References

Bauman, Z. (1992) *Intimations of Postmodernity*, London: Routledge.
Berger, A. (1997) *Narratives in Popular Culture, Media, and Everyday Life*, London: Sage.
Bollas, C. (1995) *Cracking Up*, London: Routledge.
Denzin, N. (1989) *Interpretive Biography*, London: Sage.
Giddens, A. (1984) *The Constitution of Society*, Cambridge: Polity Press.
Plummer, K. (1995) *Telling Sexual Stories*, London: Routledge.
Ricoeur, P. (1984, 1985, 1988) *Time and Narrative*, volumes 1–3, Chicago: University of Chicago Press.

Part I

Narrative and culture

Introduction

Corinne Squire

Individuals become to some extent their autobiographies and the social stories being told around them, but they become their cultural narratives too (Riessman 1994: 68–9). If narrative analysis in the social sciences is to extend beyond reading individuals' lives, then 'culture', broadly defined, is surely one of the best fields in which to develop it. Culture is by definition made up of events, representations and values that are relatively long-lasting and widely distributed. This means that cultural narratives are never just individual. Cultural symbol systems may indeed 'tell' individuals their life stories (Riessman 1994) but often, too, cultural narratives are lived through collectively. If, as with many popular media, they are experienced individually, cultural narratives still have common meanings. Even the most individualised and emotionally charged narratives belong, as Clive Seale puts it in this section, to specific communities with specific scripts. This 'top-down' perspective on narrative leads the writers in this section, in particular, to pay sustained attention to the 'cultural locus' (Denzin 1989: 73) of stories, to the personal meanings of these cultural narratives (Bruner 1986) and to their significance in civil society (Alexander and Smith 1993).

A focus on culture also makes it impossible to take a formalistic, abstract approach to analysing the structure of social-scientific 'texts'. Culture is never just a matter of abstract texts that can be analysed free of context. Culture with a small 'c' (Clifford 1990) is always lived, enacted or cultivated (Mercer 1994). It is actively made by people in specific situations, whether they are producing or consuming culture. Even when we are reading newspapers or watching TV, we are still acting on these media in order to make narrative sense of them. The writers in this part present a variety of such collective, active narratives, from self-evident examples like the everyday sequences of shopping, preparing and eating food and looking after the dying discussed in Seale's chapter or the patterns of lesbian parenting described by Walters, to less obviously 'active' instances, like the press representations of the 1991 Los Angeles uprisings whose readings are explored by Jacobs, or the television sitcom representations of gay and lesbian marriage and parenting, whose significance for viewers and the wider cultural climate is examined in Walters' chapter.

The concept of narrative in the social sciences is notoriously wide in scope, and attention to culture emphasises this breadth. The first three chapters in this part look at a range of products and activities that go to make up contemporary culture – not just what people say about their lives and their worlds, but also print news and feature articles, television sitcoms, legal judgements, medical procedures, relationships, marriages, parenting, shopping, cooking, caring for the dying. The chapters weigh up the narrative load carried by speech, but also by documentary writing, image sequences, institutional certifications, and the whole set of discourses and practices that constitute 'everyday life'. They hold in common a notion of narrative as a temporal sequencing of representations or events. The press accounts of the Los Angeles uprisings considered by Jacobs do not all tell the story of the events themselves; many are editorial or opinion pieces that try to find reasons for the events. However, they are still narratives – sequential causal explanations ending, in this case, with the apparently unavoidable 'tragedy' of African American suffering and disempowerment. In Seale's chapter, people live out narratives in their engagement with the deaths of those close to them, and, more prosaically, in how they deal with food and shopping. Both in the stories told of them and in how they are lived, these engagements take a repetitive, closed narrative form.

What does this ubiquity of narrative mean for social-scientific considerations of culture? In the last chapter of this part, Craib remarks on how concepts of narrative have become so broad that they seem applicable to every phenomenon that psychologists and sociologists take an interest in. One example he gives is causal explanation, which he notes is increasingly referred to as a form of narrative – as in Jacobs' chapter. Such breadth of definition only really becomes a problem, though, when the category of 'narrative' is transformed from description into sufficient explanation. Within this section, the writers differ considerably on whether a narrative sequence makes psychological, social, cultural or merely linguistic sense of the elements in the sequence, and on how important that sense is. Perhaps it is not surprising that this divergence should appear in relation to culture, which after all is a category that forces us to view narrative on a wide screen. Seale argues that stories make us who we are, both as individuals and in the social world. By investing social bonds with emotion, narratives maintain these bonds. Seale suggests that this function is of particular significance at moments when social bonds are threatened or weakened – ultimately, when members of social groups have to face death and find meaning in it. For Seale, lived and spoken cultural narratives of, for instance, death, food preparation, even shopping, can be forms of 'resurrective practice', turning human beings away from death itself, helping them live in and through the rituals of their societies. The life progress of the body is, he says, mirrored and sustained in narrative progress. Seale is thus a strong exponent not just of the 'top-down' model of narrative, but also of the bottom-up (Berger 1997: 34) theory of close and constitutive parallels between the stories of individuals, cultures and societies – a theory that receives its most sustained exposition in Part II. This theory is contested here most vigorously by Craib, who argues that stories do not entirely account for individuals or societies, both of which are too complex to be caught in such simple analogies. Stories that set themselves up as such full accounts are 'bad faith' narratives. In particular, Craib lays stress on how the idiosyncrasies of individual emotions, the psychic realities referred to by Freud, evade all narrative formalisations, and on how stories that claim to contain such emotions impoverish and disempower them. Between these two, Jacobs and Walters concern themselves more specifically with the mutual relationships between persuasive narratives, their audiences and their subjects. Jacobs is interested in how the semiotics of culture interact with civil society, in particular through cultural symbol systems' deployment of polarised and highly durable categories of inclusion and exclusion. The operation of the 'tragic' news narratives of the Los Angeles uprisings as a kind of implicit cultural backlash, emerging as they did at a time when people of colour were gaining social power, is an example. Like Seale, Jacobs is concerned with breaks in the usual narrative order, in this instance the Los Angeles up-rising's interruption of conventional conversations about 'democracy' in the American public sphere. Walters discusses the significance of the recent upswing in popular media narratives of gay and lesbian 'marriage' and parenting, and, while acknowledging the narratives' personal meaningfulness, argues that they are socially fairly ineffective. Their 'delusional neo-liberalism' ignores both the powerful, homophobic emotions Craib might point to, and the lived realities of discrimination and oppression.

Within arguments about the significance of cultural narratives, style holds an important place. Styles, specific linguistic forms, are a means through which the cultural saturation of narratives becomes manifest, and they are at their most obvious when we are dealing with clearly 'cultural' narratives. Of course, narrative content also expresses culture – as with the partial and contested shift, documented by Seale, from medical to self-help or 'growth' narratives of death; or with the inclusion that Walters describes of lesbian and gay partners and their children in narratives of 'family' on sitcoms, news reports, soaps and talkshows. Yet style itself narrates culture, often in subtle and contradictory ways. Many of the section's arguments about cultural, social and personal continuity and change depend upon their attention to narrative style. Seale describes the heroic, romantic closure that the bereaved impart, across different narrative contents, to finished lives. Walters argues that, in popular culture, lesbians' and gay men's stories of relationships and parenting are assimilated into mimetic narratives of heterosexual family, so that they become comfortable variants of the heterosexual norm. Jacobs suggests that, despite content similarities in media representations of the Los Angeles uprisings and the 1960s uprisings in Watts, the tragic form that characterises the plot, characters and genre of the later representations marks an important, regressive shift away from the more optimistic romance form of the earlier representations. Finally, Walters' account of lesbians and gay men living out *new* narratives of parenting points out the difficulty of describing these stories when, despite the familiarity of their contents, they are stylistically novel, genre-bending assaults on the family romance.

The plurality and instability of cultural narrative styles is for most of the writers in this part a guarantee of possibility. Unsurprisingly perhaps, an attention to culture has led them to a perspective on narrative inflected by postmodernism. Craib's scepticism about sociologists' and psychologists' 'grand narrative' of narrative could perhaps be seen in this postmodern light. In general, however, Craib is on the other side: he views paeans to narrative multiplicity as misguided. He is pessimistic about popular culture's ability to sustain genuine complexity, and sees most narratives as reducing personal and social meanings to glib fables. The other contributors, though, are also qualified in their assessments of narrative multiplicity and uncertainty. Seale values these properties, but emphasises the importance of stories' repetitions and cohesion. Like Craib, he points to the unnarratable events – ultimately, death – that drive narrative reiteration. For him, however, unlike Craib, narratives *mark* emotional excesses and complex social realities by their failures, rather than denying them. Jacobs and Walters show how narrative plurality can generate change – but not necessarily in a progressive direction. Jacobs, interested in the genre clashes that occur at times of social crisis, argues for irony, specifically, as an open, counter-hegemonic form of rhetoric within narrative, but he also recognises its potential for elitism and anomie. Walters sees the progressive narratives of lesbian and gay parenting that are performed in everyday life as existing in a tense relation with conventional narratives of family, only occasionally and with difficulty breaking away from them.

Finally, we must return the question of narrative's significance to its most concrete realm: that of narrative's material effects. Again, contributors display a range of takes on the relationship. Walters, while she has little hope of social change resulting from 'straight – with a twist' media stories of lesbian and gay partnership and parenting, thinks such stories can be transformative when they are lived out actively and consciously within lesbian and gay communities. Jacobs draws a firm distinction between popular media narrations of 'race' and the material circumstances in which racialised differences are lived. The distinction emerges clearly in his contrasting of minorities' improved material circumstances, including increased African American presence in the media, with the 'tragic' backlash representations of the Los Angeles uprisings. Craib emphasises the distinction further, regretting the tendency of narratives to become, for many, simulacral replacements of the real (de Certeau 1984: 186). Stories are wonderfully imaginative and creative products, he says, but telling a consistent, engaging story does not make everything right, at either the individual or the social level. He calls for attention to be paid less to stories' persuasiveness and more to the differences between them and the external realities to which they refer. Moving in the other direction, Seale sees narratives as coterminous with materiality. Stories create the world we live in and are themselves creatures of their material cultural context. In Seale's account, social scientists cannot tell what is a true story (Denzin 1989: 77), but they can tell which story is at odds with or agrees with which others, and which is most convincing. Even for Seale, though, stories are not the only means of sustaining the 'resurrective practice' he sees as their most significant consequence. All the contributors are, then, interested in narratives that claim to produce personal and social change. The debate is about whether and how narratives can achieve this aim.

References

Alexander, J. and Smith, P. (1993) 'The discourse of American civil society: a new proposal for cultural studies', *Theory and Society* 22, 3: 151–207.

Berger, A. (1997) *Narratives in Popular Culture, Media, and Everyday Life*, London: Sage.

Bruner, J. (1986) *Actual Minds, Possible Worlds*, Cambridge, MA: Harvard University Press.

Clifford, J. (1990) 'On collecting art and culture', in R. Ferguson, M. Gever, T. Minh-Ha and C. West (eds) *Out There: Marginalisation and Contemporary Culture*, Cambridge, MA: MIT Press.

de Certeau, M. (1984) *The Practice of Everyday Life*, Berkeley and Los Angeles: University of California Press.

Denzin, N. (1989) *Interpretive Biography*, London: Sage.

Mercer, K. (1994) *Welcome to the Jungle*, London: Routledge.

Riessman, C. K. (1994) *Qualitative Studies in Social Work Research*, London: Sage.

1 Narrative, civil society and public culture

Ronald N. Jacobs

In recent years, research on public communication has shifted its focus away from the study of propaganda towards a concern with civil society and the public sphere. Recognising that the ideal of 'democracy' has very often been a shorthand way for talking about things that take place in civil society (Gellner 1991), scholars have begun to consider more carefully the processes of communication through which citizens discover common interests and identities, assert new rights and privileges, and try to influence public opinion and public policy (Alexander 1998; Cohen and Arato 1992; Keane 1995). Arguing that these communication processes are obscured by approaches which emphasise rational-critical discourse, this chapter outlines an alternative, narrative-based approach for studying civil society. Like the chapter by Seale which follows, it emphasises the importance of narrative in constituting and changing social orders, but it applies this understanding to public culture rather than to everyday social life. I illustrate the empirical utility of this approach by drawing on a larger research project that compared African American and 'mainstream' media narratives about racial crisis, and emphasise how the dynamic processes of plot, character and genre are important factors shaping the public culture of any civil society.

The limitations of rational-critical discourse

By contrasting rational and narrative models of communication, I am following the lead of others who have challenged and revised the now-classical understanding of the public sphere formulated by Jurgen Habermas (1989 [1962]).[1] The rise of a bourgeois public sphere during the seventeenth and eighteenth centuries (particularly in the Anglo-American world) was crucial for the history of democracy and enlightenment, because it led for the first time to the 'people's public use of their reason' (Habermas 1989: 27). Claiming the space of public discourse from state regulation, and demanding that the state engage them in debate about matters of common concern, private citizens successfully campaigned to replace the dominant political practice of parliamentary secrecy with a new principle of open public discussion (Habermas 1989: 62).

While Habermas insisted that the development of the bourgeois public sphere was a crucial event in the history of democracy, he also worried that the democratic potential of public communication had become significantly reduced throughout the twentieth century. With the rise of advertising and marketing, Habermas feared that public opinion was being replaced by 'representative publicity', in which arguments were publicised but never really discussed or debated. 'Public opinion' had become an 'object to be molded in connection with a staged display of . . . publicity in the service of persons and institutions, consumer goods, and programs' (Habermas 1989: 236). In the face of these structural changes, Habermas argued that the best strategy for recovering civil society was to insist on procedural norms of rational-critical discourse, centring around the principles of symmetry, reciprocity and reflexivity. This is the 'ideal speech situation', referring to 'the rules participants would have to follow if they were to strive for an agreement motivated by the force of the better argument alone' (Cohen and Arato 1992: 348). By requiring that public discourse be subjected to the requirements of generalisable validity claims, Habermas believed that civil society would become more resistant to the corrupting influences of money and power.

As the public sphere has come under closer critical scrutiny, an increasing number of scholars have begun to question whether rational-critical discourse can really provide the organising framework for democratic spaces of communication (Baker 1992; Eley 1992; Schudson 1992). Historically, the organisation of the public sphere around such procedural norms as 'rationality' and 'objectivity' has been used to delegitimate and exclude specific groups. Claims about the putative 'undisciplined' and 'mob-like' activity of the working class, the 'natural' sexuality and desire of women, and the 'natural' passivity and indolence of non-whites have all operated to keep the public sphere white, male and bourgeois through most of its history (Eley 1992; Jacobs 1998). This dynamic has been built into the very discourse of civil society, such that criteria of inclusion and exclusion can be seen as forming a common semiotic system (Alexander 1992; 1994). Even with the removal of formal barriers to public participation, the procedural norms of 'rationality' and 'objectivity' have still worked to the benefit of privileged social groups. While in principle anyone can enter a conversation in the public sphere, 'insiders' and 'outsiders' are defined and identified by the tacit, uncodified classificatory schemes provided by the norms of rational-critical discourse, the practical mastery of which is unequally distributed among the participants.[2] Thus, while the bourgeois public sphere may have been organised according to the open and democratic principles of rationality and publicity, it has been at the same time – as Nancy Fraser (1992: 114) has argued so convincingly – 'the arena, the training ground, and eventually the power base of a stratum of bourgeois men who were coming to see themselves as a "universal class" and preparing to assert their fitness to govern'.

Fortunately, a belief in the democratic potential of public communication does not require one to invest so much hope in the procedural norms of rational-critical discourse. Rational consensus (and the procedures for achieving it) only needs to be privileged if one adopts a narrowly political view of democracy as a mechanism for reaching decisions. If one subscribes to a broader view of civic democracy, however, then participation and engagement replace decision-making as the key elements of a democratic society (Schudson 1998; Verba *et al*. 1995). From this point of view, the public sphere is important because it encourages people to participate in discussions, and to expand their discussions to include new participants and new points of view. The substantive goal of the public sphere then becomes the cultivation of ongoing public and moral conversations, and the institutionalisation of these types of practices as a way of life (Benhabib 1992). Rather than trying to determine a set of first principles about how to achieve a rational consensus, those who adopt the model of civic democracy are more interested in the empirical processes which increase public attention and engagement.

Today, when global media collapse the space and time in which people experience their lives, the possibility of public engagement in civil society requires events that concentrate public attention. Most people do not have the time to retire at the end of the day to the salon or coffeehouse, in order to discuss matters of common concern. In this sense, the bourgeois public sphere idealised by Habermas is a contemporary impossibility. But there are certain events which encourage a break from the quotidian, the instrumental, the self-focused, and orient public attention to questions of society and morality. This is not an original point, of course. Durkheim (1965) recognised that all societies needed ritual events that provoked extended periods of collective moral reflection. It is during these times, transcending the mundane moments of everyday life, that the affective bonds of sociality are mobilised, participation in the public arena is maximised, and past, present and future are fused together in an ongoing, mythic, mystical collective story about 'who we are'. The relationship between narrative and myth which emerges at such times is a crucial one. At the level of collective social movements, such as nationalism, scholars have pointed to the centrality of a shared set of origin myths, which tend to emphasise specific narrative properties: selective appropriation of historical events, romance, heroism, and perhaps even the liberation from oppression and the establishment of a unified community (Smith 1995). At the social-psychological level, hermeneutically inspired social philosophers such as Taylor (1989) and MacIntyre (1981) point to the fact that the development of a moral sense requires individuals to understand (and experience) their lives narratively, as a mythic quest.

During periods of public attention to our collective myths, moreover, social time tends to slow down, to 'linger' on specific events which serve as focal points for public discussion and reflection. In the United States, for instance, events of racial crisis such as the 1965 Watts uprisings, the 1991 Rodney King beating and the 1992 Los Angeles uprisings provided key moments of public debate and public reflection about such heady matters as the meaning of the American dream, the promise of the Civil Rights movement, and the rights and responsibilities of citizenship. These crises offered social drama of the highest order to the American public, and, importantly, the contours through which they were understood were shaped fundamentally by narrative processes.

In addition to events that concentrate public attention, overlapping networks of communication are also crucial for continuing and opening up conversations about important social matters. Because the publicity strategies of marginalised groups cannot concentrate solely on 'mainstream' media and dominant publics, civil society must also contain – and, indeed, has always contained – alternative public spheres.[3] These alternative publics offer a place for counteracting the effects of hegemony, and they do this by constructing alternative narratives which contain different heroes and different plots (Jacobs 2000). These counter-hegemonic activities are not attempts at consensus building through rational-critical discourse; rather, they are efforts to introduce new perspectives through narrative creation.

Narrative and civil society

While my concern so far has been to make a normative argument in favour of narrative communication in civil society, the primary aim of this chapter is to show how narrative analysis can be used by the social scientist as a research tool to study public communication. In the remainder of this chapter I introduce three tools of narrative analysis which I have employed in my own research: plot, character and genre.

Plot

Of all the features of narrative that influence public sphere communication, perhaps the most important is plot, which refers to the selection, evaluation and attribution of differential status to events. It is plot, more than anything else, that encourages the public concentration of attention on to specific events. Processes of emplotment encourage what Umberto Eco (1979; 1994) has called 'narrative lingering', where narrative time slows down to encourage the reader to take 'inferential walks': relating the story to one's own life, deepening the narrative to consider its relationship to events in the past and possible events in the future. As Abbott (1988) has argued, plot is the best way to study the 'time-horizon problem', where events can differ in their speed and duration. A focus on which events are selected for narration (and which events are not selected), as well as which events produce the effect of narrative lingering, provides important clues about how a given individual, group or collectivity understands the past, present and future.

For an example of how plot can shape public sphere discourse, we can turn to media coverage of the 1965 Watts uprisings in Los Angeles. This event, which lasted five days and resulted in thirty-four deaths, 1,032 injuries, over 4,000 arrests and an estimated $40 million in property damage,[4] galvanised public attention for months, and still has the ability to provoke discussion and reflection today. In the initial weeks after the uprisings, little else was reported in the American media. But the narrative lingering caused by Watts produced very different plots, depending on what other events were included as relevant to the story. In the *Los Angeles Times*, for example, the events surrounding Watts were initially connected to a larger Cold War narrative, inserting the crisis into the middle of a plot in which all criticism of the American government was deemed illegitimate. As a result of this process of emplotment, those writing and speaking in the *Los Angeles Times* were able to dismiss as communist propaganda many of the discussions people wanted to have about the possible causes of the uprisings. The following news excerpts were typical of this narrative strategy:

> President Johnson, concerned that the Communists will make propaganda hay out of American racial strife, kept close watch Monday on continued Negro violence in and around Los Angeles.
>
> (*Los Angeles Times*, 17 August 1965: A14)

> Charges that police brutality led to south Los Angeles' riot were branded Tuesday by Mayor Samuel W. Yorty as part of a 'big lie' technique shouted by 'Communists, dupes and demagogues.' In a bristling statement blaming the riots on 'criminal elements,' Yorty said that 'for some time there has existed a worldwide subversive campaign to stigmatize all police as brutal.'
>
> (*Los Angeles Times*, 18 August 1965: A3)

In such a plot, considerations of the historical deprivations suffered by African American urban residents were unlikely to be incorporated into the news narrative. Furthermore, within this type of plot, African American leaders were unlikely to shift public debate about matters of urban policy, because they would end up spending most of their time explaining why they were not communist propagandists. Faced with such an environment, efforts by African American leaders to engage in serious dialogue about racial crisis in American cities were more fruitfully pursued in other publics and other news media. In the *New York Times* as well as the African American press, for instance, the emplotment of the 1965 Watts uprisings avoided the Cold War narrative; these news publics, as a result, were much more open to historical discussions about race and urban policy, and the public statements made by African American leaders were taken more seriously.

We can see another example of the power of emplotment by considering the 1992 Los Angeles uprisings, an event that created a period of public focus and attention on race equalled by few events in recent American history.[5] A Times–Mirror opinion poll taken one week after the verdict found that 92 per cent of those surveyed were following the Los Angeles events either closely or very closely, a figure even greater than public attention to the Persian Gulf War (*Los Angeles Times*, 5 May 1992: A9). Between 30 April and 13 May, the *Los Angeles Times* wrote 290 articles about the Rodney King crisis, the *New York Times* wrote 105 articles and the *Chicago Tribune* wrote 103 articles. ABC *World News Tonight* covered the Rodney King crisis as its lead story for eight consecutive evenings, between 29 April and 6 May. All of these news organisations reported about the verdict by linking it to the 1991 videotaped beating of Rodney King, contrasting the images of the videotape with the verdict returned by the jurors, and wondering aloud about racism in American society. But there were important differences in the historical plots used to narrate the problem of racism. In the 'mainstream' press, the 1992 uprisings provoked memories about the Kerner Commission and other *political* attempts to address race and urban crisis. But it was precisely these political attempts by white elites that were criticised in black newspapers for contributing to the problems of racial injustice. For these African American papers, the uprisings provoked memories of racial injustice caused by insincere white politicians and racist white jurors: the Missouri Compromise of 1820, the California Constitutional Convention of 1847, the Kansas–Nebraska act of 1854, the Dred Scott decision of 1857, and previous legal injustices in trials such as the Emmett Till and Medgar Evers murders. The *New York Amsterdam News* went so far as to report that 'nowhere in the annals of American history has a highly publicized case of White police brutality against a Black man ended in conviction' (9 May 1992: A6). These were much more damaging historical metaphors, because they equated contemporary times with antebellum America, implied that little if anything had changed since then in the area of race relations, and openly challenged the sincerity of white Americans in matters of race.

These differences in cultural understanding can be seen most clearly through a narrative approach to studying civil society. Concerns with symmetry, reciprocity and the 'force of the better argument' obscure the fact that even the most democratically organised discursive spaces will be uneven, unequal and unfair to a certain extent. As I argued earlier, appeals to such seemingly neutral values as rationality, objectivity and formal procedure are themselves situated within a narrative history of exclusion and hegemony. The chapters by Walters and Wolkowitz (in this volume) show clearly that the circulation of certain types of narratives (rather than others) is closely linked with issues of power and hegemony. Yet despite the complicity of narrative, power and history, social actors and social groups are still able to use narrative effectively to challenge power and create social change. Because the cultural structures of narrative require knowledgeable actors, they can be generalised, transposed on to new situations, and used as resources for creating social change (Giddens 1984; Sewell 1992). Social actors are not powerless and passive subjects of narrative, but rather have the ability to challenge inequities in plot. A concern with emplotment helps the researcher to explain this dynamic process of narrative power and resistance, by uncovering in an empirical way the different possibilities of interpretation favoured in specific interpretive communities.

Character

As events become emplotted into narratives, they shape the symbolic relationships between the different characters in a story. Indeed, in Aristotle's poetics, the primary function of the characters in a narrative was to realise the 'soul' of the plot (Frye 1957: 52). I would suggest, following Greimas (1982), that this relationship between characters and emplotment provides the 'narrative skeleton' that informs any semiotic process. Because plots require protagonists and antagonists, who are arranged in relations of homology and antipathy to each other, the characters of a narrative serve as embodiments of a society's deep cultural codes. Bruner (1986: 39) has suggested, in fact, that the construal of character is the most important step in dealing with another person, and the part of social interaction which is inherently dramatic.

By arranging the characters of a narrative in binary relations to one another, and doing the same thing with the descriptive terms attached to those characters, narratives help to charge social life with evaluative and dramatic intensity. In this way, the binary structure of character relations becomes a potent resource for individuals and groups trying to gain power and influence in civil society (Alexander 1992; Alexander and Smith 1993). Public actors engage in competitive and conflictual narrative struggles, trying to circulate stories that 'purify' themselves and their allies, and 'pollute' their enemies. In order to narrate themselves as powerful and heroic, they describe their enemies as dangerous, foolish, weak, irrational, deceitful or antiheroic in some other way; by contrast, they describe themselves and their allies as rational, reasoned and straightforward. They describe the projects and policies of their enemies as perverse, futile and jeopardising, while those of their friends are synergistic, mutually supportive and progressive. These oppositions seem to regulate both reactionary and progressive political rhetoric (Hirschman 1991). Over time, these identifications of similarity and difference, which have their origins in the character oppositions so central to all narratives, develop into a cultural structure based on sets of homologies and antipathies, resulting in a semiotic system of civil society discourse. This 'common code' allows for a degree of intersubjectivity among public speakers as well as a relatively stable system for evaluating persons. Members of a civil society know when they are being symbolically polluted, and must spend a great deal of their time trying to repair the symbolic damage. Groups and associations who find themselves continually polluted, to the extent that they wish to engage in that public sphere, must continually operate from a defensive and reactive position.

While the chapters by Craib and by Abell, Stokoe and Billig show how character works in the narrative production of the self, I want to consider how character structures operate in the public sphere, by considering the narrative link that developed between Rodney King and O. J. Simpson. After the videotaped police beating of Rodney King in 1991, every possible negative description was mobilised in characterising the Los Angeles Police Department. Its police officers were described as wild, out of control, lying racists; its police chief, Daryl Gates, was described as unaccountable, racist, ego-driven and contemptuous of the American public and Constitution (Jacobs 1996a). During the 1992 uprisings which followed the return of not-guilty verdicts in the trial of the officers charged with beating Rodney King, these negative characterisations continued; the cowardly and impassive police officers, as well as the unprepared and politically motivated Gates, received much of the blame for the duration and severity of the civil disorder. As a cultural symbol, any association with the Los Angeles Police Department was taken as evidence of moral corruption. The jurors in the trial, coming from the same Simi Valley community as many of the police officers, were criticised frequently as racist police sympathisers, 'people who ran away from Los Angeles to get away from Rodney King' (*Los Angeles Times*, 30 April 1992: A18, quoted in Jacobs 2000).

Even two years after the Los Angeles uprisings, the negative characterisation of the Los Angeles Police Department, sedimented in the thousands of public conversations which had taken place since the Rodney King beating, still had tremendous power to influence the evaluative structure of public narratives. The O. J. Simpson trial demonstrated this clearly. Every move Judge Lance Ito made during the trial was understood in the media through a comparison with the first Rodney King beating trial; every mention of the Los Angeles Police Department brought back memories of the 1991 videotape. As Gibbs (1996: 200–1) has argued, one of the most significant components of the Simpson defence team strategy was to keep the memory of Rodney King vivid and recurrent: 'More than any single factor, [defense attorney] Cochran had evoked the memory of Rodney King, the innocent victim of a vicious LAPD beating, police conspiracy, and subsequent cover-up only four years previously . . . For the defense during the yearlong trial, Rodney King was indeed the thirteenth juror, unobserved in the jury box but clearly visible in the imaginations of the black jurors.'[6] Linked together with Rodney King in a common narrative of police misconduct, O. J. Simpson enjoyed the cultural rewards of the Rodney King narrative, and it became possible to see him as a victim. The prosecuting lawyers in the case, assuming that the jurors would make their decisions based on a rational determination of the facts, failed to offer any significant alternatives discrediting the common narrative link between King and Simpson.[7]

Genre

What should be becoming clear by now is that narrative provides the dramatic dimensions of public culture, which are so necessary if individuals are to participate in civil society. Plot encourages the public concentration of attention on to specific events, encouraging discussion about the meaning of those events. Character relations serve to dramatise a society's deep cultural codes, increasing the likelihood of a continued emotional investment in the social drama. What ties these two properties of narrative together – by providing a temporal and spatial link between the characters and events of the story, as well as establishing a relationship between a story's characters, audience and narrator – is genre. This relationship has been aptly described by Bruner (1986: 6):

> Genre seems to be a way of both organizing the structure of events and organizing the telling of them – a way that can be used for one's own storytelling or, indeed, for 'placing' stories one is reading or hearing. Something in the actual text 'triggers' an interpretation of genre in the reader, an interpretation that then dominates the reader's own creation of what Wolfgang Iser calls a 'virtual text'.

Craib (this volume) criticises Bruner's and others' installation of narrative as an absolute category that reduces human experience by seeming to make sense of it. In this account, however, the power of genre resides not so much in a set of textual conventions rigidly followed by producers of narratives as in a set of expectations, or family resemblances, shared by audiences and producers alike (Pye 1975). While most empirical narratives will cross the boundaries of any single analytical genre, there are nevertheless patterned consistencies in the movement of certain types of stories through narrative time and space (Neale 1990). Emphasising the intertextual aspects of culture, genre analysis has moved beyond its traditional location in literature departments to become one of the most important methods of analysis in film studies (Maltby and Craven 1995: 137), and it is becoming increasingly important throughout the social sciences.

We can understand how genre operates by considering Frye's (1957: 158–239) discussion of the four narrative 'archetypes' of Western literature: romance, tragedy, comedy and irony. This is by no means an exhaustive list; other genres might include epic, lyric, melodrama, *Bildungsroman*, picaresque and many others. Indeed, in the cultural climate of today, some might argue that it would be more useful to think in terms of the eight Hollywood cinema genres typically discussed by film critics (Maltby and Craven 1995: 116). Nevertheless, by limiting myself to a discussion of four genres, I hope to show how the structural features of genre operate as both opportunities and constraints, helping to create certain audience expectations at the same time as they block others. Furthermore, as Frye (1957: 161–2) has argued, romance, tragedy, comedy and irony are so general and pervasive in the history of Western culture that they can be thought of as logically prior to other literary genres.

In *comedy*, Frye says, the protagonists, or heroes, are viewed from the perspective of their common humanity, and the general theme is the integration of society. The movement in comedy is usually from one kind of society, where the protagonist's wishes are blocked, to another society that crystallises around the hero. Comic heroes have average or below-average power, and typically fall into three general types: the imposter, the buffoon and the self-deprecator. In *romance*, the hero has great powers, the enemy is clearly articulated and often has great powers as well, and the movement takes the form of an adventure with the ultimate triumph of hero over enemy. Romantic genres are viewed by the audience from a perspective of wish fulfilment, where heroes represent ideals and villains represent threats. In *tragedy*, the hero typically possesses great powers, but is isolated from society and ultimately falls to an omnipotent and external fate or to the violation of a moral law. Because the reader expects catastrophe as its inevitable end, tragedy is a particularly dangerous form of discourse if one values civic engagement because, as Frye (1957: 211) describes it, tragedy 'eludes the antithesis between moral responsibility and arbitrary fate'. Finally, in *irony* the protagonist is viewed from an attitude of detachment and through the negative characterisation of parody and satire. As I have argued elsewhere (Jacobs and Smith 1997), irony encourages reflexivity, difference, tolerance and healthy forms of critique in civil society.

These genres are not neutral carriers of pre-existing interests and dispositions towards public engagement; rather, genres constitute interests and dispositions at the same time as they help to express them.[8] Some genres are more likely to turn civil society into a discursive arena supportive of new narratives, new points of difference and an active citizenry; others are less likely to do so. For example, public narratives told through the comic genre tend to be relatively inflexible and conservative, defining agitators as buffoon or imposter characters, with the ultimate message serving to reinforce the status quo (see Gitlin 1980: 46 on early *New York Times* coverage of the US student movement, and Frye 1957: 165). On the other hand, where comic genres assume a singular source of knowledge and an archimedean point from which to criticise those who are 'less enlightened', ironic genres permit the formation of multiple identities and allow for the construction of multiple and overlapping reflexive communities. This is seen clearly in African American press responses to 'mainstream' media coverage of racial issues, where expressions of outrage about the latest instance of police brutality are ironically deconstructed as yet another case of false sincerity, no doubt to be overwhelmed by a recurring phenomenon of memory loss (Jacobs 1996a, 2000). Yet irony contains dangers of its own. Where positive goals and destination narratives are missing there is always the possibility of a nihilistic form of irony coming to predominate in political cultures (Jacobs and Smith 1997). Many ironic narratives reflect an elitism which can result in pain, humiliation, and ultimately, backlash (Rorty 1989: 91–2). There is also the problem, noted by Schlegel, that one becomes weary of irony if confronted by it everywhere and all the time (Muecke 1969: 201).

While comedy and irony differ in their relative openness to multiple perspectives, they are similar in that they both attribute less power to the story's characters than to the audience, and tend to encourage an attitude of detachment or distance; in contrast to these types of narratives, romantic genres tend to encourage maximal participation and active engagement in civil society. Founded upon a 'theme of ascent' in which individuals and collectivities move towards a more perfect state, romantic narratives organise powerful and overarching collective identities that unite people in the pursuit of a utopian future; not surprisingly, it is the romantic genre that is found most often in the self-descriptions of social movements (Jacobs and Smith 1997). The Civil Rights movement, for example, translated then-present circumstances through a future-oriented and romantic exodus narrative in order to mobilise its adherents to action (Omi and Winant 1994: 99–100). Early American nationalists used a similar narrative strategy, as did many successful revolutionary movements (Greenfeld 1992: 403–11; Walzer 1985). Virtually every nationalist movement, in fact, presents to its target audience a totalistic picture of communal development that ties together the community's past, present and future into a romantic narrative of common destiny (Smith 1979: 17–42). Wherever romantic narratives are present, the likelihood of translating debate into action is increased immeasurably.

Of course, this translation of debate into action does not always have positive consequences. Romantic narratives suffer from an 'excess of plot', in which the teleological power of mythically validated past origins and future destinations precludes reflexivity and the interrogation either of present or of possible destinations (Jacobs and Smith 1997: 69). This problem is most clearly identified in the instance of fascism, but less extreme versions operate in any nation. In positing common goals and identities, romantic narratives are too often insensitive to the needs and wishes of marginal groups (for an example, see Walters, this volume). For these reasons, it is often helpful to combine romantic narratives with other genres. Jacobs and Smith (1997), for example, argue that ironic narratives can help to increase tolerance and reflexivity in discursive situations typically dominated by romance. West (1989: 228) argues that tragedy helps to temper the utopian impulses and excesses of many romantic and revolutionary movements.

During periods of social crisis, the dramatic power of civil society is often heightened by the tension between two genres, romance and tragedy. Will the crisis end with unity or fragmentation? Trust or suspicion? An opening of social boundaries, or an increase in tribalism and other hyperactive forms of social closure? People who are otherwise disengaged from public life turn on their television sets and open their newspapers during a social crisis, in the process having often heated arguments about its meaning and proper resolution. During the 1965 Watts uprisings, for example, the tragic narratives of self-destruction and urban neglect were counterposed against a competing interpretation, in which the challenges of fragmentation and anomie could be romantically overcome. White indifference could be overcome through African American empowerment. Political factions could be overcome through political leadership. Mass society could be overcome through grass roots community organising. In these instances, the tension between romance and tragedy served to heighten the sense of social drama surrounding the crises, increasing public attention as well as the possibility of engagement.

On the other hand, when crisis is narrated through a single genre, there is a greater likelihood that it will end through an ideological resolution. As Graeme Turner (1993: 147) has argued for the case of film, the ideological power of movies often comes from the refusal to maintain genre ambiguity and complexity all the way through to the conclusion: 'Often the formal problems we might discern within a film are traceable to the intransigence of the ideological opposition; an unsatisfactory ending in a film may emerge from the failure to unite the ideological alternatives convincingly.' As narrative tension builds to uncomfortable levels, producers fall back on highly schematised plot structures and tropes, in order to give the audience the release they desire.[9] I would suggest that, during times of civil crisis, there is a similar dynamic at work: an increase in narrative tension, followed by a release of that tension through the use of highly schematised and ideological plot devices. Whereas crisis gets its dramatic power from the tension between competing genres, it gets its ideological power from the seemingly seamless shift to a single generic ending.

For an example of romantic consolidation with ideological consequences, we can turn to the Rodney King beating in Los Angeles where, after the release of the Report of the Independent Commission on the Los Angeles Police Department in July 1991, 'mainstream' media reports shifted into an exclusively romantic narrative that reinforced the legitimacy of existing political leaders. Acting as a bridge to unify the previously divided members of the local government and the political elite, the Christopher Commission was represented as an objective and visionary body enabling the unification and cooperation of local government leaders. Public focus began to turn to the upcoming trial of the four officers indicted, the conviction of whom would signal complete redemption for the political leaders of Los Angeles, legitimacy for its institutions and moral uplifting for its citizens. Rather than treating the trial of the officers as a separate and contingent event, the 'mainstream' news media and their publics understood the trial as the final chapter of the narrative, clearly expecting the result to be the conviction of the officers. As for the other narrative forms that had previously been used to dramatise the crisis – the tragedy of isolation, and the satire of politicisation – they appeared to disappear in a case of collective memory-loss. While all of the 'mainstream' media began their Rodney King narratives through a focus on police brutality, they ended their stories through plots which emphasised how the concerns of African Americans and African American leaders could be met through normal political channels.

The ideological effect of the Rodney King beating was related to the shift to an exclusively romantic genre; for the 1992 Los Angeles uprisings, it came from a shift to the tragic. While media narratives were initially open to new voices and new perspectives, this openness was quickly overwhelmed by a number of powerful tragic narratives: the tragedy of urban neglect, the tragedy of politics, the tragedy of racial division and legal paralysis (Jacobs 2000). For white Americans as well as African Americans, the cultural legacy of the 1992 uprisings was the tragic sense that there was an unbridgeable gap between the races, and that talk about matters of racial concern was a hopeless waste of time. The following news excerpt is a typical example of the tragic mood which prevailed in the aftermath of the uprisings:

> Six months after the worst urban unrest of this century, Los Angeles remains a city divided, its residents separated by deep fissures that have split along racial, economic and geographic lines. At a time when fragmentation and Balkanization have become civic buzzwords, Angelenos increasingly see their neighbors as being resentful or indifferent toward people of other races, more suspicious even than in the immediate aftermath of the riots.
>
> (*Los Angeles Times*, 16 November 1992: JJ4)

The tragic mode of reporting about the 1992 Rodney King crisis persisted even in the face of new events which might have led to a more positive and romantic re-emplotment of the crisis. When the Webster Commission released its report about the causes of the uprisings, it was seen as powerless to counteract the forces of political failure and racial division.[10] When Willie Williams was sworn into office as the first African American police chief of Los Angeles, news reports emphasised how he would most likely be blocked by political infighting, police factions, a demoralised staff that was too small to institute more progressive police practices, and a budget crisis that would stifle any attempts at systemic change.[11] When the federal trial against the four police officers charged in the Rodney King beating resulted in two guilty verdicts and two not-guilty verdicts, it was criticised as a 'politically correct' compromise verdict which would only exacerbate existing tensions in the city (Gibbs 1996). Regardless of the event, it seemed that nothing could shake the sense of resignation about race and civil society − racial division and distrust, it seemed, were to be permanent features of American life.

It is noteworthy that tragedy prevailed in 'mainstream' public discourse about racial crisis at the precise time that real engagement across lines of racial difference was most likely. By 1992, the writing staffs of daily newspapers were composed of more women and more minorities, came from more regionally diverse origins, and were more likely than ever before to incorporate African American voices and viewpoints into their narratives about

American civil society. The Rodney King beating and ensuing crisis of 1991 had vindicated longstanding African American complaints of excessive force by police, reinforcing the authority of those complaints through the official seal of the Christopher Commission report. The return of the not-guilty verdicts showed in a public and dramatic way that African American complaints of legal injustices, also longstanding, were still valid. All of these factors influenced early 'mainstream' news coverage of the 1992 Los Angeles uprisings, which was indeed open and sympathetic to African American voices, histories and interpretations. That the shift to tragedy occurred precisely at the moment of greatest openness to African American voices and concerns can only be understood as the operation of ideology – not in the way that propaganda models explain ideology, where military and corporate interests actively filter the news production process, but in a more subtle, cultural way, where ideology works 'behind the scenes' of conscious intent, in the cognitive ordering of events into meaningful sequences of significance. And this ideological movement can be uncovered most effectively through narrative analysis.

The point is that the outcomes of public communication depend in large part on the forms of representation used to make events meaningful. Communication cannot be considered solely in terms of its ability to produce a shared commitment to a singular vision of the good, or to some 'rational' consensus; it must also be evaluated in terms of its ability to keep a conversation going, and to protect the possibility of opening up these conversations to new narratives and to new points of difference. The shape of public narratives, then, is crucially important for democracy and civil society. Those who are or would be included in civil society engage in cooperative and conflictual symbolic 'conversations' about who deserves membership and just how far the obligations of membership extend (Alexander and Jacobs 1998). By using narrative structures such as plot, character, and genre skilful social actors are able to exert a powerful influence on the expansion or the contraction of solidarity, tolerance and inclusion.

As the 'narrative turn' continues to win over social scientists interested in culture and meaning, what is sorely needed is methodological refinement: that is, the attempt to delineate specific narrative processes, and relate them to empirical instances of cultural creation. In my discussion of plot, character and genre, I have attempted to contribute to this methodological project, at the same time as I have argued in favour of narrative analysis as a way to study public culture in civil society. As a sociologist, my emphasis has been on collective representations and the social. Ultimately, this work must be connected to other research that explores how plot, character, and genre shape the self, at the individual and psychological level. The remaining chapters in this volume go a long way towards integrating these micro- and macro-level concerns. Taken together, they should generate conclusions which are applicable to a broad range of substantive and empirical contexts, providing valuable resources for cultural scholars throughout the social sciences.

Notes

1 For an excellent critical discussion of Habermas and public sphere theory, see the collected essays in Calhoun (1992).
2 In arguing that the binary discourse of civil society operates as an open and informal system of social closure, I am relying on the excellent discussion of social closure by Brubaker (1992: 29–31).
3 For historical accounts of the plebian public sphere, see Eley (1992) and Tucker (1996a). For historical accounts of women's publics, see Ryan (1992), Baker (1992) and Landes (1988). On festive communication and the public sphere, see Keane (1984) and Tucker (1996b).
4 More detailed descriptions of the events surrounding the Watts uprisings can be found in McCone (1965) and Fogelson (1969 [1967]).
5 Of course, the Los Angeles uprisings were labelled 'riots' in most of the initial reports in the 'mainstream' media. The struggle over what to call the crisis was part of the larger interpretive struggle over narration. While riot narratives tend to describe irrational, out of control and unplanned actions, uprising narratives tend to describe active and self-conscious acts of protest and rebellion against oppression. At stake in these competing labels, then, was the description of the agency and role of the African American community in responding to racial crisis. See Crenshaw and Peller (1993).
6 Indeed, once the Simpson trial became linked to the earlier King trial, and its images of legal injustice, the entirety of Black America became the symbolic thirteenth juror in the trial. Television news media had already acted from such an understanding during the Reginald Denny beating trial, stationing cameras throughout South Los Angeles in order to get the African American reaction to the verdict (Jacobs 1996b).
7 Of course, an additional character structure helped to influence public understandings of the Simpson trial and verdict: namely, the opposition between the violent and the victimized black male. This character structure also operated powerfully during the Rodney King trial, as it has for much of American history (Butler 1993; Gooding-Williams 1993).
8 Brubaker (1992: 16) makes much the same argument about cultural idioms of nationhood and citizenship.
9 Elsaesser (1981) has argued that, in the case of film, the psychology of the cinematic experience is one of increasing tension and anxiety, demanding a cathectic release and a psychic outlet. The end of the film narrative, provided that it resolves the plot ambiguities and tensions, can offer the psychic release demanded by the cinematic viewer, even if it is a rather implausible ending. In this sense, the ideological potential of narrative is supported by powerful psychological underpinnings.
10 See, for example, *New York Times*, 18 October 1992: A32; *Los Angeles Times*, 22 October 1992: A1; *Los Angeles Sentinel*, 12 November 1992: A17.
11 *New York Times*, 27 June 1992: A6; *Los Angeles Times*, 1 July 1992: B2; 18 October 1992: M3; *Los Angeles Sentinel*, 13 August 1992: A3; 8 October 1992: A3.

References

Abbott, A. (1988) 'Transcending general linear reality', *Sociological Theory* 6: 169–86.
Alexander, J. C. (1992) 'Citizen and enemy as symbolic classification: on the polarizing discourse of civil society', in M. Fournier and M. Lamont (eds) *Where Culture Talks: Exclusion and the Making of Society*, Chicago: University of Chicago Press.

—— (1994) 'Modern, anti, post, neo: how social theories have tried to understand the "New World" of "Our Time"', *Zeitschrift fur Soziologie* 23, 3: 165–97.

—— (1998) 'Civil society I, II, III: constructing an empirical concept from normative controversies and historical transformations', in J. Alexander (ed.) *Real Civil Societies: Dilemmas of Institutionalization*, London: Sage.

Alexander, J. C. and Jacobs, R. N. (1998) 'Mass communication, ritual, and civil society', in T. Liebes and J. Curran (eds) *Media, Ritual and Identity*, London and New York: Routledge.

Alexander, J. C. and Smith, P. (1993) 'The discourse of American civil society: a new proposal for cultural studies', *Theory and Society* 22: 151–207.

Baker, K. (1992) 'Defining the public sphere in eighteenth-century France: variations on a theme by Habermas', in C. Calhoun (ed.) *Habermas and the Public Sphere*, Cambridge, MA: The MIT Press.

Benhabib, S. (1992) 'In the shadow of Aristotle and Hegel: communicative ethics and current controversies in practical philosophy', in *Situating the Self: Gender, Community and Postmodernism in Contemporary Ethics*, New York: Routledge.

Brubaker, R. (1992) *Citizenship and Nationhood in France and Germany*, Cambridge, MA: Harvard University Press.

Bruner, J. (1986) *Actual Minds, Possible Worlds*, Cambridge, MA: Harvard University Press.

Butler, J. (1993) 'Endangered/endangering: schematic racism and white paranoia', in R. Gooding-Williams (ed.) *Reading Rodney King/Reading Urban Uprising*, New York: Routledge.

Calhoun, C. (ed.) (1992) *Habermas and the Public Sphere*, Cambridge, MA: The MIT Press.

Cohen, J. and Arato, A. (1992) *Civil Society and Political Theory*, Cambridge, MA: The MIT Press.

Crenshaw, K. and Peller, G. (1993) 'Reel time/real justice', in R. Gooding-Williams (ed.) *Reading Rodney King/Reading Urban Uprising*, New York: Routledge.

Durkheim, E. (1965) *The Elementary Forms of the Religious Life*, New York: The Free Press.

Eco, U. (1979) *The Role of the Reader*, Bloomington: Indiana University Press.

—— (1994) *Six Walks in the Fictional Woods*, Cambridge, MA: Harvard University Press.

Eley, G. (1992) 'Nations, publics, and political cultures: placing Habermas in the nineteenth century', in C. Calhoun (ed.) *Habermas and the Public Sphere*, Cambridge, MA: The MIT Press.

Elsaesser, T. (1981) 'Narrative cinema and audience-oriented aesthetics', in T. Bennett, S. Boyd-Bowman, C. Mercer and J. Woollacott (eds) *Popular Television and Film*, London: British Film Institute.

Fogelson, R. (1969 [1967]) 'White on Black: a critique of the McCone Commission Report on the Los Angeles Riots', in R. Fogelson (ed.) *Mass Violence in America: The Los Angeles Riots*, New York: Arno Press and the New York Times.

Fraser, N. (1992) 'Rethinking the public sphere: a contribution to the critique of actually existing democracy', in C. Calhoun (ed.) *Habermas and the Public Sphere*, Cambridge, MA: The MIT Press.

Frye, N. (1957) *Anatomy of Criticism*, Princeton, NJ: Princeton University Press.

Gellner, E. (1991) 'Civil society in historical context', *International Social Science Journal* 43, 3: 495–510.

Gibbs, J. T. (1996) *Race and Justice: Rodney King and O. J. Simpson in a House Divided*, San Francisco, CA: Jossey-Bass Publishers.

Giddens, A. (1984) *The Constitution of Society: Outline of the Theory of Structuration*, Berkeley and Los Angeles: University of California Press.

Gitlin, T. (1980) *The Whole World Is Watching: Mass Media in the Making and Unmaking of the New Left*, Berkeley: University of California Press.

Gooding-Williams, R. (1993) 'Look, a negro!', in R. Gooding-Williams (ed.) *Reading Rodney King/Reading Urban Uprising*, New York: Routledge.

Greenfeld, L. (1992) *Nationalism: Five Roads to Modernity*, Cambridge, MA: Harvard University Press.

Greimas, A. J. (1982) *Semiotics and Language: An Analytical Dictionary*, Bloomington: Indiana University Press.

Habermas, J. (1989 [1962]) *The Structural Transformation of the Public Sphere*, Cambridge, MA: The MIT Press.

Hirschman, A. O. (1991) *The Rhetoric of Reaction*, Cambridge, MA: Harvard University Press.

Jacobs, R. N. (1996a) 'Civil society and crisis: culture, discourse, and the Rodney King beating', *American Journal of Sociology* 101, 5: 1238–72.

—— (1996b) 'Producing the news, producing the crisis: narrativity, television and news work', *Media, Culture and Society* 18: 373–97.

—— (1998) 'The racial discourse of civil society: the Rodney King affair and the City of Los Angeles', in J. Alexander (ed.) *Real Civil Societies: Dilemmas of Institutionalization*, London: Sage.

—— (2000) *Race, Media, and the Crisis of Civil Society: From Watts to Rodney King*, Cambridge: Cambridge University Press.

Jacobs, R. N. and Smith, P. (1997) 'Romance, irony, and solidarity', *Sociological Theory* 15, 1: 60–80.

Keane, J. (1984) *Public Life and Late Capitalism: Toward a Socialist Theory of Democracy*, Cambridge: Cambridge University Press.

—— (1995) 'Structural transformations of the public sphere', *The Communication Review* 1, 1: 1–22.

Landes, J. (1988) *Women and the Public Sphere in the Age of the French Revolution*, Ithaca, NY: Cornell University Press.

McCone, J. (1965) *Violence in the City – An End or a Beginning? A Report by the Governor's Commission on the Los Angeles Riots*. Los Angeles.

MacIntyre, A. (1981) *After Virtue: A Study in Moral Theory*, Notre Dame, IN: University of Notre Dame Press.

Maltby, R. and Craven, I. (1995) *Hollywood Cinema*, Oxford: Blackwell.

Muecke, D. C. (1969) *The Compass of Irony*, London: Methuen.

Neale, S. (1990) 'Questions of genre', *Screen* 31, 1: 45–67.

Omi, M. and Winant, H. (1994) *Racial Formation in the United States*, New York: Routledge.

Pye, D. (1975) 'Genre and movies', *MOVIE* 20: 29–43.

Rorty, R. (1989) *Contingency, Irony and Solidarity*, Cambridge: Cambridge University Press.

Ryan, M. (1992) 'Gender and public access: women's politics in nineteenth-century America', in C. Calhoun (ed.) *Habermas and the Public Sphere*, Cambridge, MA: The MIT Press.

Schudson, M. (1992) 'Was there ever a public sphere? If so, when? Reflections on the American case', in C. Calhoun (ed.) *Habermas and the Public Sphere*, Cambridge, MA: The MIT Press.

—— (1998) *The Good Citizen: A History of American Civic Life*, New York: Free Press.

Sewell, W. H., Jr. (1992) 'Narratives and social identities', *Social Science History* 16, 3: 480–9.

Smith, A. (1979) *Nationalism in the Twentieth Century*, New York: Penguin Press.

—— (1995) *Nations and Nationalism in a Global Era*, Cambridge: Polity Press.

Taylor, C. (1989) *Sources of the Self: The Making of Modern Identity*, Cambridge, MA: Harvard University Press.

Tucker, K. H. (1996a) *French Revolutionary Syndicalism and the Public Sphere*, Cambridge: Cambridge University Press.

—— (1996b) 'Harmony and transgression: aesthetic imagery and the public sphere in Habermas and post-structuralism', *Current Perspectives in Social Theory* 16: 101–20.

Turner, G. (1993) *Film as Social Practice*, New York: Routledge.

Verba, S., Lehman Schlozman, K. and Brady, H. E. (1995) *Voice and Equality: Civic Voluntarism in American Politics*, Cambridge, MA: Harvard University Press.

Walzer, M. (1985) *Exodus and Revolution*, New York: Basic Books.

West, C. (1989) *The American Evasion of Philosophy: A Genealogy of Pragmatism*, Madison: The University of Wisconsin Press.

2 Resurrective practice and narrative

Clive Seale

Because the experiences of dying and bereavement place us at the margin of social life, forcing us to recognise that all of our cultural life is predicated upon our material existence in bodies, and that this is the finishing point and the starting point for us all, the study of narratives told by dying and bereaved people is a particularly fertile area for gaining an understanding of how we jointly produce our sense of being human. This production is, of course, something which is normally done as a matter of everyday routine, but there are special moments which occur from time to time that reveal the socially constructed nature of this sense of being human, which are then often occasions for an activity I have called resurrective practice (Seale 1998). I intend this term to refer both to practices of a both formal and organised nature for which there exists an established expertise (such as psychotherapy, or the 'resurrective', primarily romantic, forms of rhetoric in the public sphere discussed by Jacobs, this volume) and to the fine details of everyday conversation, since these have in common an affirmation of the social bond in the face of its dissolution, enabling people to claim membership in an imagined human community. Resurrective practice restores a sense of basic security fractured by death (thus its religious connotations), but is also a routine feature of daily life.

To understand, then, how we constitute ourselves in social bonds on an everyday basis it is illuminating to see what happens to social membership when routines are disrupted. Disruptions by illness and death are particularly instructive, for they remind us that the material life of the body precedes its narrative construction. Something of this focus is adopted by other contributors to this volume (Freeman, Wengraf, Hollway and Jefferson, Malson). But it is at times omitted in social constructionist accounts of self-identity, which may then appear either to 'forget' the body, or to regard it as so endlessly mutable that it does not matter that we live in and through bodies. In fact our material, animal life underlies everything that we do and is the primary vehicle for cultural life. If we understand this then we can also understand that life involves a daily effort (of which, thankfully, we are generally unaware) to turn ourselves away from the death that we carry in our bodies.

In this analysis it will become clear that 'narrative' is something which I believe to be a pervasive feature of social life, being present in many situations that do not involve storytelling through language as conventionally conceived. I understand narratives to be constructed through many things, including acts of consumption, for example, which can be made symbolically to tell stories about tastes, relationships (whether real or desired) or social standing. Objects can be ordered in relation to the body, the household, a life, in ways that make narrative sense. The stories that people tell about the acquisition of objects, their use, disposal and value, or about selves and identities, simply assist researchers in perceiving what was already 'known' before speech. Objects and subjects, incorporated into culture via human sense-making activity, comprise a grammar and a language, so that the social life of things as well as people is a legitimate object of inquiry for those interested in narrative. For this reason I include here and elsewhere (Seale 1998) examples from a variety of human activities, including shopping, eating, warfare, media representations, medical procedures, life insurance systems, as well as bereavement narratives, which together illustrate the broad scope of resurrective practice through narrative construction.

Falling from culture

Study of bereavement narratives, in which people tell the stories of what it was like to be close to a dying relative or friend, reveals a dissolution of the social bond which everyday narrative actions otherwise sustain by allowing individuals to claim membership in the human social group (see the ideas of Sacks, expressed in Silverman (1998)). Eventually, there is the moment of final withdrawal from life when dying people and their carers may experience a stark awareness; words lose the capacity to construct realities so that people fall out of the culture that had formed their life's sheltering canopy:

> she was a bag of bones with no strength in her legs. I got her to the toilet alright and she couldn't even sit up so she had to go back to bed. Well, she just couldn't get back. I'm kind of strong but I don't think she weighed more than 85 or 90 pounds, and before I got her back in that bed, I thought I was going to die and she knew. She was well aware of everything so she didn't say anything for a long time. She just looked out in the direction of the window with this far away horrible look on her face and that, that was the worst. That was the worst.
>
> (Meares 1995: 755)

In my own analysis of bereavement narratives I have found it helpful to focus on the meanings of food as a way of exploring the fall from culture (Seale 1998: Chapter 7). I have argued that changes in feeding practices acquire a symbolic value within people's stories and are understood by storytellers to run closely in parallel with a decline and the eventual extinction of life itself.

In everyday social life, of course, food is a language, so that a semiotic analysis of meals is possible. In 'Deciphering a meal', Douglas (1975) points out that food is a code for hierarchy, exclusion and boundaries in social relations. The food served to visitors indicates the degree of intimacy a host desires. Invitations to 'drinks' as opposed to 'meals' serve to distinguish strangers from honoured guests. The manner of eating food may be closely scrutinised for markers of social status (Elias 1978, 1982). Within a sequence of meals in a household, Douglas (1975) has argued, each element (breakfast, lunch, supper; daily meals, birthday meals, Christmas meals) derives its meaning from its relation to other elements. The 'grand' meal (three courses) sets the standard by which other events are constituted as 'meals' or 'snacks'. Within the meal, too, elements (such as 'pudding' or 'starter') gain their meaning from their place in relation to other elements, so that a meal can be understood as structured in a manner analogous to a poem with verses. The example of food is incorporated into Douglas' general project of representing classificatory thinking as the imposition of order upon disorder. Food, then, sustains us not only physically but also psychologically through the operations of culture, so that the micro-rituals of commensality are an important arena for everyday resurrective practice.

Drawing on an interview survey of the bereaved relatives and friends of people in England who had died some months earlier (Cartwright and Seale 1990; Seale and Cartwright 1994) as well as similar material collected by Meares (1995) in the USA, I have analysed the meanings of food expressed in their stories (Seale 1998). The narratives often involve the progressive dissolution of structure and daily routine, as the complex reciprocities required for the performance of normal, mannered eating cannot be sustained. Alterations to the type and consistency of foodstuffs, a decline in appetite and eventual cessation of intake mirror the decline of the body and of self-control, leading eventually to the withdrawal of the self in a final fall from culture. Food items are, then, presented in bereavement narratives as symbolic tokens that tell their own story. The movement from one type of food to another is rehearsed, to indicate the declining force of the social bond:

> She went from eating solids to almost liquids. She went from eating meats and vegetables to eating sweets. You know, there were levels of that too, like she went from eating the solids I always knew she ate to eating soups and occasionally a frozen dinner. And went from that to ... just eating eggs in the morning and liquids in the afternoon ... And then she went from that stage into drinking [liquid supplements] and just eating sweets like cakes and cookies ... And then she just wanted sipping ginger ale.
>
> (Meares 1995: 9)

The efforts of the teller in preparing 'special foods' that indicate last-ditch attempts to sustain the social bond may be stressed. Here, for example, is a mother talking about her daughter's last day:

> I was with her all the time at the end. I knew it was the last day because I went out at least 20 times in the car to the shops to get her all the things she asked for. Wild cherry ice-cream, iced lollies, different drinks, it went on all day. As soon as I got back she'd thought of something else she'd like. She said she was a nuisance, but she wasn't . . . In the afternoon she asked for her brother, ex-husband, sons, her father to come. They all came and she said her farewells, and to me of course, and then she had the nurse come because the pain was so bad. The nurse said if she gave her the injection she might doze or might not wake up again, and my daughter said she had said all her good-byes and so have the injection. She didn't wake up again, she died 2 hours later.
>
> (Seale 1998: 163)

These examples gain an added poignancy when we contrast them with the more routinely established meanings of food in everyday life described by Douglas. We begin to understand the void that underlies everyday life, against which we are defended by routinely established resurrective practice, in this case the narrative order created by mealtimes. Additionally, the act of telling these stories can itself be understood as a form of resurrective practice, serving to establish the adequacy and justified pride of the speaker in having fulfilled the obligations of social bonds up to the last moment of life, preserving recognisably human behaviour in the face of dissolution. Caring for dying people is imbued with this confrontation, so that the acts of carers are often understood to be filled with triumphs of the human spirit. This is why professional carers of dying people are at times idealised and admired.

Shopping and sacrifice

Let us now turn from these intensely fateful moments to something a little more light hearted in order to demonstrate the role of narrative as resurrective practice in everyday experience. For this I draw on the work of Miller (1998) who has shown that shopping is organised to tell stories about relationships. Supermarket trips can be understood as story-making episodes, in which the choices made are imbued with significance for the social bond in later accounts. In this respect, a shopping expedition is directly equivalent to a bereavement narrative or to a family meal, since all these enable resurrective practice through a narrative ordering of social relationships.

In his ethnography of shoppers in North London Miller shows, first, that the concept of a special 'treat' is used to define the rest of the shopping expedition as being about something else, such as the collection of essential provisions. The treat is thus made to act in a manner similar to a 'pudding' in a meal, a moment of pleasurable indulgence that marks the rest as nutritious or healthy. The 'special foods' prepared for dying people are contrasted with more routine foods in bereavement narratives to produce a similar rhetorical effect of marking difference (Seale 1998).

Miller observes that shopping has ritualised elements in which, as in sacrificial ritual, there is 'a splitting of the objects of sacrifice between that which is given to the deity and that which is retained for human consumption' (Miller 1998: 7). The 'deity' in this case is thrift, a commitment to which is based on the desire and obligation to assert secure membership of the social bond by engaging in properly accountable behaviour. The act of saving money for the benefit of the family, the household, or some vaguer sense of thrift being a necessary virtue that will bestow good fortune, is being sacralised. This discharge of obligation releases the storyteller to engage in justified consumption of the goods brought home, itself a matter which is organised to symbolise appropriate family relationships (for example, the well-known gender divisions that occur in the preparation and distribution of foodstuffs within households).

It helps to see an example of someone living on the edge of this symbolic, world-making system in order to perceive what many other people routinely sustain. One of the people in Miller's study was an elderly woman living alone:

> who clearly shopped incessantly as a means of keeping occupied. The problem then arose as to how to keep such shopping going when in reality she had little in the way of goods she needed and little by way of money to buy them. In practice she develops 'projects' which fortunately are very hard to come to fruition. Several of these relate to gifts she will have to buy for Christmas, a wedding or a christening that she can start thinking about months, even years ahead. A more elaborate project revolved around an ancestral shrine. This consisted of the decoration of the flat with photographs of her parents and other deceased relatives. So, for example, she needed a particular photo frame to match exactly the one she already had, but which she could never find, combined with other elements such as the right artificial flowers that would festoon the portraits. Through such devices she manages to engage herself in daily acts of shopping where most of the time is spent considering others and maintaining the same subsumption of self that was crafted through decades of housewifery, but now returns as affection for her ancestors.
>
> (Miller 1998: 33)

This woman's shopping projects effectively tell to others and to herself a life-sustaining story about herself, her purposes in life, and her reasons for her continuing existence. The human social bond is routinely constituted in such activity, so that everyday life can be understood as imbued with small-scale rituals that place the biography of the 'teller' within broader stories or

cultural scripts, in this case stories of love, obligation, proper family relationships, and in the case of thrift, the fulfilment of properly accountable
acts undertaken to conserve resources. Shopping and associated consumption
activities, then, allow people to tell stories about themselves as much as any
verbal discourse transcribed by a researcher and designated as 'narrative' for
the purposes of a research project. It is perhaps because of the dominance of
the interview as the method of choice in contemporary qualitative social
research (Atkinson and Silverman 1997) that an interest in narrative has
become associated with the analysis of tape transcripts. Observational studies like that of Miller, by contrast, reveal that there is considerable potential
for the investigator seeking narrative material in the activities performed in
everyday life, continual sense-making activities in which we all engage for
most of the time, as we pursue projects of self-identity.

The question of motive

What, though, impels people to narrativise their daily lives, as they do in
shopping trips, and to have recourse to narrative in particularly explicit
forms at fateful moments, as they do in bereavement narratives? Defining
narrative as broadly as I have done suggests that this is a question about the
roots of the human social bond, about the basic motives that lead us to cling
together as human beings in a jointly produced cultural life. At this most
fundamental level we must look to some of the elementary parameters of
human existence, beginning from the fact that we live as bodies, that these
bodies will die, and that all of the rest of our world is built upon these
things. Human worlds are made on these foundations through emotional
life, which binds us to each other in a continually negotiated membership. It
is, then, to the sociology of emotions that we can turn for some insight into
the emotional work that is done in the resurrective practice of narrative.
Through narrative constructions of our personal biographies we formulate
self-identities embedded in social networks, whose currency is that of emotional exchange.

The work of Thomas Scheff (1990, 1997) explores the emotional roots of
human social bonds in a way that allows an understanding of the underlying
motives for resurrective practice through narrative. Scheff shares Durkheim's
perception that the maintenance of social bonds is 'the most crucial human
motive' (1990: 4). Indeed, I suggest, it keeps us alive. The link with Durkheim
is evident if we consider that suicide may be caused by pathologies of the
social bond, while collective protection against such pathologies is social
solidarity. Scheff's interest in conversation analysis leads him to propose that
talk is an essential route for intersubjective communication, but he claims
equal status for what he calls the 'deference-emotion system' that relies on
non-verbal bodily communication and emotions. Together, these systems
generate the emotions of pride in social bonds that are intact, and shame
at those which are broken, and explain our sense of moral failure when

insufficient care has been shown towards others. Attunement to these matters is established between people through almost instantaneous empathic 'mind reading'. Analysis of the minutiae of everyday conversation suggests that this attunement requires remarkably rapid shifts of attention as well as the summary of complex masses of information.

Conversation analysis supplies us with a powerful demonstration of talk as a ritual affirmation and, indeed, construction of membership. The related technique of membership categorisation analysis, derived from Sacks' work, is precisely devoted to showing how membership concerns are raised in almost every interaction in which we engage (see Silverman 1998 for an account of Sacks that draws this out). Conversation analysts have shown talk to be surprisingly repetitive. At the most obvious level, in most settings where talk occurs, answers are expected to follow questions. Summons (such as the ring of a telephone) are followed by answers (Schegloff and Sacks 1974). If they are not, 'repair' moves are made. In institutional settings, conversation analysts have observed the routine use of particular patterns of talk, such as the use of perspective-display series in medical consultations (Maynard 1991), the pre-allocation of turns in courtroom talk (Atkinson and Drew 1979), and standardised communication formats in counselling sessions (Silverman 1996). Mutual recognition of the legitimacy of the rules that govern talk indicates an acceptance of participation in a social institution. Such recognition establishes each speaker as an accredited human being, living in a community that is continually renewed in the imaginary life of members. The outrage that results from the breaking of such rules has been engagingly demonstrated by Garfinkel, whose experiments (1963) provoked emotional reactions among 'normals' analogous to the rage that lies behind the expulsion of heretics. The defence of imagined community that one sees here is therefore a maintenance of boundaries which depend on securely established narratives of membership and self-identity.

Scheff (1990) observes that basic social bonds are continually at risk at the routine level of everyday interaction, where people may manipulate claims to membership (and therefore negotiate between alternative narratives) for momentary strategic advantage (perhaps to assert distinction), or through unconscious disturbance so that misunderstandings and distorted communication takes place. Social bonds are also disrupted at moments of great personal or general social change, such as those described in major 'life events' (Brown and Harris 1978), 'fateful moments' (Giddens 1991) or social revolutions. It is at this point that a variety of repair mechanisms may be wielded, including restatements of communication, psychotherapeutic repair and societal reconstruction. Here, then, is a place for narrative reconstruction in the context of a broad theory of the elemental bonds of social life. Indeed, Scheff's ideas help to explain why discursive narratives of the self characteristically contain justifications, excuses and rationalisations for 'bad' behaviour that present the self in a morally acceptable fashion (for example, Baruch 1981; Riessman 1990). Such reconstructions depict social bonds as intact when they are in fact broken, or justifiably in tatters owing to the bad behaviour of others, restoring pride and guarding against shame, and maintaining the legitimacy of the speaker's claim to membership of an imagined moral community.

This view of the ritual qualities of everyday life must lead us to question social commentators who mourn the 'decline' of ritual in the move from tribal or traditional societies to modern and late modern societies. Clearly, allegiance to large-scale formal ritual is more problematic in a society where many of these compete, and a sense of scepticism about the truth value of any grand narrative is pervasive. Yet human social life is fundamentally ritualistic at the everyday level, as the studies of shopping and eating reviewed earlier have shown. And an essential part of these rituals involves membership claims, achieved through the persuasive 'storytelling' activities that constitute everyday life.

Community membership

I hope that I have shown by now that 'narrative' is something which occurs throughout everyday life, when we engage in actions and interactions as well as in storytelling episodes. Second, the resurrection of a meaningful narrative of self-identity, involving secure membership, in the face of loss of membership and ontological insecurity occurs on a daily basis. We have seen how the material life of the body, including its death, sets the parameters for this ongoing activity, and in the work of Scheff we can perceive the role of emotions in this. Let us finally, then, investigate some examples of community membership that are achieved through resurrective practice. 'Joining' such communities involves people committing themselves to particular versions of self-identity, yet such acts are not always understood to be choices, since people are handed down community memberships of various sorts that often appear to be natural or inevitable. These grand cultural scripts or discourses encourage people to include their more personal biographical stories within them.

In Seale (1995; 1998) I have described a particular construction of self-identity in bereavement narratives, where speakers draw on a 'revivalist' cultural script to tell stories that emphasise the heroic qualities of dying people. These stories of heroism emphasise the inner journeys of people dying in open awareness of their deaths, passing through a sequence of stages (for example, from denial to acceptance of death) often in a drama of emotional accompaniment that also involves the speaker who is recollecting events. The revivalist script is informed by iconic writings such as those of Elisabeth Kubler-Ross (1969), and performances of culture heroes in the media, for example dying 'celebrities' confessing their deaths, and is institutionally orchestrated, by hospices or bereavement counsellors for example. Yet it is a relatively recent cultural script to which there remains a degree of resistance in the Anglophone countries in which it has largely developed, so that not all bereavement narratives are written along these lines and membership in the community of the psychologically 'aware' offered by this script is not aspired to by all.

There exists also a much older script which is generally understood to be so natural and true that bereaved individuals usually have no great difficulty in assuming membership of the community it offers. In our interviews, when asked why a person died, most people quite readily provided an account of medical conditions, often reading from a death certificate as if it were the most helpful or accurate version. This easy adoption of a medical narrative speaks for the naturalising power of medical scripts in late modernity. It would have been unusual, for example, for a person to say that their relative died from misfortune or witchcraft. Speakers unproblematically asserted their membership of a particular imagined community constructed in medical discourse. To explain this, we turn first to the Foucauldian work of Prior (1989) on the cultural script that medicine writes about death, enacted in the practice of death certification by doctors.

Death certification enshrines a unified medical view of what causes death, as well as symbolising the presence of universal, essential features of human nature. Prior points out that the rules for assigning cause, dictating the physical layout of the certificate, reflect this view. The very fact that one can complain about 'accuracy' reflects consensus about what certification 'should' do, and it performs this function effectively for most practical purposes, most of the time. As Prior has observed, no longer do we find 'intemperate living', 'want', or 'cold and whiskey' written on certificates. Of more contemporary relevance, neither do we find death from a rubber bullet in a street disturbance, or from structured class inequality, or poverty; Prior notes that a Belfast coroner even ruled out 'suicide' as a legitimate cause of death at the certification stage, since this did not describe a bodily event. Certification removes human agency, and is a pure assertion of the bodily containment of death, a ritualised identification of the workings of natural disease within the body. And as medicine contains the promise of intervention into the course of natural disease, so the death certificate is an indirect promise to the living that death can be controlled (Bauman 1992).

A process of narrative incitement occurs when death is announced to people, consisting of encouragement to relatives of deceased persons to write the death into the medical script, so that secure membership of this medically defined community is established. Observations of death announcements by hospital staff (Sudnow 1967) and coroners' officials (Charmaz 1976) show this process at work. Charmaz notes that key tasks which must be achieved by coroners' deputies in notifying relatives of a sudden, unexpected death, apart from preserving composure and ensuring acceptance of burial costs by relatives, are to make the death credible, accountable and 'acceptable' to relatives. A common strategy is to delay announcement of death until details of an accident or collapse have been given as 'cues', which ideally prompt the relative to jump to the conclusion that a death has occurred:

I tell them that he collapsed today while at work. They asked if he is all right now. I say slowly, 'Well, no, but they took him to the hospital.' They ask if he is there now. I say, 'They did all they could do – the doctors tried very hard.' They say, 'He is dead at the hospital?' Then I tell them he's at the coroner's office.

(Charmaz 1976: 78)

To the question that then follows 'What must I do?' the deputy then proceeds to point the shocked recipient towards activity to deal with the death. Sudnow (1967) notes that in every such hospital announcement scene he witnessed a 'historical reference' was made to a medically relevant antecedent 'cause of death' such as a heart attack. Talk then proceeded to further elaboration on this cause, to a discussion of whether the person had 'suffered', and assurances that all that could have been done was done. On this last matter, Sudnow records occasions where this impression was made easier to sustain by artificially delaying the appearance of the medical announcer in order to sustain the impression that heroic but futile rescue attempts were made. On the matter of suffering, Sudnow notes that: 'doctors . . . routinely lie in their characterisations of death as painless' (1967: 146), an impression that relatives are often equally keen to sustain. In these various ways people 'learn' about deaths, and almost simultaneously engage in practices which repair security and sustain their own orientation towards living. Crucially, people are encouraged to tell the story of the death themselves in the terms of the medical script, aided, abetted and incited by the officials involved.

This process can be understood as similar in function to the mortuary rites described by anthropologists studying tribal or traditional societies. The task of the living is to enclose and explain death, to reduce its polluting effects, and symbolically to place individual deaths in a context which helps survivors turn away from death and towards continuing life. In other words medicine writes a cultural script that enables participants to engage in resurrective practice, involving acceptance of a particular story about the death, which then becomes incorporated into a narrative explanation of why the death occurred.

Conclusion

In this chapter I have sought to explore the underlying motives and mechanisms that make us into storytelling beings. I have argued that a root premise of human social life is the body and its death, from which just about all else arises. To orient ourselves towards life and away from death, we engage in resurrective practices of various sorts, of which narrative activity is an important part. Through narrative acts we define ourselves as members of imagined communities, with particular biographies and essential natures that we share with others. This assertion of membership is a process imbued with emotions, as Scheff's work shows, though these emotions may not become apparent until major disruptions to membership claims occur. The study of threats to narrative constructions at fateful moments provides many insights into more routinely established resurrective practices.

Additionally, I have sought to expand the notion of narrative to incorporate more than simply stories told in words. The clothes we wear, the food we eat, the words we choose and the way we understand our deaths are all crafted, in this sense, to speak volumes about the kinds of memberships we aspire to, or the identities we prefer. Some of these are explicit choices, where we know things could be otherwise. Others, though, indeed the vast majority of our narrative acts, are part of a routine, taken for granted background to our lives. Nevertheless, they are 'choices', as I have tried to demonstrate, since in any culture there is a contingent character to the scripts that are on offer. Narrative is thus a pervasive feature of human social life, since through a myriad of acts, both small and large, both routine and extraordinary, we engage in self-defining activity through the telling of our stories.

References

Atkinson, J. M. and Drew, P. (1979) *Order in Court: The Organization of Verbal Interaction in Judicial Settings*, London: Macmillan.

Atkinson, P. and Silverman, D. (1997) 'Kundera's "Immortality": the interview society and the invention of self', *Qualitative Inquiry* 3, 3: 304–25.

Baruch, G. (1981) 'Moral tales: parents' stories of encounters with the health profession', *Sociology of Health and Illness* 3, 3: 275–96.

Bauman, Z. (1992) *Mortality, Immortality and Other Life Strategies*, Cambridge: Polity Press.

Brown, G. and Harris, T. (1978) *Social Origins of Depression*, London: Macmillan.

Cartwright, A. and Seale, C. (1990) *The Natural History of a Survey: An Account of the Methodological Issues Encountered in a Study of Life before Death*, London: King's Fund.

Charmaz, K. C. (1976) 'The coroner's strategies for announcing death', in L. Lofland (ed.) *Toward a Sociology of Death and Dying*, Beverly Hills, CA: Sage.

Douglas, M. (1975) 'Deciphering a meal', in M. Douglas (ed.) *Implicit Meanings*, London: Routledge and Kegan Paul.

Elias, N. (1978) *The Civilizing Process Volume I: The History of Manners*, Oxford: Blackwell.

—— (1982) *The Civilizing Process Volume II: State Formation and Civilization*, Oxford: Blackwell.

Garfinkel, H. (1963) 'A conception of, and experiments with, "trust" as a condition of stable concerted actions', in O. J. Harvey (ed.) *Motivation and Social Interaction*, New York: Ronald Press.

Giddens, A. (1991) *Modernity and Self-identity: Self and Society in the Late Modern Age*, Cambridge: Polity Press.

Kubler-Ross, E. (1969) *On Death and Dying*, New York: Macmillan.

Maynard, D. W. (1991) 'Interaction and asymmetry in clinical discourse', *American Journal of Sociology* 97, 2: 448–95.

Meares, C. J. (1995) 'Primary caregiver perceptions of intake cessation in the terminally ill', *Oncology Nursing Forum* 24, 10: 1751–7.

Miller, D. (1998) *A Theory of Shopping*, Cambridge: Polity Press.

Prior, L. (1989) *The Social Organization of Death*, Basingstoke and London: Macmillan.

Riessman, C. K. (1990) 'Strategic uses of narrative in the presentation of self and illness: a research note', *Social Science and Medicine* 30, 11: 1195–200.

Scheff, T. (1990) *Micro Sociology, Discourse, Emotion and Social Structure*, Chicago: University of Chicago Press.

—— (1997) *Emotions, the Social Bond, and Human Reality: Part/Whole Analysis*, Cambridge: Cambridge University Press.

Schegloff, E. A. and Sacks, H. (1974) 'Opening up closings', in R. Turner (ed.) *Ethnomethodology*, Harmondsworth: Penguin.

Seale, C. F. (1995) 'Heroic death', *Sociology* 29, 4: 597–613.

—— (1998) *Constructing Death: The Sociology of Dying and Bereavement*, Cambridge: Cambridge University Press.

Seale, C. F. and Cartwright, A. (1994) *The Year before Death*, Aldershot: Avebury.

Silverman, D. (1996) *Discourses of Counselling: HIV Counselling as Social Interaction*, London: Sage.

—— (1998) *Harvey Sacks: Social Science and Conversation Analysis*, Cambridge: Polity Press.

Sudnow, D. (1967) *Passing On: The Social Organization of Dying*, Englewood Cliffs, NJ: Prentice-Hall.

3   Wedding bells and baby carriages

Heterosexuals imagine gay families, gay families imagine themselves

Suzanna Danuta Walters

Is it worth being Boring for a Blender? Gay Marriage: You might as well be straight.
>   DAM! (Dyke Action Machine) postcards and posters, New York

Just a thought. How soon before expectant parents tell their friends: 'It's twins. A boy and a girl. They're going to be gay. We're calling them Michelangelo and Martina. We've painted the nursery lavender.'
>   Sir Ian McKellen, *The Guardian*

The civilizing influence of family values, with or without children, ultimately may be the best argument for same-sex marriage.
>   William Eskridge, Jr., *The Case for Same-Sex Marriage*

Family: the final frontier?

It is no coincidence that the 'family values' debate emerges in the context of growing discussion and examination of the multiplicity of family forms. In an era when both the feminist and the gay movements have challenged the centrality and desirability of the heterosexual nuclear family, the phrase 'family values' emerges to set up an impenetrable dividing line between 'us' and 'them'. However, not only are feminists continuing to question the validity of a uniform notion of 'family' but gays and lesbians have begun to come out of the closet about both their own, often poignant, experiences in families and their attempts to form families themselves.

The very place of family is often a fraught one for lesbians and gay men. While the larger social world offers few sites of freedom, the family is often the first place where they experienced homophobia and the place where they felt most betrayed, most alone, most violated. Some of the saddest stories gay people tell are the stories of family – remaining in the closet for fear of rejection, being kicked out, being told you are no longer a son/daughter, being kept away from other kids, being beaten, being told you are sick, telling your mother it is not 'her fault', being disinherited, being shunned. It should be no surprise, then, that 'family' remains a highly charged arena for lesbians and gay men.[1]

But gay life and identity, defined so much by the problems of invisibility, subliminal coding, double entendres and double lives, have now taken on the dubious distinction of public spectacle. I cannot begin to do it justice here,[2] but suffice it to say that gay family life has not been immune from the extraordinary proliferation of books, TV shows, films, ads, magazine stories, merchandising firms, consumer expos and Internet chat rooms that have made gay identity (or a media version of it) available to all.

Beyond the odes to diversity and 'tolerance', few (except those on the extreme political right) have questioned the value of this almost obsessive 'love affair' with gay life. At first glance, these stunning changes seem all for the good. But if gays seem like the paragons of trendiness, then they are being simultaneously depicted as the Antichrist, the sign of a culture in decay, a society in ruins, the perverse eclipse of rational modernity. As religious fundamentalism grows, becomes mainstream and legitimate, so too does hard-edged homophobia. Hate crimes are on the rise – not just in numbers but in the severity and brutality of the acts.[3]

The debates about assimilation are as old as the movement itself, and echo in some ways the conversations about racialised exclusion and inclusion considered by Jacobs (this volume). What *is* new is that these debates are now taking place in full public view, around the water coolers of corporate America, the hallways of university campuses, the barbeque grills of genteel suburbia, and the streets and malls of both urban and rural areas. No longer restricted to closed-door meetings and internecine battles, these internal debates have been irrevocably externalised. If the enemy once was perceived as invisibility itself, then how is the enemy defined in an era of increased visibility? Is the penetrating gaze of the popular a sign of public acceptance or of the homosexual as commodity fetish, as side-show freak?

What profound (and new) alienation must be felt when a gay person looks at a gay wedding cheerfully depicted on TV and then has her/his partner studiously ignored at a family gathering? What does it feel like to be depicted as the cutting edge of chic postmodern style as you are getting fired from your job, rejected by your family and targeted by right-wing activists? For every successful custody suit, there seem to be two defeats. For every parent who is able successfully to 'adopt' her or his non-biological child, others are endlessly delayed or deferred. And it takes great financial resources to be able to access even these tenuous legal avenues.

For all the confusion and localism of gay family rulings and legislation, dominant themes do emerge. Whether it is marriage or parenting, both well-meaning heterosexuals *and* mainstream gays seem to stress gay sameness to straights. Our relationships, our desires, our parenting styles are again and again presented as replicas of heterosexual patterns, as if gay families exist in a sort of alternate universe that isn't really alternate at all. While odes to family *diversity* abound, real invocations of family *difference* are muted.

Honeymoon in Hawaii: the great marriage debate

Into this strange register of the visible enters the soundbite-ish 'gay marriage debate', a debate played out in the pages of gay journals but also on our TV sets, in glossy mainstream magazines, in prime-time news specials, in legal argumentation, in everyday talk. The peculiarly public display that is the wedding ritual emphasises the centrality of the visible to marriage, in a way that domestic partnerships or even commitment ceremonies can never quite manifest. Weddings are highly commercialised public signs; it is no accident that this imagery has captivated public imagination, pushing aside the more mundane and everyday images of lesbian and gay life by making visible that which we cannot have.

Nowhere is this new gay visibility more pronounced – and more problematic – than in television. Gay weddings have appeared in numerous series, including *Friends* (with Candace Gingrich, the lesbian half-sister of Republican standard-bearer Newt, playing the lesbian minister), the since-cancelled *Northern Exposure*, and *Roseanne*. For all the obvious newness of these representations, most have forgone the taboo gay kiss and presented gay marriage ceremonies as cuddly, desexualised mirrors of the more familiar heterosexual ritual. Notably absent are the odes to same-sex love and the revisions of traditional vows that most assuredly accompany many gay commitment ceremonies. The *Friends* wedding – while carefully sensitive – went out of its way to portray the gay wedding as an exact replica of its heterosexual counterpart, only with two bridal gowns. The episode focused more on the heterosexual response to the gay environment than on the gay participants themselves. Indeed, the gay wedding was framed by a secondary plot line concerning the impending divorce of a character's traditional mom, implicitly linking heterosexuality and homosexuality in a liberal scenario of sameness.

It is interesting to note that in the three major 'gay weddings' handled on TV, it is a heterosexual character who brings the nervous and fighting homosexual couple together when the nuptials are threatened. In *Friends*, *Northern Exposure*, and even the more innovative *Roseanne*, one of the series regulars has a 'heart-to-heart' with one member of the bickering gay couple and helps convince the wavering one to go through with the wedding. Often, it is the character who is initially most resistant to the wedding. The confidential tête-à-tête between gay outsider and heterosexual insider thus renders not only homosexuality but *homophobia* benign and palatable. The appalled Maurice (of *Northern Exposure*), who complains about 'tutti fruttis' ruining the very concept of marriage by engaging in a same-sex version of it, becomes not a bigoted homophobe but rather a befuddled and ultimately good-hearted traditionalist. The straight character gets reformed and redeemed through a demonstrated expertise in pre-wedding cold feet, thereby avoiding reckoning with a previously impregnable homophobia. This redemption, alongside the approving and supportive stance of all the other heterosexual characters, also avoids reckoning with the actual homophobia that surrounds such events.

In this scenario, straight people know more about family life and relationships and are needed to pass that knowledge on to their floundering gay brethren. The implication is that gays are simply not knowledgeable about the 'real-life' issues of forming families, making commitments, raising kids.[4] This reintroduces the old canard about homosexuals as childlike, immature, unformed versions of heterosexuals. This backlash scenario argues to 'accept' homosexuals, but not as full-fledged people who can handle their own lives.

In addition, there is a certain hubris in the straight homophobe playing Dear Abby to the jittery gay person. Do these gay people on TV never have *any* gay friends to consult in their travails? Isolation and assimilation are often the price of tokenism. But at least the *Cosby* family had each other. Gay people on TV appear to have sprung full-blown from the Zeus' head of heterosexuality. The social, political and cultural context that 'births' gay people gives way to the fiction of the fully formed fag, parented by bravely reconstructed heterosexuals. Homophobia is reduced to ignorance, bewilderment and discomfort. In the television land of gay life, the perpetrators of homophobia – aside from the obvious gaybashers – are basically good-hearted souls whose liberal inclinations win out in the end.

Contrast this delusional neo-liberalism with the realities of anti-gay politics. The same year that witnessed ratings-successful gay weddings on TV also saw the US Congress overwhelmingly support an anti-gay marriage bill and a putatively 'pro-gay' President sign it. State after state votes to restrict marriage to heterosexuals, and polls suggest most Americans agree with the decisions and not with the television shows they watch so assiduously. Even the extraordinary victory in Vermont – granting gays the closest thing we have to marriage-like status – has not slowed down the juggernaut of reactionary activism. For the religious Right, gay marriage is the proverbial line in the sand. A full-page ad by the Family Research Council quite explicitly locates marriage as the glue that holds society together – and keeps out the undesirables. Above a picture of a crumbling wedding cake, the ad encapsulates 'family values' rhetoric and reveals its political heritage: 'The institution of marriage was built to last . . . It was made in heaven . . . Recognized by the state . . . Sanctioned by faith and honored by the community. It has gone hand-in-hand with the rise of civilization. Marriage has survived Marxism. Outlasted Free Love. Outlived Woodstock. Toughed-out the Playboy philosophy. Even endured radical feminism.' Opponents of gay marriage link the supposed evils of same-sex love to all the other supposed evils of a secular humanist society – the ogre of sixties-style sex, drugs and rock-n-roll meets up with the shibboleth of radical feminism and encounters the Godzilla of gay marriage. Because the Right has used this as a 'wedge' issue in recent elections, gays must fight on this turf, responding to right-wing hysteria with assurances of shared 'family values' and reverence for traditional marriage. It is difficult to hear the more radical gay voices. In this truncated battle, the complicated and difficult politics of marriage evaporates in a sea of assimilationist paeans to divine coupledom.

A place at the altar: the equality argument

What are gays themselves saying about the contested institution of marriage? There are really two debates. The first is the familiar one between gays arguing for rights to marriage and heterosexuals attempting to limit legally recognised marriage to heterosexual couples. On this debate, one can take a position without much ado. The dominant and public gay argument is one of equality: how can one justify denying one group of people access to a practice, simply on the basis of sexual preference? That marriage rights would confer benefits – both social and economic – to many lesbians and gays is undeniable. Given the structure of our social and legal system (including our tax system, inheritance laws, health benefits and responsibilities, childcare and custody and parenting issues, to name just a few), it is understandable that many gay couples desire the same rights and responsibilities, benefits and assumptions, that married heterosexuals receive. Numerous writers have spelled out the financial and legal ramifications and argue that gay access to marriage is not only just and fair, but would confer tangible benefits that far outweigh additional responsibilities or burdens (Chambers 2000).

This argument is persuasive and important. However, there is a more complex issue that often gets ignored in the media, and that is the differences among gays *themselves* over marriage. The rest of this chapter will engage in a much more critical analysis of gay *desire* to join such dubious institutions, and of the ideological positions and cultural assumptions that surround such desire. No one – gay or straight – is born with some inherent desire to throw themselves on the altar, pledging fidelity to one true love and filing joint income taxes. No gene for that. So gay desire to marry must be interrogated, its seeming transparency compromised in order to reveal the complex of cultural and political imaginings that have produced a moment such as this.

To tame the wild beast: gay marriage as antidote

Many gays, such as conservative writer and former editor of the *New Republic* Andrew Sullivan, strongly believe that the right to marry is crucial to the 'maturity' of the gay movement. Writing in 1989, Sullivan argues against domestic partnerships and for legalising gay marriage. He is wary of the legal ramifications of domestic partnerships (who qualifies?) but is even more concerned that the concept undermines the centrality and hegemony of the marriage institution, arguing that 'Society has good reason to extend legal advantages to heterosexuals who choose the formal sanction of marriage over simply living together' (1989: 20). His argument, like that of many other conservative gays, is a familiar and vaguely Victorian one: marriage tames and civilises the wild beast that is Man. Without it, we would be awash in a sea of sexual depravity, flitting madly about from partner to partner, never tending to the business of the day. Like his 'family values' counterparts on the Christian right, Sullivan sees marriage as the 'anchor . . . in the chaos of sex and relationships to which we are all prone' (1989: 20).

Sullivan's arguments for marriage are framed within an understanding of the gay movement that interprets the 'Stonewall generation' as washed-out radicals, too blinded by their own perverse desire for 'liberation' to grow up and assimilate. But brave young souls like himself have reckoned with this immaturity and now agree that 'a need to rebel has quietly ceded to a desire to belong' (1989: 20). More recently, Sullivan has testified before the House Judiciary subcommittee hearings on the Defense of Marriage Act, arguing that to be in favour of same-sex marriage is to be very pro-family, pro-stability, pro-monogamy and pro-responsibility. His is, as he himself admits, a conservative argument for gay marriage, a claim that same-sex marriage will have two beneficent outcomes: forcing homosexuals into more 'committed' and monogamous relationships, and reinforcing the centrality and dominance of marriage as the primary social unit.

While heterosexual commentators give credence to the anti-marriage position, they too often end up arguing that gays should be allowed to marry in order to encourage 'harmony and stability' and in order to 'serve the common good' (Yardley 1996). Even conservative columnists such as Clarence Page support gay marriage, for the same reasons conservative *gays* do: it helps support those gays who are 'law-abiding, productive and well-educated' and who 'go to church' and believe in 'family values' (Page 1996). Gays will honour the institution and, after all, there is 'a compelling social interest and arguably a state interest in encouraging homosexuals to settle down in stable, monogamous, responsible and spiritually fulfilling relationships' (Page 1996).

Georgetown University law professor William Eskridge published a more sophisticated and nuanced treatise on gay marriage that unfortunately and perhaps unwittingly echoes the Sullivan argument. Eskridge supports Sullivan's argument about the 'civilising' influence of marriage on gay men in particular, men whose wanton promiscuity needs to be tamed (1996: 78). Eskridge also joins Sullivan in framing the argument around a very particular and truncated historical narrative. Eerily like mainstream heterosexual stories of gay life, Eskridge creates a history of radical gay activists and sexual liberationists giving way to commitment-bound, home-owning, AIDS-fearing 'guppies' for whom marriage is the bright light at the end of the tunnel. Not only does this falsely paint a picture of the demise of gay radicalism (it is still alive and well), it also completely ignores the reality of non-white, poor, working-class gays – the majority of course. So marriage will civilise nasty promiscuous gay men (and what of lesbians?) and, in so doing, will make them more 'acceptable' (his language) to straights. Like Sullivan,

Eskridge argues for marriage over domestic partnership, because 'most lesbians and gay men want something more than domestic partnership; they want to be in a committed relationship at some point in their lifetime' (1996: 78). For these gay men, marriage is the *real* sign of a 'committed relationship'. In making his argument for gay marriage as 'pro-family', Eskridge unintentionally joins in the chorus of single-mother-bashing that has characterised the 'family values' debate since Dan Quayle let fly at Murphy Brown, claiming that 'some studies have found that children of lesbian couples are better adjusted than children of single heterosexual mothers, presumably because there are two parents in the household. If this finding can be generalized, it yields the ironic point that state prohibitions against same-sex marriages may be antifamily and antichildren' (1996: 13). So, in arguing that gay marriage promotes a sound environment for raising children, Eskridge falls into the worst sort of conservative assumptions of two-parent 'stability' over just about anything else.

In this conservative argument for gay marriage, there is an implicit and often explicit denigration of radical attempts to challenge marriage and the family. During the early days of both the women's movement and the gay movement, a critique of the family and marriage was integral to a critique of patriarchy and heterosexism. The Gay Liberation Front made a statement in 1969, right after Stonewall, that was crystal clear in its denunciation of marriage: 'We expose the institution of marriage as one of the most insidious and basic sustainers of the system' (cited in Eskridge 1996: 53). For writers like Eskridge, Sullivan and Bruce Bawers (and, one might add, most heterosexuals) this kind of statement is one they would like to forget. For them it is a remnant of an 'extremist' and liberationist past that must be transcended if gays are to enter fully into mainstream society and take their rightful place alongside Mr and Mrs Cleaver. But for many others, these are glorious statements of which we are proud. They indicate a thoughtful and thoroughgoing critique of social institutions that have played a serious role in the subjugation of women and the enforcement of heterosexuality. To be liberated from these institutions – and then perhaps to create new and sturdier ones – seems a worthy and ethical goal. For if marriage itself reinforces structural inequalities within families, it also 'privileges' state-regulated long-term pairing over other forms of intimacy and connectedness. Many in the gay movement – like their counterparts in the women's movement – have been critical of marriage not only for its gender inequity and history of violence, but for the ways it *devalues* other ways of being sexual, loving and nurturing.

If gays succeed in sanctifying the couple as the primary social unit, the one that gets financial and legal benefits, does that set up a hierarchy of intimacy that replicates the heterosexual one, rather than challenging or altering it? Gay marriage might grant visibility and 'acceptance' to gay marrieds, but it will not necessarily challenge homophobia or the nuclear family. Indeed, it might demonise non-married gays as the 'bad gays', uncivilised, promiscuous, irresponsible, while embracing the 'good gays' who settle down and get married. Participation in this institution not only assimilates us into the dominant heterosexist way of relating, but gives further credence to an institution that has been built on the backs of sexism and heterosexism.

While there is no measurable correlation between desire to marry and desire to assimilate, testimonies and anecdotal evidence suggest that many gays who desire marriage ceremonies are precisely those gays most interested in demonstrating their essential sameness with heterosexuals. A piece in the *Washington Post* entitled 'Every girl's dream' describes the ceremony of two women ('On this untraditional wedding day, the traditional jitters and the traditional tears'). Like all narratives of gay mimesis, the article draws you in by describing the couple the morning before the wedding, like any other couple, then hits you with the bombshell: 'Angela is a bride. So is her fiancée' (Blumenfeld 1996: 1). Parents comment on how it is just like a 'regular wedding' and bride Elise expresses her desire to do it exactly like the 'real people'. The 'brides' observe a vow of celibacy the week prior to the 'wedding' and the whole event is recounted in loving and supportive detail. Is the dream of a seamless inclusion really so foolproof?

If, as many have argued, gay rights and women's rights are intertwined, then any gay argument for marriage that ignores or downplays the relationship of the marriage institution to institutionalised male dominance is problematic at best. Indeed, in recent years we have seen a restigmatising of single women and single mothers – portrayed either as pathetically lonely career gals gone sour (*Ally McBeal, Sex in the City*) or as the cancer in the body of domesticity, creating social havoc through reckless child-rearing and neglectful daycare. While feminists pushed legislation to make it easier to leave marriages, the push now is to make it more difficult, through challenges to no-fault divorce and a rise in fundamentalist 'covenant marriages'. If feminists are right – that marriage is one of the cornerstones of the patriarchal family and a central site for the reproduction of gendered ideologies and behaviours – then gay inclusion must be examined through that feminist lens. In other words, gay access to marriage must be understood in terms of both sexual exclusion *and* gender domination.

If granted inclusion in the marriage club, will gays and lesbians be pressured to marry like their heterosexual counterparts? Marriage is hardly a choice (Polikoff 1996). Like its partner in crime, heterosexuality, marriage is largely *compulsory*: if the economic benefits don't get you, the social ones surely will. The institution of marriage is inextricably tied to the heterosexual nuclear family, and to the merger of parenting and partnering, intimacy and financial interdependency, that is so central to our truncated vision of 'family'. Marriage is not an isolated institution, nor some innate desire. Lesbians and gays should do all they can to dismantle those conflations and to continue to envision and enact ways of caring and loving that reinvent family, intimacy, parenting. Working to end marriage as a legal institution, and to provide instead meaningful social and financial supports for relations of dependency and need, would do much more to challenge the noxious politics of family values than getting married ourselves.

Familiar families: the 'gayby' boom and family values

For many lesbians and gays, certainly those of the pre-Stonewall era, gayness itself seemed to close off the possibility of having children. Gayness seemed so outside of the realm of family that not being able to have children appeared the inevitable price to pay for a life on the margins. In earlier times, then, most gay people had children within heterosexual relationships, relationships in which they often hid their desires and led painful double lives. In story after story of older gays, one of the constant refrains has to do with children and family. The stress of coming out to parents was exacerbated by a recognition that the parent would be experiencing the loss not only of the presumed heterosexual son/daughter, but of the prospect of grandchildren as well. Parents often report this as one of their biggest fears upon hearing that their child is gay: assuming that gayness disenables reproduction.

Earlier, more pathologising renderings of homosexuality clearly marked gays as bad candidates for parenthood. If gayness was thought of as arrested development (as in much of psychoanalytic theory) then how could gays be parents? If gayness was thought of as inherited disease, then it might be transferred to progeny. If gayness was understood as predatory and inclined towards conversion, then kids would be forced into 'the life' by their recruiting parents. There were no cultural role models, no familial portraits of gays and lesbians, no inkling in the vast social landscape that it could be done.

Let's be clear: lesbians and gays have always had children. What we are witnessing now, though, is the growing phenomenon of lesbians and, to a lesser extent, gay men, having children *as gay people*, outside the conventions of heterosexuality and marriage. There have always been gay people who have been out enough – and brave enough – to live their lives the way they wanted to, including having children. The current gayby boom, however, seems to be the result of a confluence of factors: the availability of sperm banks and other reproductive technology, the growth of the lesbian and gay movement, and the emergence of couples and individuals who never were 'in' the closet and never had to extricate themselves from straight relationships, families, marriages. Gay parents are now a visible, present force to be reckoned with, forming organisations and support groups, participating in PTAs and Little Leagues.

In the midst of all the hype about the gayby boom and the happy stories of gay parenting, it is important to remember that children are still routinely taken away from parents simply because the parent is gay. The celebrated Virginia case of Sharon Bottoms is typical. A mother – living with another woman – has to undergo a custody battle with *her* mother, who claims her lesbianism constitutes her an 'unfit' mother. The court agrees, awarding custody to the grandmother solely on the basis of the mother's sexuality.

The National Center for Lesbian Rights, Lambda Legal Defense Fund and other gay legal organisations regularly defend mothers and fathers in custody cases, around visitation rights and in second-parent adoptions. Gay women are routinely denied access to alternative insemination and both lesbians and gay men are routinely turned down in attempts to foster and adopt. Legal victories are often fleeting and can be reversed at a moment's notice.

And a white picket fence: selling gay sameness

Given heterosexual mistreatment of gay parents, what remain surprising are the narratives by both gays and straights that relegate this mistreatment to a sidebar while focusing on the overwhelming 'truth' of assimilated sameness. In article after article on gays with children, the reader is presented with strikingly similar formats. Articles typically go something like this: 'Sunshine streams into the kitchen as a small, tow-headed boy and his parents bite into breakfast muffins rich with cherries from their backyard orchard in Cockeysville, Md. It's a Kodak moment of the '90's: Dad, Daddy and Duncan' (Smith 1995). In itself, there is nothing so terribly wrong with the story of Duncan: the lives of gay families often do look much the same as the lives of straight families. Kids have to be fed, diapered, bathed, loved, taught, bundled off to school, disciplined, nurtured. Barney rules, wherever you go. Yet the power of such family narratives is indisputable. Wolkowitz (this volume), for instance, describes how they operate to assimilate and neutralise even the conflicts and horrors of atomic weapons, in the autobiographies of women married to Manhattan Project scientists. And in the context of structural discrimination, things take on a different hue. Duncan is – of course – like every other kid. But he is a kid who will have to face homophobic comments (and perhaps worse) from other kids, parents, schoolteachers. He will rarely see his life depicted in textbooks and teaching aids, much less on TV. His parents do not have the same rights as other parents; they can lose jobs, be denied housing, not be promoted. He can even be removed from his parents because of their sexual orientation. In addition, it just might be the case that his parents don't *want* their lives to look like that of the Cleavers. Perhaps they want to build *new* kinds of families with *different* kinds of values.

Finally, gay parents are visible and are not made out to be lurking demons and perverts. What could be wrong with this? When the media make gays 'safe' for American cultural consumption, are they not confining gays to a new kind of closet and denying the realities of homophobia? In 'reducing' homophobia through assimilation there is a danger of making homosexuality itself invisible again – 'straight, with a twist'. Aside from the obvious and tedious attacks by the right, denouncing gay parents as immoral and dangers to the very concept of family, most reportage is supportive and steers clear of overt bigotry. What the articles do share is an almost identical narrative structure. In dozens if not hundreds of pieces on gay families the writers could be interchangeable such is the continuity of style and substance. Here are some more samples:

> To look at her, Alanna Gabrielle Handler seems an altogether conventional baby. Just 14 weeks old, she scrunches her tiny face and inspires the usual oohs and ahhs. The nursery in her family's Van Nuys apartment is pastel and girlish and graced with a banner proclaiming, 'Welcome Alanna – Grandma and Grandpa'. But Alanna is not a typical infant. She was not conceived the traditional way and her parents are not a conventional couple – or should we say trio? No, Alanna is different. She is a tribute to lesbian romance and a product of artificial insemination, a baby whose very existence challenges traditional views of nature and family. And for the gay rights movement, she is a tiny bundle of hope.
>
> (Harris 1991)

> Four-year-old Trevor wants to touch the ceiling. He leaps, grunts and tries to climb the wall, but soon figures out he's not going to get there on his own. 'If you put me on your shoulders, I can touch the ceiling', he tells his dad. Dad is dubious – but a good sport. The shouldering is successful. But the pair are still inches away from their destination. Enter Dad-dy. He lifts his son easily onto his taller shoulders and raises the little boy's arms. Mission accomplished. Innocent of the social implications of being the adopted son of gay parents, Trevor is quite content to have two fathers . . . In all but one respect, they are the classic American family. The couple say that despite what stereotypes might suggest about a male child raised by gay men, Trevor is 'all boy'. He loves trucks, guns, sports and playing in the dirt, and wants to be a policeman.
>
> (Loebs 1995)

When mainstream narratives aren't extolling the sameness of homosexual family life, they are concerned with how children of gay parents will reckon with their own sexuality. A number of articles raise the issue of whether children raised by gay parents will themselves be gay or otherwise 'do worse' than other kids. To counter hetero fears of a bumper crop of gay kids emerging from the gayby boom, gay researchers have argued that children of gay parents are 'no worse' off than kids of hetero parents: 'children born to or adopted by lesbians are psychologically healthy' (Tuller 1992). But fears of queer parents producing queer kids persist, and reporters feel compelled to comment on 'conflicting evidence' such as a 1986 study of thirty-four gay households that indicated that the children became homosexual or bisexual

15 per cent of the time; and a 1990 study that found that 16 per cent of the daughters of lesbian mothers identified themselves as lesbian. One writer sees these findings as 'worst-case scenarios', but is relieved to note that 'other studies come up with figures below ten per cent for children of gays and lesbians' (Latz Griffin 1992). This kind of discourse implies a 'natural' desire to raise children as heterosexual and figures gayness in kids raised by gays as a 'worst-case scenario'. Like the discourse that argues children of single parents fare 'as well' as children of two-parent households, it inadvertently lends itself to a reassertion of the centrality and desirability of heterosexuality and dual parenting.

And baby makes . . . two: one mother's story

As I entered the growing ranks of lesbian mothers, I was forced to reckon with the ways in which alternative families elicit the most thoroughgoing heterosexual fear. I want to raise my daughter to believe that families come in many forms, that two parents are not necessary and that couples of the same gender or single parents may provide all the 'role models' needed for healthy development. I try to raise her in a community of like-minded people and, in doing so, to break the hold that the 'Cleaver Family' model still has on our cultural imagination. Even for less politically minded gay parents, the choice to raise a child must entail a challenge to many accepted notions of family life and family formation. Times certainly have changed in this regard, and my experience of lesbian motherhood is, I believe, illustrative of some transformations and issues both between straights and gays and within the gay community itself.

I will never forget the time I brought my daughter – barely four months old – to a Kol Nidre service at the local lesbian and gay synagogue. She was dressed in her hippest outfit (leopard print pants and top with matching cap) and all eyes were upon her. From the beginning of the service, as we milled about the church (borrowed for the occasion), to the end schmoozing outside on the steps, I felt suffused – almost overwhelmed – by the warmth and beloved attention that came Emma's way. Now, I could attribute this to her exceptional beauty and charm, but – as a wee infant – her delightful manner had yet to emerge. Something was certainly going on. As hands reached out to touch her hair softly and the line formed for the post-service viewing, I was struck by the delight my community seemed to have in this child. Now most people do coo and chuckle over a cute baby. And God knows my daughter is cute. But the response to Emma seemed much more engaged and deliberate – as if to acknowledge our disenfranchisement from this option and to celebrate it at long last. An elderly heterosexual couple came up to talk with me, tears in their eyes. Their son had recently died of AIDS – he had been a member of this congregation. They wanted to thank me for bringing Emma, for having Emma. An older lesbian approached me and talked to me about 'the old days' when it was simply assumed that gay people did not parent, at least not as gay people. Her regrets were clear, even as she talked about her recent decision to attempt adoption. A thirtysomething couple approached me for info, comparing notes on sperm banks and pondering the possibility of play groups in the future. This is only one event among many and Kol Nidre is already an overweighted holiday, filled as it is with memories of those gone and the mournful tones of the cantor's invocation of Kaddish. But I was to find events like this repeated and repeated over the course of Emma's young life, as she was welcomed into the world by a newly awakened gay community. In Provincetown, the lesbian moms banded together on a section of Herring Cove, staking out baby territory amidst the friendly hordes of topless young women. In demonstrations and Pride Days, babies figure prominently, adorned with appropriate bumper stickers affixed to their overburdened strollers. And everywhere, everywhere questions. How did you do it? Did you go to a doctor? What sperm bank did you use? Did you tell them you were a lesbian? Did they turn you down? Did you experience hostility or discrimination? How did you pick the donor? What was the hospital scene like? What are you going to tell her? Many of these discussions were like any others around pregnancy and birth. But others were particular to this time and place, to this situation, to lesbians choosing children. My particular situation is perhaps unique (and perhaps not) but it does raise some important questions for how we think about family. For me, having a child was never an attempt to replicate heterosexual parenting. Because I came from a progressive family and was raised in an era of possibilities, it never occurred to me that being a lesbian would stop me having children. I was simply waiting for the right time. While more and more women are planning when and if to have children, the deliberation that goes into lesbian motherhood by choice is profound. Not dependent on the 'right man' to turn up, lesbians choosing children call their own shots, in a context where lesbian mothers still produce terror, anger, discrimination. So they make the choice with the knowledge of the hardship that will likely ensue.

Curiously, my pregnancy – and later my child – often made me invisible as a lesbian. Heterosexuals – and some gay people – wrongly assumed I was straight because of the belly pushing out in front or the diaper bag over my shoulder. A colleague looked at me quizzically and wondered if I had 'intended' to get pregnant. In disbelief I told her I just got drunk and had my way with a bunch of sailors and forgot to use birth control. So unable was she to reckon with my lesbianism and my pregnancy simultaneously, that one had to disappear and since my belly wasn't going anywhere . . . I simply didn't fit into her mainstream narrative of parenting. While this type of homophobia increased, other forms relented. As I became more recognisable to my colleagues as a woman (real women have babies, therefore I must be a woman, even if I was a lesbian – not a woman), their discomfort with my homosexuality decreased, but not for the 'right' reasons. Simply, they now *recognised* me – a pregnant woman – and that familiarity made me more accessible.

This new 'tolerance' is problematic; does it help demarcate two separate classes of gay people – those acceptable to straights through their assumption of presumably straight practices, and those unacceptable through their insistence on 'doing it their way'? Does it avoid reckoning with the real problem – the homophobia of straights? Indeed, I often feel profoundly misunderstood as a lesbian mother. I am no less radical than I was before Emma. I don't want my family 'compared' to heterosexual nuclear families and I'm angered by well-meaning studies that set out to prove that children of gay parents are 'no worse off' than children of straight parents. And I'm not really sure I see my family simply as a benign alternative in a sea of welling diversity. I see it in more grandiose terms, as forging intimacy and connection in ways that will enhance the life of the child and of those she comes in contact with. By separating parenting from socially enforced rules of partnering, I believe there are possibilities for familial constructions that are less mired in the violence, inequality and longing that characterise so many families.

Beyond inclusion: rethinking intimacy, sex, community

Anthropologist Kath Weston (1991) and others have written convincingly of the ways in which lesbians and gay men, so often disenfranchised from their families of origin, have created 'families of choice' that serve many of the personal, emotional and social functions of more traditional familial formations. In creating vast and intricate networks of friends and lovers, ex-lovers and their partners and friends, gay people have forged intimacies and connections that often seem more lasting and durable than the tenuous family of origin. Weston argues that these 'families of choice' are not merely replicas of heterosexual families but create new forms of mutual responsibility, outside the typically gendered roles inhabited by women and men in heterosexual families.

This is not a banal argument for diversity of familial forms. It is about advocating models of love, support and intimacy that actively dethrone the sexual/familial couple and present instead ever-expanding webs of relationships – ex-lovers, their partners or lovers, old friends, blood kin. Indeed, one can see this as a gay gift to the bankrupt models of middle-class white heterosexuality that 'tend to isolate couples from their larger families and sometimes from friends – especially if they are ex-lovers' (Browning 1997: 133).

Gay family issues will, I believe, be the last holdout in the battle for gay and lesbian rights. As much as straights and many gays might want to argue that there is 'no difference' between the way gays create families and the way heterosexuals do, it is hard to believe that the structures of exclusion and discrimination that surround gay life will not in some way impact gay family life. Embedded institutions are funny things. True, no institution is impenetrable or completely inelastic to change. Nevertheless, powerful and hierarchical ones such as the military or marriage are not easily altered. Is it possible that the creation of gay families through marriage or commitment ceremonies is the nail in the assimilationist coffin, linking gays irrevocably with mainstream heterosexuality? Or do these moves shake up heterosexual dominance like nothing else, permanently altering the very definition of family? If gays marry from within the dominant heterosexual frameworks, invoking dangerous ideologies of familialism, faith and fidelity, the prospect of internal combustion fizzles out. If gays claim the right to parent based on their similarity to heterosexuals, we just may find our suburbs expanding to include June and June Cleaver. Obviously, not all gay parents are hetero clones, but those are the only gay parents we see in the news. These pervasive narratives of sameness could serve to keep the brass ring of gay liberation out of reach as gays settle for simple acceptance and a ride on the family merry-go-round. I'd much rather see a utopian future of unmarried love and lust – for our heterosexual brothers and sisters too – than a dystopian future where marriage and familialism continue to trump values of community and care.

Notes

1 It is ironic that one of the coded ways gays have of acknowledging other gays is to ask if they 'are family'.
2 For a more thorough account of the explosion of gay visibility, read my forthcoming book *All the Rage: The Story of Gay Visibility in America* (Walters 2001).
3 According to statistics from the Human Rights Campaign (garnered from the FBI), hate crimes against lesbians and gays (or those perceived as lesbian or gay) increased to 14 per cent of the total of all reported hate crimes in 1997, up from 11.6 per cent in 1996. In addition, attacks against lesbians and gays are becoming more violent, indicated most dramatically by the brutal murder of Wyoming gay student Matthew Shepard in October 1998.
4 The construction of gays as congenitally unable to negotiate the vicissitudes of adulthood (read marriage and kids) is a common theme not only in TV neo-liberal discourse, but in gay conservative discourse as well. See particularly Sullivan (1997) and Bawer (1996).

Portions of this chapter are published as 'Take my domestic partner, please: gays and marriage in the age of the visible', in R. Reimann and M. Bernstein (eds) *Queer Families, Queer Politics: Challenging Culture and Society*, New York: Columbia University Press, 2001.

References

Bawer, B. (ed.) (1996) *Beyond Queer: Challenging Gay Left Orthodoxy*, New York: Free Press.
Blumenfeld, L. (1996) 'Every girl's dream', *The Washington Post* 20 November: D1–2.
Browning, F. (1997) 'Why marry?', in A. Sullivan (ed.) *Same-sex Marriage: Pro and Con*, New York: Vintage.
Chambers, D. (2000) 'What if? The legal consequences of marriage in the United States today and the legal needs of lesbian and gay male couples', in R. Reimann

and M. Bernstein (eds) *Queer Families, Queer Politics: Challenging Culture and the State*, New York: Columbia University Press.

Eskridge, W. N. (1996) *The Case for Same-sex Marriage: From Sexual Liberty to Civilised Commitment*, New York: Free Press.

Harris, S. (1991) '2 moms or 2 dads – and a baby', *Los Angeles Times* 20 October: A1.

Latz Griffin, J. (1992) 'The gay baby boom', *Chicago Tribune* 3 September: C1.

Loebs, C. (1995) 'Gay partners with children: adoption a challenge in climate of intolerance, legal ambiguities', *The Arizona Republic* 27 July: 1.

Page, C. (1996) 'Same-sex marriages strengthen the institution, not demonise it', *The Phoenix Gazette* 23 May: B5.

Polikoff, N. (1996) 'Marriage as choice? Since when?', *Gay Community News* 24, 3–4: 26–7.

Smith, L. (1995) 'Gay parents have typical worries', *Baltimore Sun* 23 July: 11E.

Sullivan, A. (1989) 'Here comes the groom', *New Republic* August: 20.

—— (ed.) (1997) *Same-sex Marriage: Pro and Con*, New York: Vintage.

Tuller, D. (1992) 'Lesbian families – study shows healthy kids', *San Francisco Chronicle* 23 November: A13.

Walters, S. (2001) 'Take my domestic partner, please: gays and marriage in the age of the visible', in R. Reimann and M. Bernstein (eds) *Queer Families, Queer Politics: Challenging Culture and Society*, New York: Columbia University Press.

Weston, K. (1991) *Families We Choose: Lesbians, Gays, Kinship*, New York: Columbia University Press.

Yardley, J. (1996) 'The march of time', *The Washington Post* 9 December: E2.

4 Narratives as bad faith

Ian Craib

Introduction

Narratives are stories. It is now a commonplace to start this sort of discussion by saying that human beings are storytelling creatures: we tell each other stories of greater or lesser complexity and for all sorts of purposes. Practically every statement that we produce about ourselves and the world is, by definition, part of a narrative, a linking of different things together in some sort of order. I recently heard a well known empirical social scientist talking about the development of 'causal narratives' linking social class and health where once the term 'causal explanation' might have been used. And 'narrative' is not a simple term: some people in the academic world are critical of 'meta-narratives' which are supposedly attempts to explain everything (Lyotard 1984). Once meta-narratives would have been called theories and philosophies, and debate between them would have provided the stuff of intellectual life, but we now find a meta-narrative which disputes the worth of meta-narratives and claims that each narrative is of equal worth. One might think that a concept which brings together the world religions, all of Western philosophy, large-scale statistical correlations in the social sciences, every biography and autobiography that's ever been written, every work of fiction and my account of losing a pet cat obscures more than it illuminates.

Narratives are stories and stories are not simple. My mother told, or rather read, me stories when I was little, and she accused me of telling stories when (usually with good reason) she doubted the veracity of what I was telling her. In all this there is a distinction between stories which are more or less true and those which are not and a question about whether the distinction matters. It might be that it is not a matter of the truth value of a narrative but something about its structure. McAdams (1993) for example, employing some Jungian ideas, argues that what is important for our psychological lives is that we construct myths or myth-based stories for ourselves and this performs a healing function – the myth is a psychological requirement and a psychological fact.

In this chapter, I want to question certain conceptions of narrative and to identify what I shall call 'bad faith' narratives. In the first half I shall question what I consider to be a naïve psychological conception of narrative – that of Jerome Bruner – and argue that there is a complexity to the way we tell ourselves stories that means that we cannot treat them in the way he wishes to treat them. We need to distinguish those that are closer to an external reality and those that are further from it. In the second part I want to use a sociological account of emotions to show the way in which social science might supply bad faith narratives.

Narratives and life

Jerome Bruner (1987) is a prime mover of our interest in narratives and typically modest in his claims, talking about the way in which different narratives can reinforce each other to give us an account nearer to what might be the truth. Bruner takes narrative structures as providing a key both to wider cultures and to individual lives. He adopts what has become an increasingly popular approach that he calls 'constructivist' but perhaps now might be called 'constructionist' or 'social constructionist': when I tell my story it is an 'interpretive feat', a construction of my life. There is no simple and unproblematic record of my life: 'there is no such thing psychologically as life itself' (Bruner 1987: 13). He goes on to talk about the dependence of these constructions on cultural conventions and language usage. Through these conventions and usages our culture provides us with ways of telling stories about ourselves and the stories *are* our lives, we become the stories we tell about ourselves. Narrative structures bind us into our culture and enable us to communicate our lives to others around us; in a strong sense he seems to think these structures produce our lives.

Bruner's paper is seminal and one can go off from it in all sorts of creative directions. This chapter will first move towards and *into* the individual and the telling of stories about oneself not only to other people but to oneself. Summing up his argument at the end, Bruner writes: 'I have argued that a life as led is inseparable from a life as told – or, more bluntly, a life is not "how it was" but how it is interpreted and reinterpreted, told and retold: Freud's *psychic reality*' (Bruner 1987: 33). I want to suggest that in this respect – and perhaps only in this respect – my mother may have been a better psychologist than Bruner for she could tell the difference between a life as lived and a life as told. In fact I think we all have an intuitive sense of this difference, otherwise life itself would become impossible since we could never know or suspect when people (including ourselves) were lying by commission or omission, trying to inform or persuade or dictate or whatever. These are judgements which I suggest we make all the time. Narratives are not sacred: they can be judged as being more or less true or false, more or less self-serving, and more or less many other things. I also want to argue that Freud's notion of psychic reality and of external reality itself is more complex than is implied in Bruner's statement and that there is a rooting of our narratives, even if only minimally, in a reality external to the narrative.

Bad faith

Jean-Paul Sartre and Sigmund Freud are not obvious bedfellows. In *Being and Nothingness* (1957) Sartre develops a phenomenology of consciousness that does not allow for any internal structures or other content. Consciousness is a pure nothingness, nothing more than a relation to the world. In the development of Sartre's ethical position, 'bad faith' is a denial of this situation. Because consciousness is a space, the nothingness between myself and the outside world, I can never be seen as determined by that world. I am condemned to freedom. There is always a choice in how I live my relationship to the world even if that world itself, including my body, is under another's control. Even if I am chained in a dungeon and left to die, there is a sense in which I choose how to live my death. At first glance this is a radical view of human freedom, very different from Freud's version of human beings subjected to a conflict between our drives and the demands of the outer world, decentred beings never clear about what we are doing and what we want – ships tossed this way and that by invisible forces which we struggle, often in vain, to manage.

However there is a point where it seems to me that the two come close together. For Sartre 'bad faith' is the denial of our human being, a denial of the nothingness that separates us from the world of objects, a denial of our choice. And the choice that we deny is not necessarily made at a reflective level, the level usually studied by the social sciences, but at a pre-reflective level. Sartre is not talking about an *un*conscious but his pre-reflective level and Freud's unconscious both share the status of not being thought, although they might be reflected upon. Pre-reflective choice and unconscious drives and conflicts share the status of being open to denial. Sartre's examples of bad faith tend towards the behavioural – the waiter in a complete identification with his role, the woman refusing to acknowledge to herself that she is in the process of being seduced, people who are denying that they are not objects, denying that they are responsible for their actions; or perhaps more accurately people assuming an object status which is belied by their active assumption of it as subjects. For Freud denial is a refusal to recognise, for whatever reason, something unacceptable about oneself, a drive, an idea, a conflict, the fact of internal complexity. In both cases, whether we deny a pre-reflective choice or some aspect of our psyche, we are denying some crucial, defining feature of our humanity. I am linking these two because I think each adds to the other: one captures the internal complexity of the psyche, the other captures the sometimes residual degree of freedom we have in relation to what happens to and within us.

For Sartre bad faith is a form of internal denial, of denying to oneself that something is happening, and the happening is a choice I make. It is a refusal to recognise the choices that are open to me. In everyday life we hear and probably perform such refusals all the time: 'I can't stop and talk to you because I *have to* do x'; 'I could not have a career because I *had to* look after the children'; 'I can't spend time with my family because I *have to* work long hours to bring in the money.' Such statements deny all options.

Freud's version of denial of course is more complex and involves divisions in consciousness, but psychoanalysts often talk about *rationalisation* as a defence which seems to me to bear a distinct resemblance to bad faith. Rationalisation is the construction of a narrative which explains a particular feeling or action in such a way that my agency does not have to be considered. I might account for my difficulty in loving my own children by saying that I had a distant or absent father myself as if I were simply a link in a causal chain and I could do nothing about it.

I am suggesting that there are classes of stories that people can tell to each other which are bad faith stories in that they deny agency – stories not about what I do but about what is done to me and what I am because these things have been done to me. For Sartre this is a denial of consciousness, of the nothingness between myself and the rest of the world. For the psychoanalyst it is the denial of a complex inner reality which processes and transforms what is done to me into something (quite possibly different) that I do to other people.

What I suggest is that in everyday interaction, listening to each other's stories, we often have an intuition that some stories are intended not as communications, explorations and developments of meaning, but as attempts to close down meaning and deny agency and the possibility of change which comes with the acknowledgement of agency. If the person telling his/her story has no choice about what he/she did, then there is nothing left to be said. Sometimes, if doubt is expressed about such stories, the storyteller will repeat them again and again, determined to convince listeners that they are true. I suspect the repetition comes not from a desire to convince the listener but from a desire to convince the storyteller him- or herself. They are a sign of self-doubt: I only want to convince others when I am myself not convinced.

What the narrative does in this situation is to cover a frightening – or perhaps fright-full – experience and possibility. I could leave my children, quit my partner and my job tomorrow; I don't *have to* pay back my loans, avoid pushing that old lady in the road, keep my clothes on while giving a lecture. I can rape, torture and kill if I wish – my only concern would be to avoid discovery or punishment and why should I even want to do that? Sartre talks about the realisation of such freedom as having a 'vertiginous' effect. Bad faith narratives avoid all such considerations: they make things normal, unproblematic with the added advantage of avoiding acknowledging or feeling guilt. At the very least they keep the problems within a recognisable plot. One might suggest that in this sense all personal narratives are to some degree bad faith narratives. In this volume we can see some of these processes at work in some of the narratives in Clive Seale's chapter (death, of course, is the ultimate disrupter of narratives, not only ending my narrative, but even worse, as Sartre points out, handing it over to others). We can also see it quite vividly at work in Tommy's story in the Hollway and Jefferson chapter.

Socially acceptable bad faith stories

I will now move on to the second part of the chapter. I am suggesting that there is a parallel between the denial of responsibility and choice that Sartre calls bad faith, and the denial of inner space and unconscious processes that Freud and later psychoanalysts talk about, between bad faith and what Christopher Bollas calls 'normopathology' (Bollas 1987) – the inability to talk about anything other than the external object world. Each denies something which can be regarded as definitively human, marking the break from external causal processes and introducing something into the world which would not exist were it not for *this* specific consciousness or psyche. For Sartre it is the nothingness of human consciousness which is denied; for Freud it is the internal conflicts and transformations produced by the human unconscious and its ability to generate meanings.

Charles Taylor (1989) has commented on the ways in which instrumental thought has been prominent in modern Western conceptions of the self. I would suggest that the 'bad faith' narratives I am talking about cohere with such thinking. They are stories in which events have causes which lie in some previous external event or in the action of some original human mover that sets off a chain of connections that result in me being the sort of person I am, doing the sort of things that I do. I make no contribution to this story, I am simply its conclusion. Several decades ago Berger, Berger and Kellner (1974) pointed to the tendency to see our personalities as bureaucratic or technological systems, but I think now computers have taken over as the dominant metaphor. In any case I would suggest that the dominant instrumental strand in contemporary Western culture makes it generally unacceptable that we should see ourselves as significant contributors to our own stories, especially when they do not have a happy ending. Human stories, of course, never have a happy ending: we just die. Elaine Showalter's recent book *Hystories* (1997) shows how reluctant we are to accept psychological explanations, and therefore *human* explanations of unease, dis-ease, unhappiness, failure or other forms of suffering, and how determined the search for external causes and/or malevolent agencies can be. Evidence has accumulated since Freud's time that there can be physical manifestations of psychological processes, yet even in areas where psychotherapies are involved in treating these manifestations, clinicians still insist on prior external causes: satanic abuse, childhood abuse and recovered memories of real events, poison gases and so on. Showalter shows how focusing on the external causes and coming together with other sufferers can provide a new and successful identity to replace old miseries and failures.

My contention is that such narratives are forms of bad faith, of the denial of the psychological processes that are a vital part of our humanity. My experience as a therapist is that people who come into therapy already equipped with or looking for such narratives are crippled by the energy they expend on the search or on maintaining their belief in the narrative. Paradoxically if they can manage to accept their particular unhappiness as a part of their personality, whatever their external situations, they begin to feel less unhappy and more capable and they can turn their energy to more satisfying tasks; they can start living with a degree of personal honesty. One of my favourite metaphors offered to me by a patient (in fact by several patients at different times) is that we are dealt a hand of cards at birth, and however bad a hand it is, it is up to us to play them as well as we can. The cards don't force us to play in one way or another.

Most narratives, if they have any worth, are multi-layered metaphors (as well as related to an external reality) and one of the more intelligent contributions to the debates about child sexual abuse and recovered memories that I have come across suggests that some, but of course not all, of these stories might be read as metaphors for experiences that are current but cannot be articulated in any other way (Haaken 1996). It might be that the difficulty in accepting such ideas and looking for the 'real cause' or 'origin' is connected to a general difficulty in contemporary popular culture in allowing the imagination to have any power or effect. There is, for instance, a ready desire to reduce novels and even poetry to the biography of the author as if all that is possible is the slightly disguised recording of 'real' external events. Even people working in the area of psychological treatment, who should be most aware of psychological processes and the role of metaphor in these processes, often seem keen to look for supposed external causes.

There is a paradox here in that, whereas there is a denial of psychological causes and the power of metaphor in popular culture, we find an over-emphasis on metaphor in some forms of social science. In some areas of sociology in particular everything is narrative and no 'real life' is to be found. My position here is that we have to look in two opposite directions at the same time – at the imaginative creativity with which people tell the story of their lives and at the reality of those lives – and also at the meaning of the difference. It should be clear that both of the human sciences with which I am concerned here, sociology and psychoanalysis, can produce 'rational accounts' of people's experiences which can be taken on by the people who have those experiences as personal narratives, and more importantly as narratives which are in some sense 'bad faith' narratives. Elsewhere (Craib 1994) I have taken an apparently personal narrative of masculinity and suggested that the author turns himself into an exemplar of a particular psychoanalytic theory in which the personal actually disappears. Here I want to investigate these paradoxes by examining the sociology of the emotions.

Emotions, bad faith and the sociology of emotions

The study of emotions enables an extension of the meaning I have given to bad faith. It is difficult to acknowledge the existence of emotions and try to pretend to ourselves that we are objects; objects, to the best of our knowledge, do not experience emotions. Sartre's short study of the emotions (Sartre 1963), however, develops his phenomenology in a predictable way by emphasising their intentionality, seeing them as a magical (non- or ir-rational) attempt to change the world. If I cannot persuade you to give me something I want very much, I start crying and screaming in the hope that it will somehow achieve my goals. This view has its element of truth, perhaps corresponding with the way in which babies communicate and experience the success of their communication.

There are of course people – Bollas' 'normopaths' – who don't seem to have any great contact with their emotional life but I am assuming that human beings are emotional beings: that emoting is a part of being alive whether we are aware of it or not and that this is part and parcel of our biological existence (Darwin 1998 [1871]). We cannot but experience emotions; those who deny feeling emotions, if they are not simply lying for some purpose of their own, are refusing part of their humanity. I am also assuming that we experience a number of possibly conflicting emotions at the same time, and that emotions, against our will, seem to drive us to do things or prevent our doing them.

Another complexity which emerges from a psychoanalytic understanding is the proximity of strong but opposite emotions (Klein 1975). Feelings of destructiveness and gratitude can alternate with each other very quickly and for some people the destructiveness of intense arguments with people they love is worth it for the confirmation of love that forgiveness and restored calm can bring. Further, we always maintain a level of anxiety about the world: it might vary in intensity and we might not like it, and we might even think that it is a symptom of mental illness, but it contributes to our survival, making us look both ways before we cross the road.

Finally, in the context of my present argument, the important lesson of psychoanalysis is that we react emotionally to internal processes and objects which might be conscious or unconscious. Our emotional life is not simply a matter of reaction to external stimuli – we can draw experiences from memory which might have nothing to do with our immediate situation, and more importantly such memories and feelings might come unbidden to our consciousness. A panic attack comes, apparently, from nowhere and we find ourselves stuffing food into our mouths, buying things we don't need and creating projects that keep us busy (see Miller's (1998) description of the elderly shopper quoted in Clive Seale's contribution to this volume). Some minor incident or comment sends us flying into a destructive rage. I wake up one morning feeling joyful, one morning feeling depressed, on another I'm angry, on another suicidal and so on. Life is such that we can always find reasons for these feelings – there are always, in most lives, enough and sufficiently varied factors to 'explain' any emotion we might feel.

This is where bad faith narratives enter into the equation. Feelings are difficult to handle: they can disrupt our often tenuous equilibrium to the point where it can take hours or days or even months or years (in the case of the break-up of relationships or death) to re-establish a new level of 'normal' anxiety. Sometimes people will express their emotions in ways in which they cannot recognise them as emotions. In one therapy group I have watched two men express what seemed like an intense affection for each other (which for a long time neither could admit to) by swapping advice about the technical problems of their trades. Alternatively we tell ourselves stories about our feelings to try and make them manageable. To try to make sense of our feelings we tell ourselves stories where perhaps there is no story to be told. We look for reasons where, if there are reasons, they are too complex and contradictory to enable a story that makes sense, but most of all we tell ourselves stories to ease our anxieties.

Now there are two levels here. First there are the processes of emotional life which make up a real life and which on occasions, if not always, are too complex and contradictory and too disruptive to be grasped in a coherent way – the reality to which narratives about emotions are related. Then there is the story we try to tell about these emotional processes to ease the anxiety and internal disruption that they cause. In the stories we tell about our feelings, then, bad faith amounts, first, to the denial of agency on those occasions when we use emotions to try to get what we want from others; second, it involves the displacement of emotions into 'unemotional' talk; third, it involves the denial of the complexity and contradictoriness of these feelings; and finally it entails a denial of their occasional disruptive and overpowering strength.

Most people with some familiarity with the sociology of the emotions will be able to see how its typical analyses provide stories which hide what I have claimed to be the real flux and difficulties of living with our emotions. By way of illustration, I want to look at a long quote from a recent book on the sociology of emotions, summing up the chapter on emotion and gender:

> The discussion in this chapter has identified the meanings and dis-courses contributing to the binary opposition of the 'emotional woman' and the 'unemotional man' and the implications of these archetypes for gendered experience . . . while certain long held assumptions around gender and the emotions remain, there is evidence of a blurring of formal distinctions between hegemonic notions of masculinity and femininity . . . women are now expected to participate in the sphere of paid labour as well as engaging actively in caring activities in the home. While it may be . . . more difficult for women to achieve the ideal of the contained, autonomous self, because of their assumed inherent tendency towards emotionality, it is still expected that they aspire towards this

ideal . . . even though men may be thought to be less capable of 'opening up' and revealing their emotions in the intimate sphere . . . they are
now encouraged (and indeed expected) to have a strong emotional presence in the family and to attempt to express their emotions to intimate
others.

(Lupton 1998: 135)

This paragraph is not untypical of the way that sociologists write about
emotions and it is a long way away from the sort of emotional life I was
trying to describe earlier. In fact it is not about emotions as such but it is
about ideas about emotions, about what are supposed to be dominant ideas
of the way in which men and women are or are not emotional. It is clear that
it is the expression of emotion rather than its experience that is important,
and the only expression of emotion that seems to be valued, or even possible,
is reflective talk about feelings. Further, the emotions which are the centre of
attention are 'caring' emotions. Since this is a discussion of men and women
in a family situation, one might ask what happens to all the other feelings
that go on there. The contemporary family, whatever its form, is frequently
an isolated hothouse of intense relationships and intense emotions where the
most vital aspects of our being are brought into play; it is where we love and
hate most strongly and where, as children, we learn to love and hate from
the moment we are born, if not before. It is still, as far as I know, within
family units that we find the majority of physical and sexual assaults on
children, that we find the majority of murders taking place, and that we find
a fair amount of violence taking place. This is not to mention the day-to-day
resentments, moments of quiet despair, sullen hostility, flaring temper, and
moments of contentment and joy that make up the emotional family life
that I have experienced (in several families) and is experienced by most of
my friends.

My point here is not that Lupton is actually wrong; she uses the word
archetype but I would prefer what I believe is the more accurate 'stereotype'
and she is describing what might be changes in dominant stereotypes. Stereotypes however do not experience emotions. Narratives concerning stereotypes can, it seems to me, enable us to avoid the experience of emotion.
They are bad faith stories.

Lupton offers me a particular story that I can take up as a man: I can see
myself as the hero in a tale in which I have been denied access to my feelings
by a society that constitutes men as not experiencing or talking about feelings. From that society I learn that the expression of feelings shows vulnerability but I am also beginning learn that talk about feelings is a desirable
thing, and that if I express my vulnerability I will not be attacked for it or
laughed at or disapproved of. I rather like this story that I can tell about
myself: it gives me a chance to be a good boy – a much better chance than
those feminist stories which tell me I am by nature violent and unfeeling. If
I concentrate on this story, on my discovery and expression of my feelings, I

can for a while keep myself away from the things that trouble me. If I work really hard at it I might find supplementary stories about the way I was treated in my childhood which explain why I might feel angry or violent, or why I might find it difficult to form a lasting relationship with a woman. I can build up quite a complex story and part of telling this story is the belief that talking about feelings modifies or even gets rid of them, and leaves me closer to those I love.

This particular sociological story, with its psychodynamic underpinnings and elaborations can make sense for a long time. I can use it to hide from all sorts of complexities of experience that I find difficult. I can believe that I am gaining in self-knowledge when I am in fact hiding from it. Psychotherapy often teaches similar narratives but a major achievement in psychotherapy comes with the realisation that such stories do not work. There is no cure for our humanity and bad faith stories attempt to reduce our humanity: to reduce emotions to feelings, the things that are talked about in problem pages. Such narratives do not necessarily work, and on balance I think it is a good thing that they do not work. The emotional confusions of our lives are the source of creativity and the attempts to cope with them as directly as possible can produce unforeseen possibilities in a life; they also produce serial killers and torturers. What I think it is necessary to hold on to against the narratives I am criticising is the often incoherent height and depths of human experience and our ability to find as much of the human condition within ourselves as possible.

A colleague who read this chapter commented that my reference to the human condition was 'trite' and added 'how can the human condition not be found in humans? Or do only certain sorts of humans understand it?' Here is the beginning of a bad faith narrative about the human condition: the implication is that if it is common to everybody it's not worth talking about – a common defence against the full force of a feeling. My point is that if we accept Freud (or Sartre) we spend much time and energy telling stories that try not to recognise our condition and we are all engaged in a struggle within ourselves around the recognition of human reality.

References

Berger, B., Berger, P. and Kellner, H. (1974) *The Homeless Mind*, Harmondsworth: Penguin.

Bollas, C. (1987) *The Shadow of the Object: Psychoanalysis of the Unthought Known*, London: Free Association Books.

Bruner, J. (1987) 'Life as narrative', *Social Research* 34, 1: 11–34.

Craib, I. (1994) *The Importance of Disappointment*, London: Routledge.

Darwin, C. (1998 [1871]) *The Expression of the Emotions in Man and Animals*, London: HarperCollins.

Haaken, J. (1996) 'The recovery of memory, fantasy and desire: feminist approaches to sexual abuse and psychic trauma'. *Signs: Journal of Women, Culture and Society* 21: 1069–93.

Klein, M. (1975) *Collected Works Volume III: Envy and Gratitude and Other Works*, London: Hogarth Press.

Lupton, D. (1998) *The Emotional Self*, London: Sage.

Lyotard, J.-F. (1984) *The Post-modern Condition: A Report on Knowledge*, Minneapolis: University of Minnesota Press.

McAdams, D. P. (1993) *Stories We Live By: Personal Myths and the Making of the Self*, New York: Morrow.

Miller, D. (1998) *A Theory of Shopping*, Cambridge: Polity Press.

Sartre, J.-P. (1957) *Being and Nothingness*, London: Methuen.

——— (1963) *Sketch for a Theory of the Emotions*, London: Methuen.

Showalter, E. (1997) *Hystories: Hysterical Epidemics and Modern Culture*, London: Picador.

Taylor, C. (1989) *Sources of the Self*, Cambridge, MA: Harvard University Press.

Part II
Narrative and life history

Introduction

Molly Andrews

When asked to describe either themselves or others, most people will launch into a series of stories which they feel are somehow revelatory (Bruner 1994: 43). Sarbin (1986) identifies this as the 'narratory principle': 'human beings think, perceive, imagine and make moral choices according to narrative structures' (p. 8). We are 'storied selves' (Sarbin 1986; Rosenwald and Ochberg 1992): the activity of being human is intricately tied to the activity of telling and listening to stories. Stories are not only the way in which we come to ascribe significance to experiences we and others have had; they are one of the primary means through which we constitute our very selves.

Human beings are inherently storytellers, and it is through the activity of narration that we create meaning in our lives. Narrative organises the structure of human experience (Bruner 1991: 21); experiences acquire meaning only when they are 'fused with' stories (Proust 1968 [1919]). Activities of daily life become imbued with meaning when they are articulated in a narrative way, because only then can one locate particular actions within a specific plot (Ricoeur 1984; 1992). The implicit meaning of life is thus made explicit through narration (Widdershoven 1993: 2).

Stories are a fundamental means of communication between people; through listening to, and telling stories we learn about others as they learn about us. As we tell stories about ourselves, the experiences of our lives acquire a certain coherence. Human beings are both authors of, and actors in, self-narratives (Sarbin 1986: 19). Through our careful selection of what parts of our pasts we conjure up, we sculpt a 'narrative identity' (Widdershoven 1993: 7) for ourselves which lends a congruence to our past, present and future selves. Thus, our stories are a cornerstone of our identity.

But personal narratives not only describe experience, they give shape to that experience; narrative and self are thus inseparable (Ochs and Capps 1996: 20). Toni Morrison, in her lecture as Nobel Laureate, identifies the synergy that is the heart of personal narratives: 'Narrative is radical, creating us at the very moment it is being created' (Morrison 1994: 22). The relationship between living and telling is a dynamic one: 'individuals do not merely tell stories, after the fact, about their experiences; instead they live out their affairs in storied forms' (Ochberg 1994: 116). Life informs and is itself informed by stories (Widdershoven 1993: 2).

Personal narratives are constructed within a wider social context; they both reproduce and are produced by dominant cultural meta-narratives. While the scripts which individuals live by may resist or conform to these 'institutionalized master storylines' (Ochs and Capps 1996: 33), they will always be influenced by them. Mark Freeman's chapter lucidly argues that personal narratives are encased in larger ideological meta-narratives (Maines 1993: 34) which individuals can accept or resist. Freeman focuses on a particular meta-narrative, 'narrative foreclosure', which is dominant in many Western cultures and offers little scope for a meaningful, productive existence in old age. In this chapter, the reader witnesses individual attempts to resist these pre-scripted narratives of decline. Ultimately, such efforts to forge a life story which goes against a dominant storyline are met with varying degrees of success and failure.

We become who we are through telling stories about our lives and living the stories we tell. The self is a story which is forever being rewritten (Bruner 1994: 53). The whole of our selves is bound up in the stories we construct about our past, present and futures, for these stories constitute the fundamental linkage across our lives. In this sense, our lives are the pasts we tell ourselves (Ochs and Capps 1996: 21); through our stories, we indicate who we have been, who we are and who we wish to become.

Zdenek Konopasek, in his chapter describing an experiment in collective autobiography with which he and a small group of Czech colleagues have been involved, recollects the dynamic relationship which exists between writing about one's life and the attempt to live in consonance with what one has written. Konopasek argues that the use of biographical method allowed him and his colleagues to resist the dominant discourse of 'the great transformation' of post-communist countries. While many statistical studies have reported on the grand sweeping changes which have been occasioned by the end of communism, this model did not match their own experiences nor those of people they knew, and so it was that they launched upon an open-ended project of collective autobiography. This collaborative effort adopts a hermeneutic approach to life story writing, incorporating the interpretations of others into the telling and retelling of personal experience. Konopasek's chapter is the only one in this section in which the author is both narrator and protagonist of the story he tells, and he considers the effects that constructing his personal narrative had on his own subsequent behaviour. While academics often interpret others' interpretations of their lives (Riessman 1993: 5), rarely do they subject their own narrations to such scrutiny. The project reported here is a bold attempt to 'conceptualize sociology narratively' (Maines 1993: 32), explicitly addressing what sociologists 'do to and with their and other people's narratives' (Maines 1993: 17).

Carol Wolkowitz's chapter on the Manhattan Project makes a contrasting point to that of Konopasek. As the structures of stories are immediately familiar to all, the act of converting experience into narrative can also have the effect of normalising that which is extraordinary. In this chapter, we hear very recognisable self-narratives about hearth and home as experienced by women whose daily lives were lived within the context of the making of the atom bomb. So engaged are we as readers with the stories these women tell, that it is quite possible to lose sight of the context of these normative family narratives. What is most fascinating about these narratives is that which has been left out. Although the bomb lies at the centre of all that is recounted – and indeed it is this connection which attracts the reader – on the rare occasions that it is explicitly mentioned, it is only in passing and not as an event of central concern in and of itself. Wolkowitz alerts us to the limitations of decontextualised narrative, emphasising that personal experiences are always and only part of a larger social nexus.

In 'Betrayals, trauma and self-redemption?' Tom Wengraf contrasts the experiences of two coal miners who become laid off from work. Using the 'biographical-interpretive method' developed by SOSTRIS which emphasises the distinction between the 'lived life' and the 'told story', Wengraf argues that the critical difference between these men is not the content of their experiences, but rather their interpretations of them. Isak Dinesen once said, 'All sorrows can be borne if we can put them into a story' (quoted in Riessman 1993: 4). The question here is not whether the very challenging experience of unemployment can be put into a story – both men are able to accomplish this – but rather into which story it is inserted. Through narrative, individuals 'situate particular events against a larger horizon' (Ochs and Capps 1996: 30). This chapter illustrates the power and consequences of emplotment.

In this part, narrative is used as both theory and method. Theoretically, all of the chapters adopt the perspective that the stories which individuals (Wengraf and Freeman) and groups of individuals (Wolkowitz and Konopasek) tell about their lives are significant. Through the use of personal narrative, the extraordinary is transformed into the ordinary (Wolkowitz), critical life events either motivate or paralyse (Wengraf), and people are suffocated by or mount resistance to dominant cultural meta-narratives (Freeman and Konopasek). But this common theoretical orientation across chapters is accompanied by a wide diversity of methodology. How do we as researchers uncover these stories? Wengraf employs the biographical interpretive method, Wolkowitz analyses written documents, Freeman combines interview material with literary analysis, and autobiography – usually regarded as the domain of individuals – is transformed into a social product by Konopasek and his colleagues, in their innovative collective autobiography.

Aldous Huxley once commented that experience is not what happens to you, but how you understand what happens to you (quoted in Kegan 1984). The way in which we make sense of our lives is through the stories we tell. People create their personal narratives as they are created by them, and it is the work of narrative researchers to narrate the narrations of others. In the chapters which follow, the reader is presented with different stories about the process and function of emplotment in the lives of narrators.

References

Bruner, J. (1991) 'The narrative construction of reality', *Critical Inquiry* 18, 1: 1–21.
—— (1994) 'The "remembered" self', in U. Neisser and R. Fivush (eds) *The Remembering Self: Construction and Accuracy in the Self-narrative*, Cambridge: Cambridge University Press.
Kegan, R. (1984) *The Evolving Self*, Cambridge, MA: Harvard University Press.
Maines, D. (1993) 'Narrative's moment and sociology's phenomena: toward a narrative sociology', *The Sociological Quarterly* 34, 1: 17–38.
Morrison, T. (1994) *The Nobel Lecture in Literature, 1993*, New York: Knopf.
Ochberg, R. (1994) 'Life stories and storied lives', in A. Lieblich and R. Josselson (eds) *The Narrative Study of Lives Volume 2*, London: Sage.
Ochs, E. and Capps, L. (1996) 'Narrating the self', *Annual Review of Anthropology* 25: 19–43.
Proust, M. (1968 [1919]) *Remembrance of Things Past*, London: Chatto & Windus.
Ricoeur, P. (1984) *Time and Narrative*, Chicago: University of Chicago Press.
—— (1992) *Oneself as Another*, Chicago: University of Chicago Press.
Riessman, C. (1993) *Narrative Analysis*, London: Sage.
Rosenwald, G. C. and Ochberg, R. (eds) (1992) *Storied Lives: The Cultural Politics of Self-understanding*, New Haven: Yale University Press.
Sarbin, T. (1986) 'The narrative as root metaphor for psychology', in T. Sarbin (ed.) *Narrative Psychology: The Storied Nature of Human Conduct*, London: Praeger.
Widdershoven, G. (1993) 'The story of life: hermeneutic perspectives on the relationship between narrative and life history', in R. Josselson and A. Lieblich (eds) *The Narrative Study of Lives Volume 1*, London: Sage.

5 When the story's over

Narrative foreclosure and the possibility of self-renewal

Mark Freeman

To the degree that the culture in which one lives fails to provide adequate narrative resources for living one's life meaningfully and productively, one's life story may be experienced as effectively over, thereby leading to what is here termed *narrative foreclosure*. The phenomenon of ageing, in certain cultures at any rate, readily comes to mind in this context: with pre-scripted narratives of decline well in place, there often appears little choice among the aged but to reconcile themselves to their narrative fate. Drawing on selected texts, both fictional and non-fictional, it will be suggested that one of the primary means of altering this fate is by challenging the cultural order, refusing prevailing endings and fashioning alternative ones. Only then, upon 'restarting' one's life story, will there emerge the possibility of self-renewal.

One significant dimension of life stories concerns what might be termed narrative 'fit', which may be understood as that measure of consonance which derives from the retrospective ordering of a life and its ability to be figured into a 'plot' of one sort or another (e.g., Brooks 1985; Ricoeur 1981; White 1987). This dimension of narrative fit can spell either pleasure or pain depending on the specific nature of one's anticipated end. What this implies is that the ends people envision for themselves – especially the expectations they may have concerning the meaning of their own death – condition the way they view their lives. In a distinct sense, the anticipated future comes to determine the past. These may be framed differently, however, as well. For the way in which one views the past also conditions the end, the 'final chapter', one envisions – whether, for instance, it is a matter of redemption or wreckage, a cause for joy or for despair.

Tolstoy's *The Death of Ivan Ilych* (1960) captures well these two moments of narrative. For a time, Ilych had seemed to be in the process of climbing steadily upward in his life. 'Everything progressed and progressed and approached the ideal he had set for himself: even when things were only half completed they exceeded his expectations' (1960: 115). 'Everything', therefore, 'was as it should be' (p. 118). After sustaining an injury that had initially appeared to be minor but that ultimately led to a terrible descent into despair, this security and comfort gave way to horror. At one point, upon beginning to recall 'the best moments of his pleasant life', he suddenly felt that 'none of those best moments of his pleasant life now seemed at all what they had then seemed'. Indeed, 'As soon as the period began which produced the present Ivan Ilych' – the beginning of his awful end – 'all that had then seemed joys now melted before his sight and turned into something trivial and often nasty' (p. 147). He can only conclude: 'It is as if I had been going downhill while I imagined I was going up' (p. 148).

On one level, Ilych's story may be construed as being about the effect of anticipated 'endings' on the shape of one's life story. Prior to his injury, his memories had retained a positive valence; by all indications, the events of the past had culminated in a positive outcome – his average but basically content adult life. As things turned out, however, the anticipated ending had changed, and with it, his past: juxtaposed against the dismal reality of his present situation, those once 'pleasant' moments appeared that much more tragic, for they pointed inexorably towards his hellish demise. On this interpretation, therefore, Ilych's past had effectively been poisoned, the meaning of its episodes becoming enveloped in the bleakness of his present situation.

Another, more standard interpretation appears to point in a quite different direction: perhaps Ilych's life wasn't so right after all, and perhaps the horror of his death was itself an index of his profound wastefulness and superficiality. ' "Maybe I did not live as I ought to have done" ' (p. 148), he had mused. However 'impossible' this initially seemed to him, Ilych eventually found that he couldn't avoid the question: ' "What if my whole life has really been wrong?" ' And at that moment, 'It occurred to him that what had appeared perfectly impossible before, namely that he had not spent his life as he should have done, might after all be true.' He thus 'began to pass his life in review in an entirely new way', such that its 'awful truth' was suddenly revealed (p. 152). Along the lines being drawn here, therefore, the problem at hand is not the poisoning of the past by the present but the poisoning of the present by the past, which is only now being 'revealed' for what it truly was (see Freeman 1997). On this interpretation, in other words, it is precisely the superficiality and wrongness of Ilych's life, heretofore mistaken for being good and right, that throws him into despair. The fact is, he will soon be dead, and there simply isn't time enough to do anything about his sorry existence. The story is all but over.

On one level, these two interpretations appear contradictory. While the first suggests that a decent enough life has retroactively become tainted by virtue of its grim conclusion, the second suggests that a quite dismal life has retroactively been cast into relief, exposed in its true dimensions. But there is another, more dialectical way of framing these two interpretations as well: even as one's view of the future conditions the meaning of the past, one's view of the past conditions the meaning of the future (Freeman 1993a). Indeed, it is precisely here, in the context of this two-way temporal traffic, that the issue of narrative fit acquires its significance. In the case of Ivan Ilych, there is, again, a dimension of finality about the situation; death was imminent, and there was precious little to be done about it. As I shall try to show in the more detailed case to follow, however, there are situations that are decidedly less final but that nevertheless become imbued with the air of finality, the sense that certain outcomes are inevitable, that things cannot be otherwise. These situations are characterised by what I am here calling narrative foreclosure – that is, the premature conviction that one's life story has effectively ended.

At an extreme, situations of this sort may lead to a kind of living death, a death in life. One such situation is that of suicide, or at least those instances of it that are tied to presumption that the future is a foregone conclusion, an inevitable reiteration of one's present suffering. Another such situation concerns those instances of ageing where there exists the unshakable conviction that it is simply too late to live meaningfully and that, consequently, there is little left to do but play out the pre-scripted ending. This conviction is often not the individual's alone. It may be a societal one as well, tied to prevailing images of development and decline or to the existence of cultural institutions that either fail to support the continued renewal of the life story or that actively promote its premature ending. In this respect, narrative foreclosure may also be related more generally to the reification of cultural storylines and the tendency, on the part of some, to internalise these storylines in such a way as to severely constrict their own field of narrative expression: the story goes this way, not that.

In order to develop further the idea of narrative foreclosure, I shall draw on the life history of a man who was in his mid-60s when he was interviewed for a research project of which I was a part.[1] He is a man who has had considerable difficulty doing the kind of art that he believes he could be doing and, in the process of narrating the story of his life over the course of the last twenty or so years, adduces numerous reasons for his troubles. Not unlike Ivan Ilych, this man's past, once a source of pleasure and pride, becomes a source of pain and shame; his own apparent ending – specifically, his anticipated failure to become the artist he had dreamed of becoming – leads to a pervasive sense of despair, which in turn taints the story he tells of his past. At the same time, there is the realisation that the glories of the past were, perhaps, not so glorious after all, that they were in fact illusory and said more about his grandiose fantasies than his real achievements. As we shall see, his own narrative foreclosure – in this case, his presumption that the story of his life as an artist has all but ended – is inseparable from his own internalisation of a number of salient cultural storylines. Indeed, it is precisely the clash of storylines that leads him to a sense of foreclosure. His story, therefore, is not only about narrative foreclosure. In a distinct sense, it is about the *dangers* of narrative itself.

Dead ends

Prior to attending art school in the early 1960s, 'Samuel'[2] had worked as an editor for a publishing company in Chicago. While in art school, he moved to part-time, and upon graduating, resumed full-time responsibilities for several years. Graduating from art school in 1964, at the age of 45, he was among the oldest students there. Several years later, he moved with his new wife to the small town she was from, which promised to be a great place to settle, raise a family perhaps, and do some serious painting. Despite the fact that his new home was about three hours from Chicago, Samuel chose not to give up his editorial job; the long commute and the hassle involved in staying in the city for several days weren't so arduous as to incite him to leave. The job remained important, both financially and emotionally; it was the one place, he said, where he was truly needed. Not surprisingly, however, he had grown more and more to feel that his life was being split into two distinct arenas: work and art. Although he continued to maintain a studio in Chicago, he felt that he was virtually unable to do anything creative while he was there; it was too unsettled, too temporary. 'I've always felt displaced. When I'm in Chicago, either I have to chat it up with whoever I'm staying with or there are other distractions . . . I've never been able to do anything really creative in that city since I left . . . It's always been a temporary situation. So I don't do anything.' The other problem with this commuting situation simply had to do with his energy level. After a day's hard work, it was difficult to turn to his art, particularly since he was getting on in years; he was tired and needed his rest. 'When I leave here', therefore, he said, referring to his home in the country, 'I'm artistically dead.'

When he had lived in Chicago, Samuel had had a number of paintings in shows and a solid gallery connection, and had even won a prize for his work. With his move, however, he was just too far away to remain involved with the Chicago art scene. As for his artistic involvement out in the country, he had been fortunate to establish a gallery connection not too long after his arrival. But after some six or seven years, the gallery was forced to go out of business, leaving him high and dry. By the time of the interview, the market situation, by his account at any rate, had become dismal. 'For various reasons, this is a terrible area to sell anything more than a watercolour . . . If you do watercolours and representational, small things, you can make a living at that – in other words, what I consider more in the realm of commercial art.' But there was not much more that could be done out there. The locals' artistic appreciation was 'nil', he explained; as for the visitors who would occasionally come through town on their country outings, they were unlikely to shell out money for such an unknown quantity as himself. 'It's too chancy.'

As he continued to reflect on this situation, the picture darkened further. He recounted an opening he had had some time ago, when the rain was coming down so hard that only four or five people showed up. 'I remember we had a lot of bottles of champagne left', he said. When it came right down to it, though, he went on to say, this opening wasn't much different than those that went on when the weather was just fine, and in bigger venues than this one. Many years back there had been another opening, at a well-known and well-respected art centre in Chicago:

> It was one of those clever shows . . . It was a black and white show –
> only black and white sculpture and painting and so on. And if you
> wanted, you could dress up in a black and white costume, that sort of
> thing. It was a lot of fun and the drinks were real good. [A critic] wrote
> later on that it was as if the world of art, that particular night, was
> centered in the Hyde Park Art Center. And there was the illusion that
> this was where it was at. And of course it wasn't at all. I mean that
> people there had the feeling that this was important. But frankly, no-
> body gave a damn two blocks away, I'm sure. Well, this opening [out in
> the country], what difference does it make? You have a good time and if
> nobody came, then so what. But this is about the way it was. And then
> you continue going back to your editorial job.

Judging by his words, Samuel had come to find it increasingly difficult to
see his former excitement as real. Despite the incredible sense of possibility
these openings had once presented, he knew now that they would lead
nowhere. His past thus appeared foolish to him, inflated with the grandio-
sity of youth. The reality, he suggested, was that he and his friends had got
caught up in the moment. And the problem was that this moment was
nothing short of mythical, or so it appears in retrospect: young artists, on
the move, living the high life, their futures wide open, there for the asking.
Whatever joy and exuberance there had been had become bathed in the
bleakness of the situation in which he had landed. Like so many others, his
plans had been 'to do a lot of painting, and attract a gallery, and be some
kind of an artistic success'. But apparently, it wasn't meant to be.

Commenting again on those people in his home town who do the 'pretty
little watercolours' he had referred to earlier, 'more power to them. If this is
what truly makes them happy, I envy them, I truly envy them . . . I think
it's great.' But 'it's not for me'. He also envied 'the person who can produce
a real good body of important work and not have any encouragement, do
this on his own and plug away'. The people he envied most, however, were
artists like Picasso, Braque and Chagall, 'who, aside from the commercial
success they all achieved . . . were able to do what they really want to do
superbly – you know, to find themselves . . . I don't care when you find it,
whether you're a Giorgioni who dies of the plague at 31 or 33, who finds it
early and dies early, or whether you find it when you're 60 . . . or whether
you're somewhere in the middle and lose it. But you've had it. At least
you've been there.' As for himself, it was unlikely that he would ever meet
with such good fortune. 'I'm distracted', he said several times during the
interview. 'I allow myself to be distracted, I think, because I'm afraid I'm
never going to find it.' Although he never quite said what 'it' was, we can

presume that he is referring to that sort of soul-ful artistic stride so integral to the romantic image of the artist – the Artist/God, seeking against all odds to locate within the interior of the self the deep pulse of things.

As Samuel went on to explain, his plight was hardly unique. Returning to artists like Braque and Chagall, he noted that,

> Hell, they touched brush to canvas and they knew basically where they were going . . . They already had a road map in their mind and it was just a matter of kind of working out the details, moving a certain amount of furniture around, so to speak, like the old religious painter of the thirteenth and fourteenth centuries . . . Well, it wasn't that simple for the modern artist . . . I think there's an element of nihilism involved . . . After Picasso, what is there left to do? In other words, it's all been done. If you want to go back to after Rembrandt or after Velázquez or Titian and so on, what is there left to do? It's been done and it's been done superbly well by these people hundreds of years ago and it's been done superbly by Picasso fifty years ago or sixty years ago. So let's not talk about that; let's do some paper clips, something Picasso never thought of doing. It's a certain element of despair, and I detect it already from conversations with instructors and contemporary artists. I mean, big deal; it's all been done; so what's new. That's the way I feel.

Samuel's search for himself and his art had become desperate. He described himself as looking frantically for that elusive formula – that magical 'it' others had been able to 'find' – which would allow him to gather both the creativity and the recognition that might have accrued to him at some other time or place. Now, as always, he was 'trying to find some new way', but like so many of his artistic forays to date, they each turned out to be 'less an avenue than a blind alley'.

Whether perceived or real, the dilemma at hand had left Samuel virtually paralysed. The ideal condition for creativity, Samuel said, is 'where art isn't beholden to any commercial considerations, where you don't have to make a living at it, where you don't have to please a customer, where you don't have to please a dictator'. If it wasn't for the lingering gaze of the public eye, in other words, the situation for artists like himself would be vastly improved; there would be no rules, no dictates; they would able to remain true to their own hearts. But then, of course, there would still remain the problems he had discussed earlier concerning the plight of the modern artist. The dilemma, therefore, was that if artists painted expressly for others, as he had sometimes done, the creative process would inevitably be deformed; by acquiescing to their demands and desires, one couldn't help but falsify the True Meaning of art. At the same time, if artists created strictly for them-selves, without attending to what was considered legitimate or valid, they would be left in a kind of vacuum, devoid both of encouragement and of those sorts of enduring traditions which, in his estimation, had once allowed artists to carry out their work with a much greater sense of certainty and security. 'The contemporary artist', he went on to ask, 'what does he have?' The answer was, 'He doesn't have anything really; he has to find his own way.'

The implication is an interesting, if familiar, one. In some sense, Samuel had implied that the entire art world could be characterised by a kind of narrative foreclosure, the postmodern era representing for some 'the end of art', the playing out of a history previously grounded in tradition but now in the process of succumbing to a vertiginous free-for-all, where it was every man – and men were certainly the dominant players at this time – for himself. For many artists (Samuel harps repeatedly on Claes Oldenburg), this would mean ceaseless repetition of one's brand image and could only yield tedium. As for himself, Samuel suggested, it meant a mad dash for the fashioning of his own artistic identity, his own unique and unrepeatable Self. His goals as an artist were modest ones, he insisted. 'At my age I'd like to make a little ripple in the art world, certainly', he said. But, 'I don't think it would be realistic to expect it.' Subjectively speaking, it was too late; judging by what he 'knew' about the process of ageing, he was past his prime and thus all but finished. Ultimately, however, he said later in the interview, after again lamenting the fact of the modern artist being 'adrift', it was all about 'the search'; that was the main problem. Even after all those years, he confessed, 'I don't know who the real me is. I don't know if I will ever know.' Alongside the storyline of the Artist/God in search of 'it' is the storyline of the Wandering Self in search of the 'real me', teasingly out of reach for those without the inner resources required. What made things more frantic still was the fact that, in his own eyes, time was running out.

The dangers of narrative

It should be emphasised that this man had remained excited by the process of painting, by handling paint and seeing what it could do on a canvas. But he was no longer able to experience his involvement in painting as part of an ongoing project, as a narrative with some promise of continuing. By all indications, his work could not possibly contribute to the future, which had already been sealed shut, or at least virtually so; it was only part of a perpetual present, leading nowhere. In his own eyes, the very factors that might allow his 'search' to lead *somewhere* were simply not operative in the world he had come to inhabit. Perhaps this is why his past, as he reconstructs it, is characterised less by a series of meaningfully interconnected episodes than by a series of fits and starts, movements in this direction and then that, all of which are permeated by the countless distractions upon which he can seize in order temporarily to prevent himself from gazing into the abyss.

Notice the similarity between the structure of his own predicament and that of Ivan Ilych, as discussed earlier. On the one hand, the very doubt of there emerging a significant ending, now exacerbated by his conviction in his own inevitable failure, leads to the fashioning of a narrative that, for all of its mini-triumphs and good times, cannot help but appear to be an exercise in futility and, on some level, delusion. It is as if he is saying, the good times *couldn't* have been that good; if they truly had been, they would have led somewhere better than here. His past, like Ilych's, has therefore been poisoned by virtue of its perceived outcome: there was a silly young man back there, so filled with his own fantasies that he had mistaken them for realities. All that might have been truly worthwhile, or that had at least appeared to be, has got swallowed up by what has followed in its path. On the other hand, however, there simultaneously emerges the conviction that maybe, after all is said and done, there just hadn't been much there to begin with. Even as the present discolours the past, the past – now perhaps being seen, as in Ilych, for what it really was, namely an illusory and somewhat masochistic exercise in futility – has yielded a present, and in turn a future, largely devoid of form. There is only a would-be story to be told, not an actual one, of the sort he had wished to tell. Narrative foreclosure brings in its wake the loss of narrative itself. There can be no story without an ending, and there can be no ending without a story.

Part of Samuel's artistic immobility undoubtedly derived from his own inflated images of the artist. As he proclaimed towards the end of the interview, when asked to reflect on the artist's place in society:

> I think that the artist is one of the principal reasons that mankind is here. When I hear about people making a lot of money or inventing marvellous labour-saving devices or whatever, I say that's all well and good. But all that is a high animal level . . . (Y)ou're not rolling around in the mud; you're not living in a cave. Say you're living in a mansion and you might have nice things even. But the artist is what it's all about, in my opinion. It's the culmination of mankind; it's the flame . . . The artist to me is god-like. He's the Prometheus pulling down the fire.

Given these sentiments, it is little wonder that Samuel was doubtful about his own future and its prospects. He was no 'God', and the odds were against his ever becoming one.

Another part of Samuel's artistic immobility surely had to do with the multiplicity of factors, from the local to the epochal, that, by his own account, had conspired to freeze him in his artistic tracks. Alongside his geographical isolation, there was the isolation that inevitably befell those modern artists who, like himself, were destined to remain 'adrift', left to their own meagre devices in a world devoid not only of meaningful artistic traditions but of *care* for what artists do. 'This isn't the era of the artist', he complained at one point. 'This is the era of the engineer, the technician.' Yes, he had to admit, maybe someone who was 'extremely gifted' or a 'wealthy dilettante' could pursue a lifetime career in fine art; he knew that there were people who had been able to make a go of it. But 'Art can be a real burden to those of us who have not supreme ability or supreme pushiness or supreme good luck or a combination to excel in "real" terms.' They were forced to 'move ahead without very much outside help, direction, or interest'.

These two storylines – the first focusing on Samuel's mythical images of the Artist/God, the second focusing on the beleaguered victim of modernity, hopelessly captive to the dizziness of freedom, the shallowness of the masses and the mechanical whir of the epoch – undoubtedly warrant consideration in trying to make sense of his life. As the text of his life story suggests, he had internalised these storylines in such a way that they came to inhabit him, to pervade his every move. Whether they finally amounted to excuses, defences designed to assuage the fact that he had been the architect of his own destiny, is largely immaterial; psychically speaking, the weight of these realities was massive. So too, I would suggest, was the weight of his own self-perception as a man growing old, staring in the face his own inevitable failure, his own inability ever to measure up to the idealised images that had peopled his imagination. Interestingly enough, he claimed to have retained a measure of hope through it all: 'Where there's life there's hope', he had said. 'I don't think all is lost.' But it was not at all clear what he could possibly do, at this moment of his life, to move forward.

Although Samuel himself made only the most oblique references to it, it can plausibly be argued that, alongside the storylines identified thus far, there was yet another one that had come to inhabit him, more surreptitiously – and more perniciously – than all the rest. I am referring here to that sort of story which is, in effect, a *non*-story. Put another way, I would suggest that Samuel had internalised a storyline so utterly devoid of possible future episodes as to lose direction and momentum. We might think of the process of reading works of literature in this context. Often, it is only after we have finished reading that we are able to understand why things happened as they did; the ending reverberates backward, serving to provide a measure of interpretive closure to what had previously been fundamentally open. There is a corollary here as well. And that is, if we already *know* or *believe* we know the ending of the work ahead of time, there may be little motivation to continue reading; whether rightly or wrongly, we may become convinced that there is little more to be had by lasting until the very end. Returning to Samuel for a moment, it might be said that he is both a writer and a reader who believes he knows how the 'work' that is his life will end. Far from being the blaze of glory he had hoped for, there will be ashes of disappointment, regret and shame. This failed ending he envisions for himself magnifies his inability to create, both as an artist and a person. Indeed, functionally speaking, the inability to create is one way in which the idea of narrative foreclosure may be operationalised: in so far as the final chapter of one's life is a foregone conclusion, one can no longer move creatively into the future. The only story to be told is the one that is over.

I earlier suggested that narrative foreclosure may be defined as the premature conviction that one's life story has effectively ended: there is no more to tell; there is no more that *can* be told. For some people, there is little to lament about this situation. For those like Samuel, however, narrative fore-closure brings in tow the futility of seeking to contribute to a future the meaning of which has already ostensibly been determined. It is therefore the death of narrative desire, the shutting down of the possibility of there ever emerging a different ending than the one envisioned now. The question is: What might one do in such a situation? More precisely, what can be done to 'reopen' a foreclosed narrative of the sort presented here?

It is at this juncture that we return to the 'two-way temporal traffic' referred to earlier. In so far as one's view of the future conditions the mean-ing of the past, there is the need to reimagine, indeed to *rewrite*, the future. For Samuel and others like him, the fixity of the present is such that the future, the inevitable victim of repetition, becomes closed off. Some way or other, therefore, the chains of the present must loosen their hold. This process appeared unavailable to Samuel; he was held too tightly in the mythical stories he had internalised to break their spell; at the 'ripe old age', as he had put it, of 63, he seemed to feel that he was on the way out. In part, this was surely his own problem, a function of his own self-perceived limits. At the same time, however, the forces at work extend well beyond the boundaries of the sovereign self. Narrative foreclosure, therefore, is not to be framed in purely individual terms; it is an eminently social phenomenon, brought about, in some instances at any rate, by people having been unwit-tingly relegated by the images and discourses surrounding them to the status of the living dead. Some, were they made aware of this problem, might, again, elect to live their lives in much the same way; they simply may not be bothered by the supposition that their lives have effectively ended. Or, they may not feel that their lives have ended at all; they have just changed, in a certain way. Others, however, may seek to call a halt to their own 'self-determinism', in the hope of fashioning somewhat different ends, and endings, than the one they had envisioned. Hence the importance of rewriting the future.

Just as the future must be rewritten in order to break the stronghold of narrative foreclosure, so too must the past. The first, very difficult step in doing so is somehow to become more aware of the storylines one has inter-nalised. To take but one example relevant to Samuel's case, many artists have become the unwitting 'hosts' of the artist's mystique and its associated story-lines during the course of recent decades, with the result that the pursuit of their work has been sacrificed to the pursuit of an image – most often, either of the Artist/God or of the struggling, beleaguered hermit, holed up in a garret, hungry and alone but free (Freeman 1993b). As such, only when these artists have been able to identify how these storylines have been opera-tive in their own lives, how they have taken them unawares, does it become possible for them to carry out their artistic activities in less alienated fashion. I have referred to this process as one of *desocialisation*, and it essentially involves identifying, becoming conscious of, the ways in which one has been constructed as a social agent and carrier of culture. This process is at one and the same time a process of *reconstruction* as well, of rewriting the past and thereby achieving some measure of self-renewal. Along these lines, one way Samuel might have been able to mobilise himself as an artist would have been through identifying the ways in which his own larger-than-life images of the artist had permeated his desires, and turning to different stories, different ways of emplotting the movement of his life.

Even this, however, may not suffice to counteract the pull of narrative foreclosure. As Smith (1988) has suggested in this context, there is a tendency towards 'claustrophilia' within the very process of narrativisation, by which he means a tendency to seek closure by fashioning stories that 'make sense of it all', that encapsulate the vagaries of a life in totalising fashion, thereby rendering a false identity out of difference (see also Shotter 1993). Narrative, therefore, is not only a vehicle of articulation and expression; it is potentially stifling as well, serving to constrict and delimit the scope of meaning. The implication is an interesting and significant one. Finally, it could be that the only way to break the stronghold of narrative foreclosure is to move beyond narrative itself. Is it possible to do so? Can there be a human world apart from stories? These questions might serve as a valuable point of entry into exploring both the dangers and the limits of narrative understanding.

Notes

1 The case history information used in this paper was gathered as part of a research project funded by the Spencer and MacArthur Foundations that was conducted at the University of Chicago under the direction of Mihaly Csikszentmihalyi, J. W. Getzels and Stephen P. Kahn.
2 'Samuel' was given the same name in Freeman (1993b), an exploration of the sociopsychological conditions of artistic creativity.

References

Brooks, P. (1985) *Reading for the Plot: Design and Intention in Narrative*, Ithaca NY: Cornell University Press.
Freeman, M. (1993a) *Rewriting the Self: History, Memory, Narrative*, London: Routledge.
—— (1993b) *Finding the Muse: A Sociopsychological Inquiry into the Conditions of Artistic Creativity*, Cambridge: Cambridge University Press.
—— (1997) 'Death, narrative integrity, and the radical challenge of self-understanding: a reading of Tolstoy's *The Death of Ivan Ilych*', *Ageing and Society* 17: 373–98.
Ricoeur, P. (1981) *Hermeneutics and the Human Sciences*, Cambridge: Cambridge University Press.
Shotter, J. (1993) *Cultural Politics of Everyday Life*, Toronto: University of Toronto Press.
Smith, P. (1988) *Discerning the Subject*, Minneapolis: University of Minnesota Press.
Tolstoy, L. (1960) *The Death of Ivan Ilych*, New York: New American Library.
White, H. (1987) *The Content of the Form*, Baltimore, MD: Johns Hopkins University Press.

6 A cautious ethnography of socialism

Autobiographical narrative in the Czech Republic

Zdenek Konopasek with Molly Andrews

Between 1991 and 1995, eight Czech academics conducted a sociological experiment of collective autobiography.[1] It all began very simply: we decided to write our life stories, and to pass them to one another, hoping that in so doing we might come to understand better the dramatic changes through which we were living. During the discussions that followed, we decided that this autobiographical production should not cease, but rather be extended to sequential, thematic writings.[2] Thus was born the project that we who are involved in it call SAMISEBE (roughly translated from Czech to 'Ourselves' Selves'). During the years immediately following the downfall of communism, the environment in which we lived and worked was ideally suited to this special blend of personal and sociological reflection. As Bauman writes:

> The new situation[3] shapes its own demands for a social-scientific exper- tise. It calls for a sociology resonant with its own structure: that is, a sociology as a flexible and self-reflective activity of interpretation and reinterpretation, as an on-going commentary on the many-centred pro- cess of interplay between relatively autonomous yet partially dependent agents (dependency and autonomy being themselves important stakes of the game).
>
> (Bauman 1992: 90)

If I were to characterise generally the SAMISEBE project, I would use those very words.

Through the years, we developed an extensive series of autobiographical texts from each participant. As mentioned above, SAMISEBE is a collective endeavour, as our narratives are produced interactively, and the success of our work depends upon mutual cooperation. The exchange inside the group, however, is not limited to the use of this shared 'database'. The members of the group also discuss, categorise, and interpret their gradually expanded narratives. This does not mean that all work together on a single theme or sociological text. Within the framework of solid rules of mutual coordination and protection, SAMISEBE participants have significant individual freedom.

Not only can each participant keep to slightly different methodological preferences, but he/she even formulates his/her own theme or problem and concentrates on it at length. The project is an interactive one, in that the individual members of the team make use of biographical and sociological feedback from all the other participants. In this sense, one member's research problem is the research problem of the others only to some extent. The project can be considered as composed of several partial thematic sub-projects, connected mainly (though not only) by the commonly produced, shared and refined database.

The SAMISEBE group is highly diverse.[4] It includes six men and two women, spanning a forty-year age gap, who vary in terms of their positions in the institutional hierarchy, methodological orientations, professional experience and political inclinations (both past and present). Personal relations within the team differ, and they change in time. Naturally, our expectations of the SAMISEBE project also differ and evolve. What unites us despite everything is this adventure in which we need each other. With the passage of time, we also share a peculiar intimacy, due to the fact that we have come to learn so much about each other – not because our autobiographies reveal secrets, but rather because the process itself is a revealing one. When we discuss events, places and persons in our narratives several times, we come to see very clearly how our perception itself, our narrative style and approaches to topics have changed during the last few years; this forms the basis of our special intimacy.

SAMISEBE is a rather unusual sociological project, and any one who is engaged with it must confront, not only theoretically but actually, that what we do as researchers is intricately connected to our personal lives. For instance, when our team discusses how to continue with the project, we are in fact holding a debate about the next difficult test to which we shall expose our personal identities/biographies and our relationship to others. The narrative form of the project tends to emphasise, rather than decrease, this close connection between (differing) personal lives and (common) research work.

A provocative sociology: the method of SAMISEBE

The marginal significance granted to personal experience is allegedly a common trait of modern society. Sociology, as an academic discipline, has been a most powerful means through which this marginalisation has been realised. But what does this mean? What is 'personal experience', and to whose advantage is it that it be stripped of its significance? Phrased differently, what is not personal experience? Only one answer can be given: the counterpart of personal experience is an 'experience' that we know as impersonal knowledge, an experience that is transformed, through numerous carefully camouflaged translations, into 'universal facts' or 'objective knowledge', knowledge which is not dependent on a particular person or the set of social practices of a particular knower.

Our project is built on the guiding principle that there is a reflexive relationship between personal experience and expert knowledge. Within this framework, massive intensive translations take place, in both directions. But how are such translations realised? The fact that objective knowledge is made up of particular transformations of personal experience is understandable: every researcher has direct access to 'ordinary' personal experience. But it might seem that not everyone has access to the experience of the researcher, to his/her objective knowledge. How, then, can the personal experience of the non-expert absorb the logic of objective facts? Quite easily. Knowledge constructs and transforms the world that we live in and endure. Modern knowledge, science, thereby acts on an unprecedented scale and functions as a powerful transformative discourse. Scientific information is experienced on the level of everyday life, through the various technologies that surround us. We absorb specialised concepts and scientific jargon into common language, because we sense their constitutive relation to various 'new' – hybrid – realities everywhere around us.

It is increasingly apparent that the descriptive and analytic categories of modern sociology do not give a full definition of the social world; moreover, classificatory and normative categories of modern social institutions are becoming less convincing. Whole segments of reality become fragmented, undecipherable, they disappear, overlap and do not fit in the established boxes. Modern sociology may indeed have transformed social reality in a significant way – but transforming does not necessarily mean successfully controlling (as has been demonstrated only too well by the experience of state socialism).

This has its consequences. As soon as the conceptual frameworks of sociology are acknowledged as insufficient, limited or relative, the self-referentiality and transformative character of social study is perceived more and more clearly, and, for many, more and more like a disgrace: it looks either as though sociology deals with some artificial, unreal problems (problems that it itself created), or as though it deals too much with itself, unable to turn its attention to the 'real' world.

There are many approaches to contemporary sociology that attempt to overcome this crisis. One of the radical efforts to arrive at a new treatment of sociological practice is our SAMISEBE project. This sociological exercise is actually an attempt to achieve an alternative sociological analysis based on collective processing of our own autobiographies. Let us try to summarise what significant contributions this attempt makes towards a better understanding of the possibilities and limits of sociology.

One of the key quasi-methodological theses of the SAMISEBE project can be summarised as follows: let us stop being ashamed about the fact that sociology is partly about itself – this was always entirely appropriate. What is problematic is that sociology is ceasing to be also about 'society' as such, that is, about the significant social relations by which people live. It therefore seems that it is necessary to maintain some measure of control. This control is available in the form of personal social experience. Not someone else's mediated personal experience, but my own direct, lived experience – as a sociologist.

A basic way by which it is possible to bring the sociologist's personal experience into play is, obviously, the use of his/her own autobiography as 'sociological data'. One can, of course, keep to this simple scheme; but only very few people will consider it to be sociology. It is certainly appropriate to go beyond this purely autobiographical/self-interpretive framework. One can, then, interpret one's own autobiography, in confrontation with other auto-biographies. These represent empirical data compatible with one's own life narrative, appropriate 'partners' for the sociologist's own personal experience transposed into biographical texts.

So how did SAMISEBE actually work? We agreed at the very beginning on the following experiment: we would write for each other our own auto-biographical narratives and attempt – each on our own, and yet, in a way, all together – to interpret them. The agreement was simple. The texts that we would write would be considered confidential working material of the group. Each of us would write an autobiography according to his/her own wishes, deciding what to include – and, by implication, what to exclude – where to begin and where to end. Participation in the experiment was clearly defined: only those who presented their own biographical texts would be given the texts of the others.

I remember that the writing of the first autobiographical text caused me, personally, terrible anguish. Who am I actually writing for? What can I tell *them* – this handful of more or less close acquaintances – about myself? Will I fall more or less within the same genre, level of intimacy, thematic orientation, as the others? It would be embarrassing if I did not, if I stood out from the ranks too much. It was also a moment of realisation: how desperately little a person knows about him- or herself at first! And how much of his/her past he/she is able, in the end, to extract from his/her memory! It is like a carefully rolled up ball of yarn: if one picks it up, all one has is an impenetrable round shape, no actual yarn. Only once one finds an end and begins to unroll does the ball produce yarn.

The presence of our own autobiographies (the biographical narratives of each one of us) in a collection of analysed texts compounded the rather common interpretive difficulties of every sociologist-biographer. Precisely because of the presence of our own autobiographies in this gradually accumulated collection of biographical texts, we felt a very immediate and intimate connection of sociological analysis with the sum of our personal experiences, with our own 'biographical knowledge'. This connection has a double effect. On the one hand, the socially relative and contextual character of knowledge becomes fully exposed. At the same time, the explicit investment of one's personal experience in sociological interpretation greatly stimulates research sensitivity regarding nuances, traps and hidden promises of all empirical material. This is why one often gets the impression of being dazzled by the thematic and interpretive potential of the text at hand.

One's own autobiographical texts thus have, as sociological data, an enhanced vantage point: they comment, illustrate, inspire, and even directly provoke sociological knowledge with great ease and mastery, but they themselves seem somehow impervious to this knowledge. Instead of providing holds for possible sociological reinterpretation, their reading only evokes more and more moments in one's life. It is as though the SAMISEBE biographical texts resisted with particular strength the various attempts of sociological reason to subjugate them and make them into obedient servants of the researcher's analysis; as though they could engage in a productive dialogue only with the researcher's own biography.

Still, as sociologists, members of SAMISEBE were committed to working our way from personal narratives to explicitly sociological texts. We felt that it was not enough to understand 'privately', personally, a comprehensive interplay of individual lives with the history of the broader community, with the background of social structure, or to offer the opportunity of this kind of understanding to others. It was important to make this 'private understanding' accessible to the theories and concepts of our discipline.

Much of the biographical texts which we collectively produced seemed to be a provocation regarding some sociological myth of the 'transforming' society. The biographies contained a surprising amount of quasi-theories, of spontaneous autobiographical interpretations and their convincing illustrations, and seemed to provide a comprehensive representation of what we were living. Our narrative texts read like closed, compact discourses, to which a sociologist could add hardly anything. It was as though we suddenly had to relearn all of sociology, laboriously and at length: to learn how to read social relations, categorise and define them, and reflect one's own participation in these relations.

The great transformation, statistical representation and biographical method

In the course of our project, it became clear to us that concerns ostensibly about our lives in our post-communist country were indeed shared by many of our contemporary colleagues in the West in their interpretations of their own social environments. Only gradually did the suspicion mature in us that there is something wrong with the silently predicted specificity and absolute uniqueness of socialism. The particulars of socialism (and of post-communism) – notably the quiet but powerful mechanisms of informal networks under the formalised front of the regime and the ubiquitous ambivalence of relations between people and their institutions in general – began to come apart in front of our eyes. Through discussion at an international seminar we held on the SAMISEBE project, we came to realise that our effort to contrast the confused, hybrid and network logic of state socialism with the transparent, easily differentiable and clearly structured societies of the West was deeply flawed. The description of state socialism refused to contrast with the reflections of contemporary capitalism; in a perhaps somewhat caricatured form, it mirrored them!

Thus another great division that helps build the theory of so-called social transformation of the post-communist society, the strict distinction between HERE (transforming socialism) and THERE (stabilised capitalism), gradually decomposed. All that remained were relatively fine and sometimes mutually contradictory differences and asymmetries. The result of this has been that the essential dichotomy between the East and the West has been discredited for us. What has been described as the subversive habits of everyday resistance of subordinate groups may be generally understood as something very typical for all relationships between people and their institutions. The study of state socialism, precisely, shows this very well. Thus the study of socialism is valuable not only because it helps us understand state socialism itself and our own past, but also in making us better understand the quasi-modern reality of contemporary capitalism. That is why the phenomenon of socialism is as important for theorising about the current post- or non-modern West as the early stages of industrialisation and the philosophical projects of the Enlightenment are for theorising about classic modernity.

As sociologists, we were convinced that the study of an unconventional society (socialism) required an unconventional methodological approach. Standardised methodological procedures developed when studying 'well-ordered' modern capitalism cannot avoid failing when confronted with a transforming post-communist society. Biographies, in contrast, connect the private and the public, the universal and the singular, what changes and what lasts, precisely what was needed to understand the strange amalgam of tradition and modernity which we call socialism. Moreover, the issues presented to us by the downfall of state socialism interested us both personally and professionally: the issue of the various dimensions of time, especially the interweaving of biographical, generational and historical time; the relation between private worlds and their institutional frameworks; the problem of individual and collective identity in relation to the reconstruction of the past; shadow economic and political strategies and practices. In short, we were enchanted by the theoretical potential of biographies and life histories.

The strongest factor contributing to the birth of the project was a deep dissatisfaction with conventional sociology in general, and, in particular, with the way it formulated, at the time, its new great theme: the Transformation of the Post-Communist Countries of Central and Eastern Europe. At the time of SAMISEBE's formation, sociological research on state socialism and on Central and Eastern Europe tended to avoid the biographical method[5] preferring, instead, large, often 'comparative', surveys.[6] Fresh data from the transforming countries were exported in a jumble to the West, where they could then be worked into various theories of transformation.

The ambition of SAMISEBE was to strengthen the use of biographical method from a sociological perspective as a tool for examining 'really existing socialism' and its decline. The members of SAMISEBE originally came together as a working group of a large interdisciplinary team that was meant to study the changes in the structure of Czechoslovakia at the time of the downfall of the communist regime. Theoretically, the biographical approach was intended to offset the dominant logic of mass survey. It was supposed to act as a corrective to the bold and self-assured explanations of the transformation, expressed in terms of the 'statistical existence of the masses'. We expected that, by working with biographies, the social changes at hand would be projected by their subjects themselves on the background of local contexts of everyday life, of the experienced world and of individual life histories; and that we would acquire a certain distance from the existing theoretical equipment, which was partly mechanically taken over from standard Western sociology and other social sciences and partly extracted from the political rhetoric of the post-revolutionary period.

Therefore, our debates in those days naturally included attempts to reconceptualise the so-called transformation of our society. It seemed to us that most of the research on transformation ignored the problem of state socialism. Socialism often was only slightly present in the conceptual schemes of the researchers, as the entirely self-evident, and thus not very interesting, point of departure of all transformation processes. We were convinced that questioning about the nature of transformation could not be separated from the question 'What is actually being transformed?' and we believed that socialism as it was lived could not be captured by statistical representation.

It is often considered that, in a socialist regime, the 'public' (in the shape of abstract, gross and violent state power) dominates the 'private' (in the shape of the fragile and thin fabric of personal relationships). But the opposite is closer to the truth. Under socialism, the domain of the 'public' – the domain of political and economic institutions, official documents, formal rules and concepts, that is, everything that could potentially make up the backbone of statistical construction – is made much more problematic than the fragile 'private' world: the world of informal social networks, personal experience and face-to-face encounters. The private networks overwhelm public institutions. Truth, the basic principle of representational realism, functions just as contextually, or locally. As statistics cannot easily represent these non-universal conditions, we thought that the biographical approach would be particularly appropriate for the sociology of socialism.

In the early stages of SAMISEBE, we were bothered, above all, by the generalising concepts connected with standard research procedures. In particular, the dominant rhetoric of discontinuity sat uncomfortably with our own experiences and observations. This is why, from the very beginning, we were fascinated most of all by everything that clearly did not transform. As soon as you look at individual people, their fates and everyday lives – and later, at the relevant institutional frameworks – it becomes quite difficult to maintain the belief that we can cut ourselves away from our past. Indeed, it soon became clear that one can discover a far greater continuity, closeness and temporal reversibility between the 'socialist' *then* and the 'transforming' *now* than we ourselves had expected. The complete break with the past, in the name of the Great Transformation in the East, is simply not taking place. People, words, things and their mutual relations in a 'transforming' society – though basically identifiable at a single time and place – belong inescapably to many different periods, scripts and trajectories.[7]

Such a perspective complicates the concept of transformation – at least as it is used by most sociologists. Indeed, a sufficiently convincing notion of transformation is possible only through careful conceptual purification of a given 'past', which is put in radical opposition to some equally purified 'present'. It must be made entirely clear that the basic framework of behaviour of individual actors is 'now' (during transformation) incommensurable with the one that existed 'then' (during socialism). The very concept of transformation is therefore an attempt to break away radically and totally from the past. Of course, the issue is not at all that the notion of such a radical dividing line would imply only sudden, immediate, one-time changes. Nevertheless, even the most long-term and complex changes currently occurring – for instance those, over several decades, expertly predicted by Dahrendorf (1990) who attributes them to the gradual maturing of civil society – belong, from the point of view of the transformation, to a single complex process, which began almost instantly, as a whole, with the downfall of communist regimes in Europe. The world has simply changed: now we are no longer a 'socialist' society, but a 'transforming' society: we therefore belong to an essentially different time, or to a different historical cohort; we belong to a different world, which is, in fact, incommensurable with the past one. We are, we are told, a post-communist society.

In other words, to make it unnecessary to consider even slightly post-communist societies in terms of state socialism, we consider them in terms of transformation. This is why, in transformological texts, the differences and asymmetries between the former socialist and the current situations are emphasised in all possible ways, whereas similarities and analogies are suppressed. Current events and situations are thereby liberated from the logic of the communist past. This is possible because the transformation perspective has given them a new logic: other objectives, other strategies, other lives are at play. Though it may seem, at first sight, that the concept of transformation interconnects the past and the present (and the future) of post-communist countries, in fact it disconnects and isolates them from each other.

Through the perspective of biographies, however, the various conceptual incommensurabilities and impressions of radical difference tend to be decreased and relativised. The solid and unambiguous borderline between state socialism and the transformation period is broken by the perspective of the biographical approach. The impressive and well-defined dividing line between the historical 'present' and 'past', which is implied in the notion of transformation, dissolves into the many divisions and breaking points identifiable in the recounted individual life stories. Other differences come to the surface, and prove to be all the more important the slighter and more fragile they are.[8] Therefore, the rhetorical construction of the radical break between (transforming) 'present' and (socialist) 'past' functions like a sociological myth, which enables the development of the now popular genre of Great Research on the Social Transformation in the East. But careful reflexive thinking works against this myth.

From autobiography to collective autobiography

It is very useful when one has, for one's autobiography, more than just oneself for a public. And it is just as useful when the sociologist has the possibility of working on a particular problem together with other colleagues who are just as interested in the matter. An indisputably elegant solution can then be provided by a sort of autobiographical group of sociologists: not only does the sociologist include his/her personal experience within a broader empirical field, but that experience itself is regarded as a sociologically legitimate basis for interpretation. The fact that it is not a one-time event but a long-term interactive process of progressive writing, discussing, categorisation and interpreting of our own autobiographies enhances the possibility of respecting the principle of permanent openness in sociological practice. The principle of gradual saturation of the theoretical concept by the addition of more and more analysed cases, common in the grounded theory-driven biographical approach, is transformed and – in a way – radicalised: the understanding of the given phenomenon is nourished by the addition of more and more continuations of the interactive team-writing and by the analysing of autobiographical texts.

The central assumption is no longer: 'if I look at others, I will necessarily also see something about myself', but rather: 'examining myself is actually the best way to examine others'. What is at stake is more than just the moral import of reflexive sociology. The sociologist's personal experience – unpurified and deromanticised – is so dangerous for modern sociology, because it mixes the sociological and the social with exceptional and irresistible intensity. The sociologist's personal experience endangers the notion of an authentic Society and an autonomous Sociology, on which the modern ideology of representational realism is dependent. This ideology prevents sociology from understanding, or even seeing, many interesting and influential aspects of contemporary life. The principles of realism permit a nostalgic and, in fact, quite unreal notion of what is the 'object' of sociological interest, and what is its 'subject'. They make us sociologists examine with ever more care and refinement that which does not exist – or rather, that which exists only in our theoretical expectations.

The mobilisation of the researcher's personal experience by means of collective autobiographical practices gives one the opportunity to understand the highly intimate reflexive relation between the sociological and the social. For members of SAMISEBE, it is not so important that we work with (our own) autobiographies, but rather how we work with them. The opportunity outlined above can really be used only if one combines the autobiographical approach with radical or constitutive research reflexivity. We shall not penetrate into the reflexive loops of the relations between sociology and modern social reality (whether we call this reality 'subjective' or 'objective') unless we enter them ourselves – if possible right at the level of reflexive relations between autobiography and the reality of life.

Through the presence of the others, each participant has him/herself continuously in sight. Each examined subject is at the same time a colleague-sociologist, and each colleague-sociologist is also an examined subject. We are 'insiders' and 'outsiders' to each other. This is particularly valuable from a more conventional epistemological perspective. The SAMISEBE design allows the project's participants to see auto/biography in action: we see (in each other) the processes of autobiographical and sociological writing and reading, 'from the inside' and 'from the outside'. When we study each other, in the context of SAMISEBE, we also study – however implicitly or incidentally – how, inside the group, socially relative criteria of autobiographical and sociological truth are created, and also how we try to respect these criteria when we want to produce for each other both trustworthy 'personal-experience stories' and 'social selves' on one hand, and convincing sociological testimonies on the other.

SAMISEBE's open nature is a fitting embodiment of the fact that the practice of autobiography is always, in principle, unfinished. Each extra step, each additional continuation opens, of course, ever new horizons. In this sense, SAMISEBE's autobiographical production resembles the writing of a diary. In many places in our narratives, the chronology and timing of the individual levels is reflected. More and more events are added to our perception of our own lives and are also reflected in our biographical production. At the same time, the continuously present possibility of more levels of biographical text, of some always accessible 'next time', decreases – to a certain extent – the pressure that is otherwise put on every biographer: the necessity of completing the biographical picture. Moreover, it has gradually become clear that the distinction between one's own research and 'normal' life weakens and gets more complicated. Not only do we, for instance, talk about our life in the past in such a way as to make it trustworthy with respect to what we know about each other now from everyday situations; we increase and maintain the trustworthiness of our narratives the other way around as well. We behave in our 'normal' lives in such a way that our identities, narratively constructed within the context of the project, may not be threatened.

Now that we are familiar with our sociological experiment, we exclaim in astonishment: but we are actually all (including you) doing SAMISEBE! All sociologists, not only those of us involved with SAMISEBE, are mobilising personal experience in a similar way, betting unwittingly on the same assumptions. We all interactively create and maintain criteria of biographical and sociological truth, and perform all sorts of witchcraft with the borderline between fact and fiction. We all deepen our research reflexivity through our knowledge of other researchers' practices. We all have to face continuously doubts about the status of our own practices. We all are continuously the studying and the studied.

Reflexive autobiography, in the SAMISEBE style, actually means that much of what sociology has historically hidden is exposed, made explicit, and even fully exhibited as the basis of sociological work. While many trends of contemporary sociology are oriented in much the same way, SAMISEBE is exceptional in its scope and the simple method by which it turns the whole situation upside down – or rather, as it appears in the end, right side up.

Notes

1 The SAMISEBE project has not ended in a formal sense, although our involvement with it after this period has been more sporadic. For this reason, I use the present tense when speaking about the project in this article.

2 Altogether, we have now written eleven levels of autobiography, of which two are introductory free narratives and nine are on mutually agreed topics. The size of the individual texts differs considerably both from person to person and from level to level, according to style and topic. Among these texts, we have narratives which range between three and one hundred pages; some are very sober biographical outlines, where austere descriptions of events, persons and times merge with sociological commentary, while others are more emotional biographical testimonies. In order to maintain some clarity in the common progression, we have co-ordinated at each level both the biographical writing and the biographical reading, regarding the interplay between the two as an integral part of a single process.

3 The 'new situation' to which Bauman refers here is not post-communism, but postmodernism. However, if we admit that the former is at least partially built on the latter, then we feel justified in taking licence to reinterpret the original meaning of Bauman's statement.

4 Most of us who are now participating in SAMISEBE met in 1990–1, at the then newly established Faculty of Social Sciences of Charles University, in Prague. The encounter was not entirely by chance. Some of us already knew each other from before, either as former colleagues or even as childhood friends; for others, however, this was the first meeting. We were brought together by our interest in the use of life stories and autobiographical accounts in sociological research, and in the spring of 1991 we thought of working systematically on our own autobiographies.

5 Since that time (1991), there has been considerable growth in this area (e.g., Passerini 1992).

6 Within Czech sociology, this preference for standardized, empirical research has a historical basis. 'Marxist-Leninist Sociology', as the discipline was labelled in Czechoslovakia in the 1970s and 1980s, devastated the already weak tradition of sociology; only statistical research, which was ideologically harmless, managed to survive unscathed. Interpretive paradigms and sociological theorising were regarded as threatening to the communist doctrine, and accordingly fared much worse. Thus in the past few decades, there has been little evidence of, or support for, biographical methods in Czech sociology.

7 This is, of course, a more general point and does not apply exclusively to state socialism. See, for instance, Bruno Latour (1993) on (non)modernity.

8 I believe that this biographically generated suspicion about unquestioned distinctions and asymmetries is amplified even more by the reflexive design of SAMISEBE.

References

Bauman, Z. (1992) *Intimations of Postmodernity*, London: Routledge.
Dahrendorf, R. (1990) *Reflections on the Revolution in Europe*, London: Chatto & Windus.
Latour, B. (1993) *We Have Never Been Modern*, London: Harvester Wheatsheaf.
Passerini, L. (ed.) (1992) *Memory and Totalitarianism*, Oxford: Oxford University Press.

7 'Papa's bomb'

The local and the global in women's Manhattan Project personal narratives

Carol Wolkowitz

This chapter examines the personal narratives written by a few of the women who participated in building the American communities in which the first atomic bombs were developed, focusing in particular on middle-class women's accounts of wartime Los Alamos, in the south-western state of New Mexico.

Examining women's personal memoirs of the Manhattan Project provides a distinctive slant on the relation between gender, war and science. These women authors wanted to record their experience, at a time when most accounts barely mentioned them, but their vantage point as community-minded women who made husbands and children the centre of their lives produces a picture of the Manhattan Project which seems to contain it within a bubble of positive human values (Wolkowitz 2000). Whatever their intentions, their domestication of the bomb can be read as a gender-specific coda on the succession of 'official narratives' identified by Lifton and Mitchell (1995) which over time have explained (away) the use of atomic bombs in Hiroshima and Nagasaki in ways which excuse the US from moral culpability or introspection.

What became known as the Manhattan Project – the term was originally the wartime code name for the making of the atomic bombs – was developed after university-based research demonstrated the atomic bomb's feasibility. Under the command of General Leslie Groves, the US Army established three main sites, which for practical and security reasons were geographically dispersed. (All three are still important centres of scientific research of various kinds.) Los Alamos, where most of the key scientific personnel were located, became by 1945 a community of some 6,000 persons, including several hundred civilian scientists and their families. The other two sites were much larger, located near the large amounts of cold river water and electricity which the new industrial complexes required: Hanford, in the north-western state of Washington, where plutonium was manufactured, and Oak Ridge, Tennessee, in one of the south-eastern states, where over 40,000 people were employed in various processes which separated uranium isotopes. My own father, then a young American soldier, was stationed in Oak Ridge, where he worked in the laboratories and my mother taught in a secondary school. It is partly this personal connection that has stimulated my interest in the conflicting emotions incorporated in representations of the experience of these communities.

In this chapter I examine the women's gender-specific narratives as a particular instance of a wider problem: the privileging of the personal and the local as against global considerations or connections. I examine what the accounts' concentration on the local as against the global achieves, and how it is narratively produced and defended, as against other possible rhetorical strategies which might have forced the writers to consider the experience of the bombs' victims alongside their own experience.

Although the narrative focus on the local can be attributed to the particular context and quandaries of the authors, it also raises issues about the use of personal narratives in sociology more generally. In particular it has led me to re-examine my tendency to privilege the 'partial truths' offered by auto-biographical accounts bounded by the subjective experience of the writer. Like many postmodernist and feminist sociologists, I had come to favour 'micro-narratives' focusing on 'the local, on daily life', as against 'conventional forms of history' (Rosenau 1992: 22; see also Clifford and Marcus 1986; Stacey 1991; Stanley 1997), and I still find them fascinating and essential. But since immersing myself in Manhattan Project literature, I have become less satisfied with this approach, drawn instead to Lovibond's wish to push towards what she terms a more 'coherentist' view, one which seeks to 'bring all perspectives on reality into communication' (Lovibond 1990: 163). I would argue that we need to go further towards recognising the interconnections between our personal experiences and explaining the relation between social context and ways of narrating personal experience.

Telling the story

Telling this particular story has always been a highly political matter. Even before Hiroshima, the American military employed journalists to put to-gether the materials which would flood the American press with its version of the history of the construction of the bomb and the need for its use against Japan; afterwards the wartime censorship machinery prevented cir-culation of film and photographs which showed the full effects of the bombs on human beings (Lifton and Mitchell 1995; Wyken 1984). Since then personal narratives have become central to the debate on the legitimacy of nuclear weaponry. For example, the controversy over the Smithsonian Insti-tute exhibition in Washington, DC, commemorating the fiftieth anniversary of Hiroshima, pivoted partly around the value of personal testimony. Once analysis of recently released archival evidence had identified rivalry with the Soviet Union and other reasons for the decision to use the bombs, apologists emphasised what they saw as more significant: American veterans' own recollections of their relief that the bombs had led to the end of the war (Freedland 1995; Goldberg 1995). In contrast, some journalists and photographers have used personal narratives to challenge US government subterfuge, for instance regarding the health and environmental harm caused by the nuclear weapons industry (Gallagher 1993; Tredici 1987).

In the US, at least until very recently, the story of the making of the first atomic bombs was almost always told as a story about human creativity and co-operation, not as a story about destructive violence. Although the narratives I am examining describe occasional instances of disaffection, taken as a whole they seem to me to be clearly located within the first of these discourses, with the addition of the women's own particular family and community concerns. For this reason I disagree with the reading of these accounts offered by Hales (1997), who sees the Los Alamos wives as 'profoundly subversive' (p. 221). His cultural history of the physical and metaphorical spaces of the Manhattan Project also sees 'the local' as conceptually crucial, but sees it as a site of opposition to US national military and industrial bureaucracies and their global ambitions, especially by the farmers and other countrypeople who were displaced by the Army. They and those 'others' (Hales' own term) who tried to maintain autonomous belief systems, based on locality, or concern for family or community, were seen by the military as necessary evils, threatening military discipline and the successful outcome of the project. But although Hales' analysis of contemporary archives demonstrates that the military top brass saw the scientists' middle-class wives as a problem (along with the African American and Native American workers, who were an important part of the workforce) (Wolkowitz 2000), I would argue that the women themselves did not challenge the project's *raison d'être*, seeing themselves rather as its human face. Indeed, many anecdotes related in their narratives were later readily incorporated into museum exhibitions in both Los Alamos and Oak Ridge celebrating the 'birth of the bomb'.

However, their narratives are not simply public relations fodder. I know from my parents' experience that many participants in the Manhattan Project became very attached to the communities they helped to create. This may be one reason why, as Smith (1965) documents, in so far as atomic scientists and their families challenged nuclear weaponry it was through trying to alter the control of nuclear power and weapons development after the war, rather than questioning or regretting their role in its development. What became known as the Federation of Atomic Scientists in effect built on scientists' longstanding suspicions of and alienation from military discipline and concerns rather than rethinking the role of 'pure' science.

Although the women's narratives I want to examine have a chequered publishing history, their tone is so similar to contemporary clippings my mother saved at the time that I feel we are justified in treating them as products of the immediately post-war period. For example, one of her newspaper clippings – unfortunately undated – notes an Oak Ridge columnist's frustration that publishers were not interested in their autobiographical accounts. These accounts were 'collective impressions' based on a 'felt need to tell and share stories' which demonstrated an 'appreciation of each other': '[W]e who have been in Oak Ridge know that it has been quite a story. If we never get a chance to tell it to outsiders, we can at least tell it over and over again to each other' (Oak Ridge Journal, late 1945).

Rejection by the press in the years after the war seems also to have been the fate of several of the Los Alamos narratives. This is why although most of the narratives I examine here were written in the immediate post-war period their dates of publication stretch into the 1980s or later. The first edition of *Atoms in the Family* (Fermi 1982), Laura Fermi's account of her life with her husband, the Nobel-prize winning Enrico Fermi, was published commercially in 1954 but the others languished in archives or attics. The preface to *Standing By and Making Do: Women of Wartime Los Alamos* (Wilson and Serber 1988) suggests that the articles and Introduction were first drafted in 1946, but were unable to find a publisher. Available to the public in the archives of the Los Alamos Historical Society for over a decade, the manuscript was eventually published by the Society in 1988. Similarly, according to her daughter-in-law's Appendix, Eleanor Jette had written the first draft of *Inside Box 1663* (1977) by 1949, although the final draft is said to have been completed in the early 1960s. Bernice Brode's *Tales of Los Alamos: Life on the Mesa 1943–1945* (1997) was first published only in the 1960s, in a Los Alamos Laboratory newsletter, but she had written the first draft 'shortly after the end of the war', and may have revised it in the 1950s, when she again failed to find a publisher. All the authors seem to intend to give an accurate picture, but Jette's (1977) admission that her account occasionally departs from strict accuracy for literary effect or other reasons, including continuity and security considerations, may also apply to the others. Almost all the manuscripts are said to have been edited slightly, the prefaces say, but in ways which are not explained.

The existence of two accounts by working-class women should also be mentioned. Eleanor Roensch's (1993) very short anecdotes about her time as a WAC switchboard operator in Los Alamos portray Los Alamos as a special community – in much the same way as the scientists' wives – a place where exceptionally long hours of work and spartan living conditions were relieved by the larger-than-life personalities of key figures, *joie de vivre*, romance and friendships. *Lest I Forget* (Downs 1997) is rather different. During the war Martha Downs and her second husband, a construction worker, drove their trailer caravan first to Hanford, and after his job there finished, looked elsewhere for work before settling for good in Los Alamos in 1945. Written by Martha Downs for a university writing course when she was over 70, her matter-of-fact account of a succession of family crises, leavened by small pleasures, pays little attention to the distinctiveness of Los Alamos' way of life, or the special talents of its people. The contrast between Downs' frequently expressed surprise that anyone might be interested in her story and the assumption guiding the scientists' wives accounts, that their narratives are highly significant, hints at the extent to which these narratives are inflected with class-specific assumptions, but space precludes further exploration of this point.

Privileging the local

As I have already implied, reading most of these Los Alamos narratives now, a particularly striking aspect is their determinedly personal and local frame of reference. Although the making of the bombs is recognised as what makes the narrative of wider interest, it is rarely mentioned, functioning within the narratives mainly to infuse the details of daily life with deeper, even heroic, significance. For many reasons the usual equation of work with public life, with what is open to view and discussed, and private family life with what is hidden or secret, is effectively reversed.

The choice of the local and personal as vantage point in the narratives is clearly overdetermined, not simply by the memoir form, but by many other factors, in particular the relative isolation of the site and the secrecy of the project. The famous Scientific Director of the Project, J. Robert Oppenheimer, is said to have known already of the Los Alamos Ranch School for Boys, a prep school for wealthy easterners' sons whose parents thought they would benefit from the rigours of healthy outdoor pursuits, and its Western-style log-cabin-type school buildings could be used for office space and housing while new facilities were being constructed. (Mention of the prior existence of this school occurs in almost all accounts of Los Alamos, perhaps a way of signalling that although the mesa had already been appropriated by the eastern establishment before the war the region was felt to retain a kind of noble innocence.) The remote wooded hilltop mesa met the Army's criteria for secrecy, while the surrounding sparsely settled desert provided testing grounds nearby. This relative isolation of residents meant that local relationships and issues inevitably dominated their concerns. Army security insisted on isolation of the inhabitants from the outside world through fences, entry and exit gates controlled by Army MPs, censoring of post, severe restrictions on travel and other measures. The Army insisted on compartmentalising knowledge of various aspects of the bombs, preventing information-sharing between research groups and, especially, between the main sites. Although scientists often broke these arrangements among themselves, especially within Los Alamos, there were circumlocutions (the bomb was always referred to as the 'gadget') and there was little public conversation about the scientific work. Not only did patterns of conversational reticence among Manhattan Project staff persist after the war, in the 1950s security measures actually intensified (Howard 1987; Taylor 1987). This in part reflected McCarthy-era suspiciousness about the loyalty of scientists, something which would also have made it difficult for authors associated with the project to express any doubts.

Although the peculiar relationship between the public and the private inhabited by the narratives is due partly to factors like these, it also needs to be read as a response to the other ways of telling the story which were circulating at the time the narratives were written. After Hiroshima the makers of the bomb were seen as superhuman in the wider American press, and sometimes even to their own children (Chapter 1 of Claudio Segrè's (1995) account of his relationship with his father, Emilio Segrè, is titled 'Son of Superman'), as over-life-sized 'gods from hell' (Jungk 1958: 218). Aside from the wider attention, Manhattan Project scientists and their families received letters from relatives and friends, many thanking them for ending the war. Others were more ambivalent, but in ways that did not challenge the makers' superhuman image. For instance Enrico Fermi's sister wrote from Italy:

> Everybody is talking about the atomic bomb, of course! . . . All, however, are perplexed and appalled by its dreadful effects, and with time the bewilderment increases rather than diminishes. For my part I recommend you to God, Who alone can judge you morally.
>
> (Fermi 1982: 245)

Los Alamos scientists had more information about the effects of the bombs than was available in the censored accounts elsewhere, and many scientists and wives were distressed by their use against civilian targets. In a recent autobiography by a Los Alamos scientist, Robert Serber (1998) mentions giving a talk there based on his visit to Japan in the autumn of 1945, along with several other scientists and Army doctors, including the Los Alamos obstetrician. Indeed Serber's first wife, Charlotte, who co-edited the original manuscript of *Standing By and Making Do* (Wilson and Serber 1988) but died before it was published, had expected a more adverse reception from the American public than actually occurred. Many joined the Association of Los Alamos Scientists (later amalgamated in the Federation of American Scientists), which attempted to build on the atomic scientists' expertise and heroic reputation to gain a political platform for internationalising control of atomic energy.

But the atomic communities also seem to have found comfort in the ordinariness of themselves and their colleagues. For instance according to one of my mother's local newspaper clippings (2 January 1947), headlined 'Oak Ridge normal town, Times man surprised to know', a *New York Times* reporter who 'talked to numerous residents in an effort to "get the feel of the place"' decided 'the place was populated by more or less normal people' who did not spend all their time talking physics. Laura Fermi insists in her book that 'Our husbands were not different from other generations of scientists' (1982: 242) and her success in humanising the scientists was very evident to one reviewer, who saw the book as: 'A major contribution to bridging the gap that separates people in general from the select group of scientific gen- iuses who created atomic physics and its fearful by-product, the atomic bomb' (David Dietz, on the back cover of Fermi 1982).

Looking at the narratives in depth provides numerous examples of the contributions made by the wives and mothers whose roles were missed out by other contemporary reports, which concentrated either on military matters or the 'scientific geniuses'. But they are also highly contradictory: the women think that their involvement in the Manhattan Project should be of wider interest because of its global historical significance, yet they are understandably reluctant to tell the whole story; moreover, their own experience was confined not only to Los Alamos, but mainly to Townsite rather than Tech Area, i.e., 'outside the inner wall' (McMillan in Badash *et al.* 1980). Thus the telling of what appear to be frank and amusing insider anecdotes was constrained and shaped in numerous ways.

Framing the story

The form taken by the women's narratives carefully brackets the years in Los Alamos as a special experience, tightly bounded in both time and space. This no doubt captures the feelings of wartime and explains the narrators' access to the 'inside story', but also contains what they can say within their personal experience.

The two-page introduction to Bernice Brode's *Tales of Los Alamos* (1997) starts with the Brodes' conversation with J. Robert Oppenheimer, when he invited them to join the Manhattan Project in Los Alamos, and ends with the public announcement of the dropping of the Hiroshima bomb. A kind of glow which suffuses all of the narratives – the warmth of the isolated community on 'the Hill', the privilege of participation in what Oppenheimer tells them will be a 'high adventure' as well as 'patriotic duty' – is heavily foreshadowed in the picture of what many accounts compare to the fictional hilltop Shangri-La:

> It was wartime Washington early in March 1943 when our friend J. Robert Oppenheimer came to see us in our chilly living room. Heat was rationed and our rented house in Chevy Chase was cheerless and damp . . . Oppenheimer burned with an inner fire as he told us about his new project . . . high up in the mesa . . . almost a kind of Shangri-La.
>
> (Brode 1997: 1)

She then simultaneously claims ignorance of the nature of the work at Los Alamos, personalises it utterly, and defines the denouement of the story. Brode says that she and her children were boarding a bus in California when they read the newspaper headlines about the dropping of a new kind of bomb on Hiroshima. Her elder son, Bill, said very quietly, 'This is Papa's bomb, you know, Mama' (Brode 1997: 2). Previously 'forbidden words', for example terms for the bomb's components, now appeared in the newspaper, although she herself had known nothing of them. By the time she returned to Los Alamos a week later, she says, 'all the children were calling the new weapon "Papa's bomb" and bragging to each other how much they knew about it all along. The wives were talking excitedly about leaving our ramshackle community and returning to civilian life' (Brode 1997: 2). Nagasaki is not mentioned at all, and neither Hiroshima nor Nagasaki appear in the main body of the text, although the formation of the Association of Los Alamos Scientists and women's participation in it does.

In the last chapter of the book Brode describes how in August scientists and their families were beginning to return to university jobs. Christmas 1945 was 'gloomy', the flat filled with packing boxes and 'parts' from the Army dump her son had collected. The book finishes with their departure, shortly before New Year's Eve, 1945: 'I could not face any farewells' and they left without saying goodbye to anyone (Brode 1997: 150).

The account by Laura Fermi is slightly different, since it covers her and Enrico's lives in pre-fascist Italy (and his career after the war) – although they too wanted to go home for the New Year, leaving Los Alamos half an hour before midnight on New Year's Eve. But the other Los Alamos narratives bracket the experience in a similar vein. Wilson's Introduction to *Standing By and Making Do: Women of Wartime Los Alamos* (Wilson and Serber 1988) places the narrator among those workers and wives who gathered on top of the local Sawyer's Hill – where residents used to ski on their days off – to try to catch a glimpse of the Trinity test blast taking place about 200 miles away. This couches the only atomic explosion described in the book within the immediacy of personal experience:

> Perhaps something was amiss down there in the desert where one's husband stood with the other men to midwife the birth of the monster ... Four o'clock ... Five o'clock. Five fifteen. Then it came. The blinding light ... The mountains flashing into life. Later, the long, slow rumble. Oh, something has happened, all right, for good or ill. Something wonderful, something terrible.
>
> (Wilson and Serber 1988: x–xi)

Although the different articles take up different aspects of community institutions – Town Council, housing allocations, leisure pursuits – the story is truncated: neither Hiroshima nor Nagasaki is explicitly mentioned in this volume of essays, never mind described; at heart it is a personal story: 'This is the story of three years of working and marrying and dying, of giving birth, of getting drunk, of laughing and crying, which culminated in that successful test at the Alamogordo bombing range' (Wilson and Serber 1988: xi).

Eleanor Jette's (1977) mediated vantage point as wife is established from the very beginning of her account, when her husband tells her one evening after dinner that he may be taking up a war job in the Southwest. Jette describes Los Alamos and introduces her cast of characters in a somewhat literary way, by reporting (real or imagined) conversations with her husband in which, based on a prior visit, he tells her what to expect in Los Alamos. She is instructed to keep quiet about it, even to their ten-year-old son, who was withdrawn from school without his knowing he would not be returning.

However, she makes it clear that she was a full partner in the undertaking (rather than being merely the accompanying wife) by mentioning that it was she who drove the car to Los Alamos. Since she and her husband remained in Los Alamos until the mid-1950s, her narrative concludes with their move from the four-family block of flats into one of the group of original Ranch School houses known as 'Bathtub Row'.

All the narratives also include, in addition to their introductions, an arrival story detailing the authors' first impressions as they enter the new environment. What is presented in all the accounts as a kind of *rite de passage* was arriving at the Project office in Santa Fe at 109 East Palace Avenue, before being sent on up to 'the Hill'. The office was run by a woman noted for her warmth and hospitality, Dorothy McKibben, a locally resident widow with wide connections in the region, who was employed by the Project as a kind of liaison worker. Civilian newcomers almost invariably passed through this office gateway, where their 'misgivings [were] replaced by trust in the unknown' (Brode 1997: xx). The warm welcome usually continues when newcomers reach their own apartment. For example, the Brodes are surrounded by the families of Robert Brode's old colleagues and new neighbours eager to welcome them; Eleanor's neighbour invites her to a 'tea party' and in the evening she and her husband dine at Fuller Lodge and then watch the square dancing at the theatre.[1]

All three of these books cover a lot of the same ground. Each of Brode's chapters deals with some facet of life in the community. Although some topics are given more space than in some other narratives, many are set pieces in almost all the narratives: character sketches of famous scientists; Sunday skiing, riding, hikes and picnics in bewitching scenery; an account of Edith Warner, a Northerner who had created a simple but charming hostelry in her home where she provided special dinners for the scientists and their families; relations with the local Native American community, including relations with the Native American cooks, janitors and maids who were bussed into work; the party their *pueblo* gave for the scientists; another, much grander party and stage revue presented by the British Mission before its departure. The impression given is of something akin to a college campus, but better. Much is made, for instance, of the informal dress of Los Alamos – where both men and women often wore shirts and jeans – as against the formality of university life in the 1940s. This young community – the average age was 26 – of intellectually adept and energetic people found a lot to poke fun at, including the Army and its rules, and necessarily spent their Christmases and other holidays with each other, rather than with kin.

Although the narratives acknowledge a down side to life in Los Alamos, and are sometimes cynical about the Shangri-La analogy, their complaints focus on the laughable irrationalities of rationing, primitive housekeeping in the small flats, and the absence of privacy rather than the larger purpose of the venture. Jette (1977) is more honest than most, but partly in order to show that they too suffered from the hardship of war. She speaks several times about the way in which the pressure and secrecy of her husband's research work affected their relationship. She said to another woman at the time:

> I'm glad someone's husband can talk. Eric doesn't say anything, he comes home late and I report my activities for the day, he snaps Bill's head off and lies down . . . [in] the living room . . . to count the nails in the ceiling.
>
> (Jette 1977: 27)

Her son too was affected by the secrecy of the project:

> [Bill's] main problem, and one which wasn't solved for many years, was his underlying resentment at the way he was deceived when we moved. Had the security restrictions permitted us to prepare him for the move, there would have been no problems. As it was, he was desperately restless and homesick. Eric was preoccupied with war; all the men on The Hill were preoccupied with war.
>
> (Jette 1977: 45)

Although the accounts are ambivalent about the succes of the effort to make the bombs, they never attempt to develop a critical discourse or try to address moral dilemmas. Jette's writing captures an underlying sense of desperation, but mainly at the personal level: she includes news on the progress of the war mainly because her soldier brother was stationed in the Pacific. Her comments on the Trinity test first seem to recognise the scientists' involvement in creating the potential for atomic destruction: 'After the first wild elation, the men were thoroughly chastened by the success of their work and the depression was contagious' (Jette 1977: 107). But she then goes on to distance themselves from its actual use. She says that the Oppenheimers gave a party a few days later 'for the bomb-makers and their wives', where they danced and played a little,

> before we faced the desperate reality of what was to come. There were a number of military men at the party whom we had never seen before, but who were present at Trinity. Their presence served as a grim reminder that not only we, but all humanity, had passed the point of no return at dawn on Monday.
>
> (Jette 1977: 107)

The text then moves immediately to her brother, but the association of the destructiveness of nuclear power with the military clearly foreshadows immediately post-war politics, when even the more radical scientists thought in terms of removing control of nuclear power from the military rather than its inherent dangers.

The responsibility of the nuclear scientists for atomic destruction is both accepted and evaded. When the bombing of Hiroshima is announced on the radio, and the Jettes' son asks what an atomic bomb is, Eleanor tells him 'That's us, dear' (Jette 1977: 109). But her husband responds to the broadcast news of Nagasaki differently, first by bowing his head, but then exclaiming 'Christ, dear Christ, why don't those fools surrender!' (Jette 1977: 109). The whole passage on the dropping of the bombs takes less than a page, and the text then moves with no break to the local water crisis, locating all the events on the same plane of experience.

Conclusions

In reading the narratives we are drawn into their local compass and experience mainly the camaraderie, mutual support and high spirits of the writers. In so far as the personal was seen to exemplify human feeling, in contrast to military and scientific indifference, Hales (1997) is justified in seeing in these women's narratives a counter-discourse. But it seems to me that theirs is a rather limited and limiting one. It is not simply that their personal experience is inevitably partial, it is rather that the chatty tone of the narratives and the self-image the authors project – warm, charming and concerned – can be consistently maintained only if the narrative scope remains local. The restricted focus of the narratives does not so much subvert the military project as retreat from its consequences; were the narratives to climax with descriptions of the bombs' effects they would have to have been written in a different way and would tell a different story. Indeed, the publication of the narratives without new prefaces which would set their apparent naïveté in context is perhaps their most disturbing quality.

For present-day readers, the personal experiences of the Los Alamos community need to be set in the context of research based on traditional methods of archival research, which tells us about decisions made in Washington, as well as within the Manhattan Project sites (Alperowitz 1995; Hales 1997). But the most interesting example of an alternative perspective, one which incorporates but is not limited to the local, is the publication of a volume of photographs by Fermi and Samra (1995), Rachel Fermi being the granddaughter of Laura and Enrico. Part of the book juxtaposes snapshots people at the Manhattan Project sites took of each other and their families with photographs of the devastation in Japan. For instance, the first page reproduces a page from a family photo album showing toddlers playing in the snow in Los Alamos, the second shows six pictures of Hiroshima and Nagasaki arranged in the same lay-out, possibly from Robert Serber's own personal album; all pictures taken by Los Alamos personnel but by being placed together presenting the history of nuclear power within a wider, more inclusive framework than the earlier women's narratives had felt able to adopt.

Note

1 So typical of Los Alamos' reputation was this abounding 'hectivity' – the term
Brode uses for the heady social atmosphere – that Joseph Kanon (1997) begins
his novel set in wartime Los Alamos with his fictional spy-catcher protagonist
attending an evening cultural event. Interestingly, whereas friendship and support between women is a central theme in the women's accounts, in Kanon's spy
story the only contact between two women is seen as hostile and obstructive.

References

Alperowitz, G. (1995) *The Decision to Use the Atomic Bomb*, London: HarperCollins.
Badash, L., Hirschfelder, J. O. and Broida, H. P. (eds) (1980) *Reminiscences of Los Alamos, 1943–1945*, London: D. Reidel Publishing Company.
Brode, B. (1997) *Tales of Los Alamos: Life on the Mesa 1943–1945*, Los Alamos, New Mexico: Los Alamos Historical Society.
Clifford, J. and Marcus, G. (eds) (1986) *Writing Culture: The Poetics and Politics of Ethnography*, Berkeley: University of California Press.
Downs, M. B. (1997) *Lest I Forget*, Santa Fe, New Mexico: Sun Books.
Fermi, L. (1982 [1954]) *Atoms in the Family: My Life with Enrico Fermi*, Chicago: University of Chicago Press.
Fermi, R. and Samra, E. (1995) *Picturing the Bomb: Photographs from the Secret World of the Manhattan Project*, New York: Harry N. Abrams, Inc.
Freedland, J. (1995) 'Memories deaden Enola Gay's lustre' *Guardian*, 30 June.
Gallagher, C. (1993) *American Ground Zero: The Secret Nuclear War*, Boston: MIT Press.
Goldberg, S. (1995) 'Smithsonian suffers Legionnaire's Disease', *The Bulletin of the Atomic Scientists* 51, 3: 28–33.
Hales, P. B. (1997) *Atomic Spaces: Living on the Manhattan Project*, Chicago: University of Illinois Press.
Howard, T. (1987) 'Secrecy in the fifties', in J. Overholt (ed.) *These Are Our Voices: The Story of Oak Ridge 1942–1970*, Oak Ridge, TN: Children's Museum.
Jette, E. (1977) *Inside Box 1663*, New Mexico: Los Alamos Historical Society.
Jungk, R. (1958) *Brighter than a Thousand Suns: The Moral and Political History of the Atomic Scientists* (trans. J. Cleugh), London: Victor Gollancz in association with Rupert Hart-Davies.
Kanon, J. (1997) *Los Alamos*, New York: Dell Publishing.
Lifton, R. J. and Mitchell, G. (1995) *Hiroshima in America: A Half Century of Denial*, New York: Avon Books.
Lovibond, S. (1990) 'Feminism and postmodernism', in R. Boyne and A. Rattansi (eds) *Postmodernism and Society*, New York: Macmillan.
Roensch, E. S. (1993) *Life within Limits*, New Mexico: Los Alamos Historical Society.
Rosenau, P. (1992) *Post-modernism and the Social Sciences*, Princeton, NJ: Princeton University Press.
Segrè, C. G. (1995) *Atoms, Bombs and Eskimo Kisses: A Memoir of Father and Son*, New York: Viking.
Serber, R. (with R. P. Crease) (1998) *Peace and War: Reminiscences of a Life on the Frontiers of Science*, New York: Columbia University Press.

Smith, A. K. (1965) *A Peril and a Hope*, Chicago: University of Chicago Press.

Stacey, J. (1991) 'Can there be a feminist ethnography?', in S. Gluck and D. Patai (eds) *Women's Words: The Feminist Practice of Oral History*, London: Routledge.

Stanley, L. (1997) 'Introduction', in L. Stanley (ed.) *Knowing Feminisms*, London: Sage.

Taylor, E. (1987) 'The many faces of security', in J. Overholt (ed.) (1987) *These Are Our Voices: The Story of Oak Ridge 1942–1970*, Oak Ridge, TN: Children's Museum.

Tredici, R. D. (1987) *At Work in the Fields of the Bomb*, London: Harrap.

Wilson, J. and Serber, C. (eds) (1988) *Standing By and Making Do: Women of Wartime Los Alamos*, Los Alamos, New Mexico: Los Alamos Historical Society.

Wolkowitz, C. (2000) 'Nuclear families: women's narratives of the making of the atomic bomb', in S. Ahmed, J. Kilby, M. McNeil, C. Lury and B. Skeggs (eds) *Transformations: Thinking Through Feminism*, London: Routledge.

Wyken, P. (1984) *Day One: Before Hiroshima and After*, New York: Simon and Schuster.

8 Betrayals, trauma and self-redemption?

The meanings of 'the closing of the mines' in two ex-miners' narratives

Tom Wengraf

Introduction

In Great Britain, the miners' strike of 1984–5 was one of the most violent and crucial industrial disputes of the late twentieth century: a crucial part of the struggle to subordinate Old Labour. In this chapter, I examine the narratives of two ex-miners from South Wales in order to expand our understanding of the different personal histories on which these historical social transformations impacted and of the different social worlds in which these personal histories were lived out. In particular, I wish to demonstrate the value of close attention to the mode of narration.

These narrative interviews were collected during research into social strategies in risk society (see Chamberlayne and Rustin 1999 for details of the Sostris project). Some 250 life story interviews were collected across Britain, France, Germany, Greece, Italy, Spain and Sweden, 1996–8.

The interviews were analysed according to the 'biographic-interpretive method' (BIM). The key feature of this method of interpreting narrative interviews and other materials is that it distinguishes the *lived life* of its subject from the *told story*, and describes and analyses these first separately and then together in a complex series of procedures (for details, brief accounts in Chamberlayne and Rustin 1999, Rosenthal 1998: 2–7; slightly enlarged accounts in Breckner 1998; Wengraf 1999, 2000; a full account in English is in Wengraf 2001). We analyse the 'lived life' to understand the sequence of the non-controversial 'objective' life-events of the person in their historical context; the 'told story' to understand the structure and the modality of the narrative account, the significance of the way the story is told. The distinction will become clearer in its use in this chapter. In our tradition of research, we 'read' narrative accounts by individuals of their own life history as potentially symptomatic and revelatory expressions of historically evolving psychologies in a historically evolving context of micro and macro social relationships. We say 'potentially' because cautious reflection in the light of background knowledge and research is required to make valid inferences from the texts of the narrative accounts plus answers to further questioning.

The generic BIM methodology described in the previous paragraph was focused in Sostris upon the strategies – not necessarily conscious, almost always at least to some extent unconscious[1] – which had brought the individual to the point in her life where she narrated her life history in the way that she did.

For reasons of space, I provide a very abbreviated account of the life histories of the two miners so as to provide more space for an exposition of their told stories, and comparison between the two.[2]

Donald[3]

Donald's life

Donald was born in 1944 into a Welsh mining family and first went into the mines when he was 16, working as an apprentice coalface worker and then joining a maintenance team. In 1969 he married a librarian, and they had what was to be their only child in 1976.

From 1984 onwards, when most of the pits in Wales were being closed down, and because Donald's back had become troublesome, he moved to the surface as a maintenance worker. In 1994, when British Coal closed down the pit in which Donald was working, Donald was made redundant, at the age of 50. Since then he has suffered from physical and mental health problems, including immobilising back pain. He takes psychiatric drugs and he began psychotherapy in 1997.

Donald's biographical self-presentation in the interview: a 'sociotechnical love story'

Donald presented his life story from the perspective of his professional identity as a miner. Other themes of his life – his family and his leisure time activities – are scarcely mentioned. In analysing the narrative, it seemed to us that Donald tells his life story as if it were a love story, from the perspective of somebody who has lost the love of his life, who is searching for the reasons for the loss, and who is struggling to create a life afterwards. The following quote illustrates his passion:

> I was a good worker, you know, I'm not an admin person, OK, getting my hands dirty didn't-, didn't-, didn't-. I loved it, you know er it's my job. I wasn't interested in- I'm not interested in reading a book or I'm not good at writing letters and I'm the world's worst speller, but I'm a good fitter . . . And I mean, I just loved it.

Asked to tell his life story, Donald's self-presentation began with the following insightful comment: 'how do I consolidate, 36 years (2) it's a task, basically erm, I've worked in Pillar Colliery all my life, it was, a second home basically'.

Bear in mind, that, at the time of this interview, he had not worked in the colliery for four years. The shift of tenses 'I was a good worker . . . it's my job . . . I just loved it . . . I've worked in the colliery all my life . . . it's a task . . . it was a second home', the impossibility of describing 'that life' in a consistent past tense, suggests the nature of his current equal balance between struggling to put his colliery life and identity behind him, and still being identified with that life and identity.

Donald's love relationship with mining was based partly on his fascination with technology. The first few minutes of his narrative focus in great detail on the early and subsequent mechanisations of the mine. The danger of the work contributed to his commitment, and the money he made gave him the reward for his physical and emotional investment. But the most important part of his relationship was the comradeship he had experienced as a face worker, as he stated at the end of the interview, once more in the present tense: 'You know, it's er (2) wonderful, erm, friendship in the industry':

> I just miss, I miss my mates. I miss being chased because I was (I used to be a bit wicked) you know in work and er (2) I miss being called you little B, get out of the way or get off the phone and, go and do this or, pull your finger out, you miss going to bed, tired, physically tired though I mean.

When asked about experiences at work, Donald told a story which illustrates how much he valued physical contact with his workmates. He describes his relation with one of these men:

> I got dirty through fighting below ground, you know . . . We used to fight, he's 6 foot 16 stone whereas me what 10, 11 stone 5 foot 4, he used to throw me on the engines and we was rolling in the dirt. We were like the black (TAPE UNCLEAR) coming out . . . coming up the pit we'd start arguing, because I mean we were always arguing. He used to sit me on his lap, saying we looked like a ventriloquist type . . . we used to physically fight, you know, like kicking and punching, he used to sit on me, sit in the coal dust. Oh, that was just one of the things.

Physical struggle with his mates was part of the physical struggle by him and his mates with things, often in extremely dangerous conditions, and he recounts several such incidents with gusto in great narrative detail.

It is clear that Donald's personal identity is connected with physical work and his enjoyment of male physicality. In the enclosed dangerous world of underground work, this brought not only a strong emotional bond with his mates but also a neglect of other comparable activities. Playing neither football nor rugby (customary contact sports), Donald was a miner, first and last. So committed was he to his work, he could not believe he would be rejected. The shock was immense. The occasion and the manner of his being 'let go' he narrates below:

> to go to work and be told your services weren't want=weren't wanted any=anymore . . . I just couldn't believe, I just, I don't know, I just became (2) numb I was I think er for the want of better words, I just went through a process of packing all my tools up, put them all in the boot of the car . . . and then, and I think one of the most (2) one of the most, one of the most different=one of the worst culture shocks I had was when I had to sign, for the redundancy, now (4) I know I was a=outspoken person but as I said before=I have to reiterate I was also a loyal employee and I don't want to sound as if I'm blowing my own trumpet but I was (2) and when I went to sign, I saw the personnel manager because he was dealing with it, and he was the only person who shook my hand, after almost 36 years, and that really hurt me, the engineer, engineer never even said to me 'all the best Donald', you know, I'd lived with different engineers coming into the pit, landing good jobs because the likes of myself and other people in the pit had stayed with Pillar and kept it open (2) and er that's it that's it in a nutshell and not to be said, I know you might think it's, trivial then, I'm only looking for a pat on the back but if they'd just said 'well the best of luck' and if the manager had shook my hand and said 'look best of luck Donald you know, thanks for all you've do=done' I might have felt better, but the personnel manager shook my hand and said 'tara, off you go (2)' that, that was very hard, very hard, and to this day I=I think it was . . . (3) sentence unfinished.

Although an oppositionist prepared to speak his mind, he had idealistically expected management to appreciate his value. He was loyal to the Pillar mine as a business, and wanted non-business political concerns excluded – for him, both the Tory government and the NUM conspired to politicise the situation, and so ruined a still-profitable mine. The psychoanalytic theory of Melanie Klein distinguishes a 'paranoid-schizoid condition' in which accounts shift between 'idealisation' and 'demonisation' of salient entities. When recounting how the mine management refused to keep him on, his narrative shifts temporarily from an 'idealising position' earlier in the text to a more 'demonising position' that British Coal was determined to sack him because of earlier 'speaking-out'. His account focuses upon the manner as much as the fact of his redundancy. He cannot accept the possibility that he was removed casually without thought.

Home life never seemed a viable option for Donald or his wife. He was liable to be called out for maintenance emergencies at all times: week-ends, Christmas and the New Year. He was 'always away' at work and his wife 'didn't know what it was to have me there at home at the weekend'. Now that he is at home, the situation is reversed, and it is she who is hardly there.

He says that her exhausting work 'is torture', but this might refer less to her experience and more to his being 'tortured' himself by her absence at work: retired himself, he wants her to stop working and stop being 'such a careerist'. In his story of his life in the mines, he narrates from the point of view of *enjoying* always being away from home and down the mines, coming back totally exhausted and rushing off again; when telling of his current life at home, he narrates from a different position; it is difficult for him to see that his wife may get the same amount of 'buzz' from her pattern of practice now, so similar to his practice then.

He hates being at home but gets panic attacks in public. One possible explanation is his firm conviction even now that he 'should be at work': perhaps, for him, to be out in public with people seeing him 'not working but shopping' (not male but female, not working but lazing) is to make himself vulnerable to shame. But being at home doing nothing except domestic labour is also intolerable.

He was 'completely devastated' by the recent suicide of a close friend, another ex-miner. Talking about the pressure of not working, he implies that the friend committed suicide because 'he didn't have anyone to talk to'. Donald *is* currently having talking sessions with a psychologist, and this he thinks of as being crucially important in helping him change his perspective and 'move on'.

There is a second detectable counter-theme in his narration of the love affair with the mine. Ambivalence did not just start with dismissal. He says that 'at one point' he had a low period at work when he 'may have been tempted' to leave the industry: 'I became very unstable but it passed over, things settle down'. This early suppressed desire to break away from 'the love object' is matched by his current very explicit perspective that his psychic survival now depends on breaking these affective ties: giggling, he half-seriously wishes that the colliery – currently reopened and run by a workers co-operative – should shut down, so he, Donald, could 'shut the book' on it.

The final words of his narrative are a statement that 'if I had a son and if mining was about now, I wouldn't stop him going into the mines: it's a wonderful thing, friendship in the industry'. This positive statement involves evading the reality that his child is a daughter, that the mines are mostly closed down, and that – apart from being a shareholder – he has virtually left the industry and is struggling to leave it subjectively . . . but the only rosy future he can imagine, of his wife also retiring and them travelling together, is too far away and conjectural to pull him out of his attachment to the mines.

He struggles to get away from the mine, he struggles to put it behind him, he struggles to be 'strong enough' to *not miss* it, but 'I just miss working because I don't want to be at home'. He knows he 'must move on' but both his explicit theory of self and the mode of his narration 'concur' that he is still strongly stuck.[4]

Harold[5]

Harold's life

Born in 1960, sixteen years younger than Donald, Harold also entered the mine as an underground worker at the age of 16. Harold's mother died when he was 11. Widowed, she had brought three children from her previous marriage to the new home with Harold's father, who was a miner. Harold was the second of the three boys they had together, and when the mother died he, together with his step-sister, did the housework, while the father fell temporarily into unemployment and alcoholism. At school, he became, as he puts it, the 'top bully'. About the time Harold left school and entered the mines his father remarried.

After a coalface accident, he worked as a crane driver, and was active in the union and in the 1984 strike. He travelled quite widely. In his early 20s he developed a relationship with a woman with a small child. They stayed together as a family, and eventually married in the 1990s.

After the 1985 strike, Harold moved pits and stayed until that pit was soon to close. Taking redundancy in 1990 at the age of 30, he then did jobs as a mobile crane driver in the private sector. After a year, he took a job working with people with learning disabilities. Between 1991, when he was 31, and 1997, having taken several GCSEs and a BTEC with distinction, he became a full-fledged community care officer, with plans to start a degree.

Harold's self-presentation: a Bildungsroman

While Donald's interview took the form of a love story, told with speed and panache, Harold's was in the guise of a *Bildungsroman*, a personal development history, tracing through and reflecting on his experience of life, constantly (and often, though not always, very consciously) switching between past and more recent perspectives.

His interview begins with an acknowledgement of his own style:

> Obviously, when we're talking about my life-history there may be times when I may have to backtrack . . . I hope I'll try and be as precise as I possibly can . . . there may be occasions when I may get slightly confused and think aha that's not quite right.

His very long narrative continually oscillates cause-periods and effect-periods, shifting between his responses then and his judgements now. In this process the painful story of the 11-year-old and the period between his mother's death and going into the mines only receive bare reporting, and the regression backwards is constantly forcing false starts on the attempt to go definitively forward.

'The death of our err mother' is mainly spoken of from the standpoint of his father's 'burden'. Note the uncertainty of tense and referent in the first sentence:

> er I think there were a lot of pressures on on my father indeed as there was the family and I think at such a young age of eleven even though I did consider myself and still do now consider myself a very mature eleven year old I had to grow up very quickly. (4) And I think that it taught me some it taught me a few things em my father did struggle quite a lot and I would describe him as turning into an alcoholic at at a stage not long after em which was very difficult he was never never ever abusive he was not an abusive, alcoholic em I think what it was was that he was very depressed he saw more of the negatives rather than how can we move on from here.

Harold does not talk immediately about strong and painful events, but finds it easier to shift focus to the experience of others, taking the view of the carer concerned for others. Yet simultaneously, he is trying to tell the story of himself at the time. In a passage that significantly confuses past and present as it struggles for expression. he represents himself as:

> having had to grow up very very quickly . . . I think it's just that I was kind of it it delayed my er development my em my educational development em by a number of years but I think from from . . . maturity wise I think I'm far ahead of my er I was far ahead of myself.

The difference between his stepmother's previous family and the joint family of his dead mother's children is spoken of in a strong argumentation which lays stress on difference and on the lack of bonding, but which also indicates the importance of and capacity for bridging differences (even if the 'we get on very very well' slightly clashes with the 'no kind of bonding' assertion and may represent a slightly tricky achievement rather than a 'state of nature'): 'We have no kind of bonding there because we were never brought up as children that's not a problem we all get on very very well and I think that's vitally important.'

The painful pre-history of his early adolescence and of his mother's death is a necessary 'explanation' of going into the mines, which is when he starts to narrativise beyond the bare reporting. The first day of going to the pits, standing at the bus-stop, is when his history becomes 'tellable as a continuous story'.

Despite its greater flow and narrativity, however, Harold's intended linear progression within the period 1976–85 is always interrupted by an explanatory reference back towards the trauma of the mother's death or a slip forwards towards the divided community in the aftermath of the miners' strike in 1984/5, and his second betrayal, his second disillusion.[6] Thus what he thought then – 'at the time I thought you couldn't come across better characters' – is constantly compared with his post-strike position in which he developed 'such a dislike for some people because of the deeds that they did', and his realising 'how naïve I was and how people can be manipulated'.[7]

This continues in his account of the mining period, particularly through the key role of his industrial and union mentor and quasi-foster father Len. From Len, Harold gains a sense of family and community history, as through his sense of lineage with Len's own mentor, an uncle who was excluded from mining jobs for thirteen years after the 1926 strike and defied conscription in World War II. Like the teacher at school who challenged Harold to question: 'how do you know those astronauts are really on the moon?', Len in the workplace and the union stimulated Harold's independence of mind, often by teasingly setting Harold and his peers against each other in argument. Travel greatly widened his horizons: 'after that first trip it em I had this em urge . . . I needed to go I wanted to go other places, I want to meet other people . . . I wanted to go further.'

At the same time, and again in contrast to Donald, Harold was energetically involved in rugby and community social life:

> my social life was like very many others in the valleys and that was a hard-drinking hard-playing, rugby training (1) and generally socialising you know in pubs and clubs . . . in fact if you didn't participate in that kind of social behaviour then you would be deemed perhaps as being rather strange.

The break in community life erupted 'overnight or certainly within a week' with the scabbing during the miners' strike. The 'social treachery' still, over a decade later, greatly exercises Harold's mind and impinges on his daily life and his professional work. His reaction if passing a 'scab' in the street is to:

> keep on walking and that's my immediate thought I have no other interest in them whatsoever (1) again that that may seem rather cruel and rather hard but I think what went on during that dispute I think I'm well justified in doing so . . . I think I was em I was deceived by many (1) they may say the same thing about me it has to be said there's always two sides to the story and I certainly wouldn't deny that . . . I still see it now you know and I (didn't) I honestly believe to the day I die you know I'll still maintain that . . . not bitterness . . . you know I wouldn't wish them to walk down the street I wouldn't wish anything to happen to their family you know . . . I wouldn't care if it happened to them but I wouldn't wish it on them.

In his current professionalism as a social worker, he prides himself on managing to overcome these feelings. He tells the story of being sent to assess a former 'scab' who was 'physically and emotionally in a pitiful state', offering him the choice of an alternative assessment officer, the man saying 'do your bloody job', him doing a properly professional job, and the man's wife ringing up Harold some time later to thank him.

This is not the only difficulty Harold experiences in his current position. His emphasis on his 'luck' is a means of maintaining solidarity and identity with the former mining community, many of whom are now unemployed and in what he sees as being 'in a very broken state'. The 'jolt' of going into the mines at 16 brought him from a position of individualistic bullying into values and practices of collectivist solidarity, but he sees these as being already inaccessible for his daughter's post-mining generation. He also feels the precariousness of life: at any moment he or his wife could lose their jobs, and against that danger he regards education as an important resource.

Conclusion

Classical Marxism (e.g. Gramsci 1971) distinguishes between two types of class-consciousness: corporatist and hegemonic. Corporatist consciousness is characterised by a concern for an instrumental collectivism primarily oriented towards making economic gains for a particular social category, corporation, within the system. Hegemonic consciousness is characterised by a project of class alliances oriented towards overthrowing and replacing 'the system' in the long run, a project seen as more important than making short-term transient economic gains within it.

Interestingly, Donald's relatively corporatist and masculinist trade-union consciousness oriented to exciting challenge and interaction in the 'emergency team' and to making money for his family (by overtime at weekends, public holidays, etc.) tunnelled him into an excessive reliance for his social needs on employment for life in the mines.

Harold's more active union activities within and beyond his particular mine and his wider social networking which emerged from his more hegemonic consciousness served him better in the transition to the post-mining epoch. Donald was deeply shocked by the brutality of his ejection by the mines management; the more militant Harold had no such unconscious expectations of capitalist industry being other than brutal and exploitative, and so had no sense of management breaking any 'implicit moral contract'. Their 'normative narratives' of management and worker action were quite different.

In Harold's narrative, he sees 'luck' as playing a major role in enabling him to go beyond the emotional trauma caused by the loss of his mother and subsequent educational failure, and make a positive and fulfilling transition out of mining into a profession in which he can retain a sense of public responsibility and service. Yet in doing so, he could and can deploy a much wider range of biographical resources than Donald. Harold steadfastly refused to do overtime or weekends, always maintaining an active sphere of sociability and interest beyond work itself, in his family and beyond. His proactivity and many of his social skills, such as his ability to meet and exercise authority and his confidence in tackling difficulties, derive from the collective environment of the mining industry and the labour movement as he located himself within it.

Donald is also an outstandingly knowledgeable, skilled and authoritative figure. In meeting emergency situations in underground conditions he exercised ingenuity and versatility, as well as engineering and team-action skills. Despite his age – 54 at the time of the interview – 'objectively' he has many capacities to equip him to find a new orientation in life. Currently, however, his narrative shows him still 'paralysed' by his subjective attachment to the mines, to which he has given his life and an identity which he has not yet emotionally retrieved. However, his determination to 'shut the book' on the mine and minework 'and move on' means that, unless too handicapped by his physical problems or too blocked by the difficult readjustment of his relation to his wife, he may well succeed in doing so.

Both feel bitterly betrayed, but differently: Donald at 50 by the employers at the moment of dismissal; Harold, at 25, at the moment of the miners' strike not by the mine-managers but by the scabs. Harold is still seething with anger and perplexity, yet he is simultaneously able to move on and negotiate particular situations, just as in his youth he learnt from his emotional difficulties. Donald's more practical skills did not prepare a basis for such proactive subjective work – he reports no traumatic experience until the day of his expulsion from the mines – though his current recourse to professional psychologists means that he is determined, at a late stage, to import such 'reflexive capacity'. He now sees himself as having previously neglected his wife and daughter and psychically overinvested in the mine. His and his wife's struggle for a new relationship and a new beginning is at an earlier stage and is more difficult.

In this chapter, I have tried to show how a close analysis of the way that a person recounts his life story in conjunction with an understanding of the life that he has lived so far, and of the contexts in which he has lived it, can shed significant light on his predicaments and his strategies. Although both of the individuals studied are responding to the 'collective event' of the 'end of the mining industry', their stories show that the ways in which this impacted upon their lives and the meanings that they gave to this 'collective event' were very different: we need to *know* such individual narratives to understand what such social and historical 'macro-happenings' actually are.

Notes

1 See Hollway and Jefferson (2000) on the concept of the anxious 'defended subject' for whom self-knowledge is always incomplete and aspects of relevant reality liable to be ignored or mis-recognised.

2 I have anonymised details to preserve confidentiality. In the quotations, numbers in parentheses indicate a pause of x seconds; the '=' sign indicates a significant pause, or change of tempo or pitch.

3 This is a modified version of part of 'Stopped in their tracks: the British National Report on Ex-traditional Workers' by P. Chamberlayne, S. Rupp and T. Wengraf (1999). The interview was carried out by Prue Chamberlayne and Tom Wengraf. Analysed first by Susanne Rupp, it was reanalysed for this chapter by Tom Wengraf.
4 In some interviews, the explicit self-theory in the text and the mode of narration are strongly incongruent. Not in this case.
5 Two interviews were conducted with Harold, both by Tom Wengraf, who also undertook the main analysis.
6 It may be that this resonated with two earlier 'betrayals': by his mother by dying and by his father by losing his job and being at least temporarily an alcoholic. This is speculation.
7 While family relationships remain marginal in Donald's account, Harold's narrative starts with those of his family of origin though his relations with his partner (now his wife) and her daughter are only integrated into his life story in his second interview.

References

Breckner, R. (1998) 'The biographical-interpretive method – principles and procedures', in *Sostris Working Paper 2: Case Study Materials – the Early Retired*, London: Centre for Biography in Social Policy at the University of East London.

Chamberlayne, P., Rupp, S. and Wengraf, T. (1999) 'Stopped in their tracks: the British National Report on ex-traditional workers' in *Sostris Working Paper 6: Case Study Materials – Ex-traditional Workers*, London: Centre for Biography in Social Policy at the University of East London.

Chamberlayne, P. and Rustin, M. (1999) *Sostris Final Report*, London: Centre for Biography in Social Policy at the University of East London.

Gramsci, A. (1971) *Selections from the Prison Notebooks*, London: Lawrence and Wishart.

Hollway, W. and Jefferson, T. (2000) 'Biography, anxiety, and the experience of locality', in P. Chamberlayne, J. Bornat and T. Wengraf (eds) *The Turn to Biographical Methods in Social Science*, London: Routledge.

Rosenthal, G. (1998) *The Holocaust in Three Generations: Families of Victims and Perpetrators of the Nazi Regime*, London: Cassell.

Sostris Working Paper 2: The Early Retired (1998), London: Centre for Biography in Social Policy at the University of East London.

Wengraf, T. (1998) 'Sostris at the level of the comparative interpretation of cases', in *Sostris Working Paper 3: Case Study Materials – Lone Parents*, London: Centre for Biography in Social Policy at the University of East London.

—— (1999) 'Contextualising subjectivity in the exploration and presentation of cases in biographic narrative research', in *Sostris Working Paper 6: Case Study Materials – Ex-traditional Workers*, London: Centre for Biography in Social Policy at the University of East London.

—— (2000) 'Uncovering the general from within the particular: from contingencies to typologies in the understanding of cases', in P. Chamberlayne, J. Bornat and T. Wengraf (eds) *The Turn to Biographical Methods in Social Science*, London: Routledge.

—— (2001) *Qualitative Research Interviewing: Biographic Narrative and Semi-structured Method*, London: Sage.

Part III

Narrative and discourse

Introduction

Shelley Day Sclater

This final part of the book contains chapters that, in their different ways, consider the dynamic relations between narrative and discourse. Since the 'turn to language' in the social sciences, studies employing a diversity of discourse-analytic techniques have proliferated, asking new questions and providing new insights into the complexities and nuances of sociological and psychological phenomena (see, for example, Burman and Parker 1993; Tonkiss 1998). A focus on the social discourses that traverse texts has enabled social scientists to begin to address the complexities of individual–social relations;[1] it permits an engagement with the contingencies of social structures and power relations while, at the same time, opening up new avenues for understanding the ways in which human agents forge their identities as subjects within the constraints and possibilities afforded by discursive frameworks.

Like 'narrative', the term 'discourse' evades any general definition; as the chapters in this section illustrate, it has a range of meanings depending upon the theoretical and methodological framework in which it is employed. At a broad level, 'discourses' are frameworks of understanding that organise the social world and make a difference to it. Laclau and Mouffe (1985), for example, see discourses as arresting the flow of differences, and as constructing centres around which certain kinds of social relations crystallise. In providing frameworks for understanding things, people, events and relationships, discourses constitute structures that afford certain kinds of readings; they therefore function, partially and temporarily, to fix meanings. In the context of narrative work, discourses exert a structuring influence on narrative accounts, at the same time as those accounts provide the broader parameters within which discursive meanings are negotiated and realised, even if partially and temporarily.

According to Foucault (see Gordon 1980), discourse and power are, ultimately, inseparable. For him, power is not confined to institutions or to the powerful, and does not act just to repress, but is multiple and productive and dispersed across a range of discursive sites. Discursive structures therefore act to express, legitimate and maintain particular power relations. But discourses cannot, ultimately, be determining, as they are always more or less open to contest and change, and oppositional discourses can and do emerge to challenge the dominant and privileged ones (see Fairclough 1992; Plummer 1995). Furthermore, discourses demand the engagement of active human subjects. Althusser (1971) reminded us of the ways in which ideologies interpellate, or 'hail', individual subjects while, more recently, Davies and Harré (1990) set out a framework for the 'discursive production of selves'. Occupying particular discursive positions, they argue, has profound implications for meaning, self and identity. But, crucially, as the chapters in this section show, human subjects, far from passively slotting into the positions provided for them by a range of dominant discourses, are more likely actively to interpret and negotiate, or even challenge and resist, the prescriptions for acting, thinking and feeling that dominant discourses imply.[2]

The concept of discourse, then, has been useful in generating new understandings about the individual-in-society and has illuminated the complexities of the dialectical processes whereby 'the social' both constrains and facilitates subjectivities and human action, at the same time as indicating how individual subjective engagements with discourse are, in important ways, unpredictable and creative.[3]

From a psychological point of view, as Parker (1992) points out, discourse-analytic work leaves many questions unanswered: it cannot tell us, for example, what is going on in people's heads when they use discourse. What is it, for example, that induces people to accept, negotiate or resist the particular 'positionings' that Davies and Harré (1990) talk about? Does a commitment to human agency, in this context, necessarily presuppose a subject anterior to the text, who exists prior to discursive engagement, rather than being constituted and reconstituted by those engagements? If there is subjectivity beyond discourse, what form does it take, and how might we have access to it?

It is this kind of ontological dilemma that Wendy Hollway and Tony Jefferson explore in their chapter. They report on a series of interviews with 'Tommy' during a project that investigated 'fear of crime'. We see that Tommy draws heavily on a discourse of 'respect', and the authors show how Tommy's subjective investments in this discourse, and the social effects and personal consequences of his engagement, cannot adequately be understood with reference to his deployment of the discourse alone. Hollway and Jefferson show how the discourse of 'respect' both structures, and is structured by, the dynamics of Tommy's personal narrative account of his 'fear of crime'. In doing so, they highlight what might be called the 'emotional sub-texts' of Tommy's interview, and show the ways in which a close analysis of those sub-texts illuminates our understanding of the discourse of 'respect' that Tommy negotiates his way around in his narrative.

In order to make their analysis, Hollway and Jefferson have to provide a new conceptualisation of the narrating subject: Tommy is presented as a 'psychosocial' subject who tells his story within the constraints provided by his immediate social nexus, his broader cultural location and his own biography. It is within the complex matrix provided by these aspects of 'context' that Tommy tells his story. Importantly, Tommy's 'psychosocial' subjectivity is seen to involve hidden, unconscious as well as conscious elements.[4] The authors argue that it is only with reference to these multiple dimensions of subjectivity (Henriques *et al.* 1984) that Tommy's discursive negotiations make sense in the context of his personal narrative of 'fear of crime'. Importantly, too, these insights depend on the employment of a particular interview technique, and particular analytic processes; methodologies clearly matter, and neither discourse[5] nor narrative analysis (Riessman 1993) alone could have facilitated the insights into the sense that Tommy makes of his life that Hollway and Jefferson provide.

Similarly, in her chapter, Helen Malson addresses the crucial question of research method. She provides a reflexive account of her empirical work on 'anorexic' subjectivities and scrutinises her discourse-analytic method with the benefit of hindsight. She argues that there is a sense in which the research method she chose predisposed particular outcomes. For her, a discourse analysis that requires the fragmentation of the personal narrative into its constituent discourses predisposes a vision of a fragmented subject, whose subjectivity is dispersed across a range of sometimes contradictory discursive sites. What, she asks, might have been the outcome of her research, had she maintained the integrity of the speaker's 'whole' narrative'?

But, she goes on to argue, what is a 'whole' narrative? With reference to the discourses that structure the text, she illustrates the fallacy of imagining that any text can be boundaried and complete; individual narratives are necessarily structured by broader social scripts and are traversed by discourses that make reference, explicit or otherwise, to other discourses and other texts, *ad infinitum*. Therefore, the idea of a 'complete' narrative is rendered problematic in Malson's account. Further, she points out that narratives produced in social-scientific research interviews cannot be considered to be the product of the narrator; at the very least, they are the joint product of the interviewer and the interviewee, the researcher and the researched, and the interaction between them. The myth of the originating author is exposed in Malson's work, raising questions about the status of personal narrative accounts (are they 'truth' or 'fiction', or something different altogether?) and about the ethical dilemmas that researchers face.

Perhaps the nature of the narrative as a 'joint' product, arising out of a particular interactional situation, is best illustrated in this section by Marion Smith's chapter. Smith reports on a conversational exchange between two researchers and four 9-year-old boys who have come together to discuss issues of 'punishment'. In her analysis, Smith treats the narrative produced in the classroom as a 'drama'. She makes no attempt, as Malson did in her work on 'anorexic' subjectivities, to fragment the text into its constituent discourses but, instead, imposes a dramaturgical structure through which it is possible to make visible the boys' engagements with wider cultural discourses of masculinities and punishment. The two interviewers quite clearly play their part in the drama, initiating and concluding the 'Acts' and presiding over the action as it unfolds.

This chapter raises the important question of what it was that was driving the boys' performance. Their negotiations around the discourses of masculinity and punishment are very much a group response that can be understood with reference to the peer-group, and to the presence of the adult researchers; the classroom setting for the drama produces particular discursive readings by the boys, such that the discourses they employ, and the ways they employ them, are best understood with reference to their 'performance' in this setting. Smith presents us with a 'drama' that helps us to understand not only what these boys had to say about punishment, but also what they, as children, perhaps were thinking about their own relationship to the adult world. Again, neither discourse nor narrative analysis alone could have provided the kinds of insights that Smith's dramaturgical analysis provides.

The question of narrative as performative also looms large in the chapter by Jackie Abell and her colleagues. They provide a thoughtful and insightful analysis of sections of text from the late Princess Diana's televised *Panorama* interview. They highlight what it is that telling this particular story, in this particular way, achieved for Diana. Their concern is with the rhetorical functions of narrative accounting. The authors show that Diana's choice of discourses, and the way she interweaves them into her narrative, have the effect of winning the sympathy of the audience as she negotiates the complex path between her private self and her public persona. Perhaps, of all the chapters in this section, the work of Abell *et al.* illustrates the complex relations among form, function and content; how the narrative is structured by its constituent discourses, at the same time as those discourses are strategically deployed to give the narrative its form as a persuasive text.

Together, the chapters in this section address the complex interrelations between narrative and discourse, and raise questions not only of what is going on in people's heads when they use discourse (Parker 1992), but also of what discourse is doing in any person's use of it. The authors, in their different ways, present challenging ideas about interview method and data analytic techniques. The value of combining discourse and narrative, methodologically and analytically, must lie in the possibilities it holds for addressing the dimensions of subjectivity as a cultural phenomenon. On the one hand, as Rustin (1998) argues, personal narrative accounts are not merely personal but, on the contrary, provide us with the means to think in new ways about broader sociological and political phenomena. It is through attention to the discourses that traverse narratives that we can bring out, in analysis, these kinds of insights. On the other hand, narratives also provide us with a route into the realm of the psychological (see Day Sclater 1999). Through attention to the discursive positions negotiated by the 'characters' in stories, and through attention to the narrative 'plot', we can catch glimpses of narrators as psychosocial beings.

Notes

1 A breakthrough came with the publication in 1984 of *Changing the Subject* (Henriques *et al.*, 1984).
2 For a discussion of these processes in relation to divorce, see Day Sclater and Yates (1999), Neale and Smart (1999).
3 Wetherell and Potter's (1992) discourse-analytic study of racism is a good example of the subtle workings of discourse in texts; cf. Rustin's (1991) psychoanalytic 'take' on racism, where he examines its psychological undercurrents.
4 The 'hidden' dimensions of Tommy's subjectivity are 'revealed' through the authors' analytic technique that utilises psychoanalytic ideas.
5 A prominent social psychology text on discourse analysis is Potter and Wetherell (1987). See also van Dijk (1985; 1997).

References

Althusser, L. (1971) *Lenin and Philosophy*, London: New Left Books.

Burman, E. and Parker, I. (eds) (1993) *Discourse Analytic Research*, London: Routledge.

Davies, B. and Harré, R. (1990) 'Positioning: the discursive production of selves', *Journal for the Theory of Social Behaviour* 20: 43–63.

Day Sclater, S. (1999) *Divorce: A Psychosocial Study*, Aldershot: Ashgate.

Day Sclater, S. and Yates, C. (1999) 'The psycho-politics of post-divorce parenting', in A. Bainham, S. Day Sclater and M. Richards (eds) *What is a Parent? A Socio-legal Analysis*, Oxford: Hart.

van Dijk, T. A. (1985) *Handbook of Discourse Analysis*, London: Academic Press.

—— (ed.) (1997) *Discourse as Structure and Process*, London: Sage.

Fairclough, N. (1992) *Discourse and Social Change*, Cambridge: Polity Press.

Gordon, C. (ed.) (1980) *Michel Foucault: Power/Knowledge: Selected Interviews and Other Writings 1972–1977 by Michel Foucault*, Brighton: Harvester Press.

Henriques, J., Hollway, W., Urwin, C., Venn, C. and Walkerdine, V. (1984) *Changing the Subject: Psychology, Social Regulation and Subjectivity*, London: Methuen; 2nd edition 1998, London: Routledge.

Laclau, E. and Mouffe, C. (1985) *Hegemony and Socialist Strategy: Towards a Radical Democratic Politics*, London: Verso.

Neale, B. and Smart, C. (1999) 'In whose best interests? Theorising family life after separation and divorce', in S. Day Sclater and C. Piper (eds) *Undercurrents of Divorce*, Aldershot: Dartmouth.

Parker, I. (1992) *Discourse Dynamics*, London: Routledge.

Plummer, K. (1995) *Telling Sexual Stories*, London: Routledge.

Potter, J. and Wetherell, M. (1987) *Discourse and Social Psychology: Beyond Attitudes and Behaviour*, London: Sage.

Riessman, C. K. (1993) *Narrative Analysis*, London: Sage.

Rustin, M. (1991) 'Psychoanalysis, racism and anti-racism', in *The Good Society and the Inner World: Psychoanalysis, Politics and Culture*, London: Verso.

—— (1998) 'From individual life stories to sociological understanding', paper presented at the Conference on Biographical Methods in the Social Sciences, Tavistock Clinic, London, September 1998.

Tonkiss, F. (1998) 'Analysing discourse', in C. Seale (ed.) *Researching Society and Culture*, London: Sage.

Wetherell, M. and Potter, J. (1992) *Mapping the Language of Racism: Discourse and the Legitimation of Exploitation*, London: Harvester/Wheatsheaf.

9 Narrative, discourse and the unconscious

The case of Tommy

Wendy Hollway and Tony Jefferson

Introduction

Our aim in this chapter is to use the narratives produced with Tommy in two research interviews to demonstrate how these can best be made sense of once Tommy is conceptualised as a psychosocial subject. This requires an analysis in terms not only of his circumstances and positioning in socially available discourses but also of his investments in those positions. The notion of investment (or motivation) implies commitment over time and thus entails a biographical dimension. Psychoanalysis offers a framework that not only takes biography seriously, but also the contradictions with which lived lives are riddled. We found that by attending to both – Tommy's discursive constructions and his investments in them – we were able to make sense of the complexities and apparent contradictions of Tommy's interview data.

The Foucauldian idea that subjectivity is a product of positioning in discourses is now a sociological commonplace. However, the increasing tendency to read subjectivity only through the discourses that subject it, has resulted in a discourse determinism. The approach of Abell *et al.* (this volume) is one such example; it brackets off the question of how the narrative (in this case Princess Diana's) is related to lived experience. In line with Craib (this volume), we want to address, rather than avoid, this question. Where Craib approaches the question through Sartre's concept of bad faith, we use psychoanalysis as part of an approach to a psychosocial subject.

If we are to understand subjectivity in other than a socially determinist fashion of discourses producing subjects, we have to address the issue of how discursive positions are occupied by subjects. To do this in a way that does not simply replace discourse determinism with the idea of individual subjects voluntaristically choosing positions entails a more complex understanding of subjective positioning. Psychoanalysis, with its core notion of a dynamic unconscious, can conceptualise people's actions as unconsciously, as well as consciously, motivated and conflictual. This is an essential step if the psychic side of the psychosocial equation is to be given equal weighting with the social.

All psychoanalytic models are based on theory which claims that subjectivity needs to be understood biographically. In other words, the contemporary experiences, actions, relations and identities that make up subjectivity achieve their meaning and influence with reference to the way a person's past is sedimented into unconscious (as well as conscious) mental processes; a past which itself signifies through fantasies of those earlier events, both at the time and subsequently.

Theorising a psychosocial subject will be affected by which version of psychoanalytic theory is applied. A Freudian psychoanalysis locates motivation in libidinal drives which are cathected on to a range of objects. Kleinian psychoanalysis, in contrast, locates primary motivations in object-seeking rather than pleasure-seeking and thus posits an essentially relational subject. The struggle to survive in the real conditions which confront the infant (not just material but also psychological conditions) generates fantasies and defences against anxiety which, for Klein, are central in simultaneously structuring both the self and its relationship to outside objects. These unconscious defences are intersubjective in the sense that they operate between people – through splitting, projection and introjection – rather than within an individual. Our analysis of Tommy's narrative illustrates how Kleinian concepts illuminate his account and enable a psychosocial analysis.

Our interest in narrative emerged during our search for a research method that was adequate to a psychosocial subject. The traditional question and answer method of interviewing tends to suppress the respondent's agenda in favour of that of the interviewer (Mishler 1986) and to invite discursive rationalisations. Our interest in individual biographies meant we were attracted to approaches, like the biographical-interpretative method (Rosenthal 1993), which put interviewees' life stories – their experiences, their relevancies, their ordering – to the fore. Consequently, we adopted the following principles (Hollway and Jefferson 1997). Interviews were designed in such a way that the interviewee has primary responsibility for structuring the account, generating its content and moving the narrative onward. This requires asking few questions, which are open-ended, but which elicit concrete stories related to a person's experience. In following up, the interviewer stays within the interviewee's meaning frame by using both the ordering and the phrasing of the interviewee. After the first interview, we both listened to the audio-tape, paying particular attention to incoherences and contradictions in the text; places where a less unitary and less rational subject erupts through what is typically an attempt to produce a coherent narrative or life story. Out of this we generated a further set of questions designed to elicit stories for interview two.

We conceptualised the structure of a narrative by free association (Hollway and Jefferson 1997), where links in the account are understood through their emotional significance, rather than through chronology or logical sequencing.[1] We found that, without continuous intervention from the interviewer, interviewees' narratives revealed preoccupations, meanings, conflicts and defences of which the interviewee was probably unaware. It is to do justice to our psychosocial subjects' interview data, and to distinguish it from standard narrative interviewing and analysis (Riessman 1993), that we call our method the Free Association Narrative Interviewing method (Hollway and Jefferson 2000).

Two interviews, plus notes that the interviewer took following each meeting with Tommy, constituted the core of our data, but not the whole. They are supplemented by data from two interviews each with Ivy, Tommy's mother, and Kelly, his youngest sister. The 'whole' of our data also includes our impressions of the family via meeting with these three members and spending time in their homes and experiencing the flow of their daily lives, as children and others came in and out during the interviews. Nonetheless, this 'whole' is a small and partial representation and this raises the question of what claims can be made on the basis of these data.

The partiality of the data is not only a function of the short time the interviews took. It is a product of the specific relationship of the interviewer (Tony J) and Tommy and also the way that Tommy related to our questions in the light of what he knew about our research interests. Elsewhere we have discussed the dynamics of the research relationship and their effects on the production and analysis of data.[2] Here we shall focus on the effects of our method and the claims that may be made about the 'real' from the narrative.

The use of a psychoanalytic theory of subjectivity problematises the assumption that research participants are experts in the veracity of their own accounts and therefore the arbiters of the researcher's representation of them. We did not check our pen portrait or our analysis with Tommy, nor any of the others, since our theoretical stance suggests that he might well have disagreed with those things he had difficulty acknowledging.[3]

This principle also implicates our own involvement as researchers, which must be understood within the same perspective. Psychoanalysis does not, however, simply claim irrationality and multiplicity where once stood the rational, unitary subject: it provides an approach to human subjectivity which can help work out the difference between honesty and fabrication, between reality and phantasy and between ambivalence and splitting. Like clinical psychoanalysts, we tried to pay attention to the counter-transference as well as the transference dynamics, to our defensive blind spots as well as the research participants'. We used each other as the equivalent of clinical supervisors here, triangulating our different perspectives on the data. As in the clinical literature, it is worth seeing unconscious dynamics as being a source of insight, rather than worrying only about them as a source of bias (Aron 1996).

Tommy: a pen portrait

Forty-three-year-old Tommy was one of thirty-seven interviewees in our research project,[4] each of whom we interviewed twice, approximately one week apart. Tommy is an unemployed man who has lived most of his life on the 'rough' end of a high-crime estate in the North of England. He moved there as a 9-year-old, as part of an inner-city slum clearance programme, and thought it was 'brilliant'. Now, although he recognises that the endemic burglaries, joy-riding and drug-taking make it 'terrible', he still would not live anywhere else. Coming from a big, 'well-respected' family, he thinks he is protected personally from being a victim of crime.

Despite the poverty and privations of his childhood, Tommy remembers it as 'fantastic'. Teen years spent hanging around the estate were followed by a seven-year apprenticeship. Then the firm 'went bust'. Unemployment interspersed with some periods of nightwork followed; then, in his late twenties, permanent unemployment. He spends his time doing sport, getting involved in community affairs (refereeing, coaching, running the local working men's club), taking his son and other kids to and from school and visiting his housebound, elderly mother. He also enjoys walking his dog, meeting people on his daily rounds and being known by all the local kids.

Family life too is important to him. Though he now sees little of his original three children, who went with his first partner after the breakup of their relationship, he looks out for his 5-year-old son and worries about the incipient delinquency of his 15-year-old stepson. When Tommy's eldest stepson asked Tommy, rather than his own father, to be grandad to the new baby, Tommy was thrilled.

Tommy's own father was strict and would take a belt to the boys; but Tommy 'appreciated 'im for it', and loved him. When he died prematurely, Tommy was devastated, especially since, unlike all the rest of the family, he could not bring himself to kiss the dead man. This resulted in a nervous breakdown. Now he takes pride in the love and respect accorded his father by those who knew him.

Despite the 'brilliant' memories of his childhood, and his claim to love all of his siblings (save youngest sister Kelly who has become 'a big 'ead and such a liar'), Tommy remains puzzled by the family's lack of closeness. Though most of them continue to live nearby, there are no regular family get-togethers, even at Christmas, like big families 'should'; on the rare occasions they do, 'there's always a big argument'. Characteristically, Tommy 'ain't bothered'.

Class, gender and the discourse of respect/ability

At one time, the notion of the respectable working-class man connoted permanent (not casual) skilled employment, heterosexuality, marriage, clean living, sobriety, moderation and reliable provision for, and protection of, the family. Tommy belongs to a generation many of whom have never experienced long-term employment. Yet, the discourse of respect,[5] as we shall show, remains crucial to him.

What can be revealed by a reading that is alert to Tommy's social location as well as the discourses available to make sense of his world? Respect recurs like a motif throughout the two interviews: his memories as an excited 9-year-old first moving on to the estate are focused through the term, as is talk about both his father's and his own standing in the community. At one level, the importance of respect is not difficult to explain. Tommy comes from a large, poor family who, like many such families, manifestly had a battle to be regarded as respectable, rather than 'rough'.

When Tommy was asked how it felt moving on to the estate, he said:

> It were brilliant feeling, to move into . . . a big 'ouse, 'cos it 'ad got a parlour, parlour-type room . . . It were fantastic. And I felt right, right cocky . . . the estate were unbelievable . . . To walk up on this estate, I felt right proud.

Moving from inner-city slums on to a much sought-after estate (as it was at that time) helped to establish Tommy's family as 'respectable' rather than 'rough'. Tommy's pride can be seen as him sharing in the family pride. Later, Tommy is keen to affirm this positioning: 'We've been well respected on this estate ever since we've moved up.'

Tommy uses identical terms to talk of his dead father: 'He were, he were well-respected chap . . . They still talk about 'im in in club where we go into na. "There were nobody, there were nobody better than your dad, your dad were fantastic." '

Whether 'well respected' here connotes masculine honour (this was a working men's club Tommy is referring to) or family respectability (in the sense of 'features of life and conduct'), or both, is unclear. However, the fact that Tommy's father was a steadfast, hard-working family man who was strict with his children probably qualified him for the term respectable on the estate (despite the fact that many of his children got into trouble).

If, as we think, one basis of his father being well respected was the fact that he worked thirteen-hour shifts in the local steelworks to support a large family, and died too young to enjoy the fruits of his long labours, this basis for respect was denied to Tommy who has hardly ever worked. So, as one of the early casualties of deindustrialisation, Tommy had to seek alternative bases upon which to build respect. Tommy's involvement in the community provided one such alternative, which intensified after he met his current partner. He stopped going to clubs and pubs off the estate, became very involved in the local working men's club, and 'got a reputation'. Now he is President of the club and, like his father before him, well respected there.

The importance of the community to Tommy's sense of self-respect is also evident in the following extract:

> I don't think anything will 'appen to me while I'm on this estate . . . 'cos I've, I've confidence I've . . . got respect. I respect everybody on this estate. There's, there's kiddies all o'er this estate all call me by me first

name . . . It's brilliant . . . I'm well respected. And I respect, I respect all families on estate. I know . . . what they are, but you can't do anything about it. All you do is, you go and see their parents.

What does it mean to talk not only of being respected but of respecting 'everybody'? Given that he knows 'what they are', a reference to the rampant delinquency of many of the youngsters on the estate, this apparently universal respect can be read as an indication of the depletion of resources personally available to Tommy for the acquisition and maintenance of respect: knowing others and being known on the estate (despite 'what they are') becomes part of what being well respected means. Tommy has respect in the sense that everybody knows him; he respects everybody, meaning he knows everybody. Tommy's worklessness helps us make sense of such a discursive position.

For many, probably most, men, family life provides one of the most readily available sources of societally approved respect. Many have argued that the most common, transcultural, hegemonic discourse of masculinity involves 'procreation, provision and protection' (see, for example, Kersten 1996). In other words, it involves a benevolent, patriarchal father, rearing, protecting and providing for his family. While work was traditionally central to respect, often going hand in hand with being a family man, as for Tommy's father, for men like Tommy, for whom work has ceased to be a very viable option, family life (in Tommy's case, his second family) can take on a special importance. This is captured in Tommy's proud response to being asked whether he would be 'grandad' to his eldest stepson's first child: 'And I went "I'd love it." I just broke down. 'Im asking me. 'E's got 'is own dad. 'E said "you've done more for me than what my dad's done, and I'd like you to be our Chris's grandad."'

Beyond the social, towards the psychosocial

The above reading takes us a long way in explaining the importance to Tommy of respect. In a sense, we gain our respect where we can; the more depleted our resources for its achievement, the more significant each becomes. But what does such a reading fail to explain about Tommy? Clues to this fuller picture can be gleaned from the following extract where Tommy remembers his childhood:

Tony J: What was it like growing up in such a large family with
    Tommy (interrupting): It were great . . . You know wi' us being a big family . . . and all at school . . . We, we always used to race 'ome for cow pie . . . big meat potato pie . . . we all used to race 'ome at tea time, to see who got (laugh) biggest plate and everything. We used to 'ave some right arguments . . . 'is there, any more, is there, is there any more?' It were brilliant. And sleeping arrangement . . . it were brilliant. (Tony:

(laugh)). There were . . . six of us. Three in one double bed, no, two, two
in each double bed. (Tony: Yeah.) And in, well, you know then, we were
skint. (Tony: Yeah) . . . To get a blanket to get covered up were unbelievable. To get big . . . overcoats. (Tony: Yeah, yeah.) What me mother
used to do, you, you know plates in oven – she used to put some bricks
in. Get bricks out – t'warm . . . bottom of the bed. And get plate out
of oven, wrap it up in a er, a, a, a sheet and put it in bottom of bed . . .
it were, it were, it were 'orrible in the morning 'cos it were, it were
freezing cold. (Tony: Yeah.) Y'know plate and brick. There were no
double glazing, no central 'eating or anything. All we, all we lived for
were coal fire . . . They were tremendous years.

If we attempt a purely discursive reading of the above, it would see Tommy
as positioned in a 'we were poor but we were happy' discourse; it's an
everyday story of life in a big, crowded, but happy household. In other
words, such a reading is alert only to the overt content of the discourse; how,
despite plenty of evidence of deprivation, Tommy appears to have thoroughly enjoyed his childhood: words like 'great', 'brilliant', 'unbelievable',
'tremendous', echo like a chorus throughout his account.

One problem with this reading is that it is insufficiently attentive both to
detail and to contradictions. The detail of how and when Tommy first utters
'it were great' is revealing since it bursts forth from Tommy's mouth, inter-
rupting the interviewer's opening question. Why? One explanation is that
Tommy is pre-empting any hint of pity that the interviewer might be
harbouring or thoughts of a less positive image of the difficulties of life in
large, poor families. What Tommy did not know was that the interviewer
was also from a large family which was never well-off, a position which
assisted a reading of the subsequent chorus of how 'brilliant' it all was as
defensive. Read in this way, in a way which gives more weight to the
''orrible' dimension of these memories, we might be less convinced about
how 'great' it all was.

Thorough familiarisation with all our interview material produced lots
more evidence supporting the idea that Tommy's childhood was difficult and
harsh, and little evidence to the contrary. In addition to food, warmth, space
and money being in short supply, Tommy could not remember being kissed
as a child, an indication that parental affection of a physical kind may well
have been in short supply too. However, physical punishment was not in
short supply (Ivy: 'They've 'ad some 'ammer off me – them I've got'), which
included getting 'whacked' with his dad's belt. It was a family where mum
was out a lot ('I never stopped in once before I were ill . . . I used to go out
seven nights a week to bingo') and was both a fighter ('Oh I used to fight.
They take after me') and a drinker ('I used to be a big drinker . . . I used to
be drunk every night'). Dad was either working nights, sleeping days or also
out drinking after the day shift (Ivy: ''E went out for a drink you see when
'e came 'ome at night, which as you couldn't blame 'im'). Later, the shame of

two of Tommy's older sisters' teenage pregnancies appeared to precipitate their mother's breakdown and subsequent agoraphobia, and at least four of the children got in trouble with the law, two seriously enough to warrant terms of imprisonment.

There is also evidence that Tommy is able to recognise that his family is less than ideal in not being close-knit. This fact he finds puzzling yet compelling (he returns to the theme twice in the second interview, each time unprompted) since it contradicts his fantasy of what big families should be like:

> You'd think families 'ud be close knit family wun't ya? You'd think they'd meet every weekend . . . or go on 'olidays every year wi' each other. Er, I 'aven't seen one of my brothers na for 18 month, and 'e only lives at [a place nearby] . . . We *never* meet. And it is a big family . . . Always every time we meet there's always a big argument . . . If your mother's 'ad all these kids, you should all be together.

Tommy seems unable to accept the mixture of good and bad, love and hate, envy and gratitude, that constitutes family dynamics. His consistent inability to acknowledge the bad, painful emotions associated with family life leaves him either puzzled, as it does here, or with only his one-sided memories of how great, fantastic or brilliant it all was.

What this broader look at the whole of the evidence revealed, consistently, is Tommy's inability to acknowledge the emotional reality – the pain – of these memories, unlike his sister Kelly who 'hated' her childhood and could not get away soon enough. If, then, the evidence suggests that Tommy's judgement on his childhood should not be taken at face value, and that his characteristically upbeat memories of his childhood and family are one-sided, how can we interpret this evidence in a more satisfactory way?

By positing an anxious, defended subject we can begin to make sense of Tommy's idealisation of his childhood. Psychodynamically speaking, what Tommy is doing by denying the harsher realities of his past is splitting off the bad from the good in order to protect his present self. The concept of splitting originated in Freud's view of the mind as conflicted and capable of producing inconsistent thoughts and beliefs. Klein's work on splitting of the object developed this, emphasising how objects are often given unrealistically good and bad characteristics. Later Klein emphasised the splitting of the ego, where parts of the self that are feared as bad are split off through projection and usually identified as belonging to an outside object (or person) (Hinshelwood 1991: 433–4).

The above extract shows Tommy adopting two inconsistent points of view (one in the detail and an opposite one in his generalised claim). If the good and the bad have been separated, and the good has become located in an idealised version of childhood, where has the bad ended up? Perhaps surprisingly, given the role of family in his defensive idealisation, it was a family member, his younger sister Kelly, who seemed to be the recipient of the 'bad' side of his splitting: 'the only one in the family I 'ate' (a point he makes three times). 'I love everybody else.' It is through such splitting that his investment in his fantastic family can be sustained, which he 'explains' through the common-sense discourse about all families having one 'black sheep: There's always one in a family . . . there's my sister in my family.'

Why did Tommy hate Kelly so? Perhaps Kelly had done terrible things. Only when we had exhausted other possibilities did we begin to see his hate as an invested denigration; as an example of Tommy's defensive splitting (see Hollway and Jefferson 1999). Understanding his hate required us to incorporate knowledge of his defensive splitting with what we had learned of his positioning in the discourse of respect; in short, it required a psychosocial approach. Briefly, he hated Kelly because of her different relationship to the estate: what for Tommy is a source of pride and respect holds bad memories for Kelly. For all its problems, the estate is where Tommy is known and belongs, like his father before him; it is where he feels safe; it is where he's destined to remain; and, as a long-term unemployed man with few prospects of meaningful work, it is his best prospect of achieving respect. Being unable to move, either geographically or socially, reinforces Tommy's habitual pattern of denying the negative features of his family and the estate. Because Tommy's self-respect depends on the very family and community that Kelly has rejected, he cannot afford, either psychically or socially, to recognise why Kelly must embrace her particular version of respectability, which is to distance herself from the estate. Since the identity costs would be unbearable, he pathologises her choice, hating her for rejecting him, them, the estate. Her big-headedness (one of his stated reasons for hating her) is just that: too big for these things he is invested in. Kelly is not only rejected, but hated for aiming for what he does not, and cannot, have.

Paternal identifications and the lost object

We have now managed to account both for Tommy's positioning in a discourse of respect and for some of the investments underpinning such a positioning. What is already apparent is the central significance of his father in this. Albert's status on the estate is tied in with Tommy's own, and the respect for Albert important for his own self-respect: "E were well respected'; 'we're well respected' (the family); 'I'm well respected.' The different pronouns, attached to the same discursive claim, suggest an identificatory elision between Tommy, his family[6] and his father.

To unravel Tommy's identifications with his father, we start with an extract which tells a startling story about Tommy's reactions to his father's death. We then argue that his identifications with his 'respected' father are important in creating and sustaining his own identity and motivating his life-style and relationships in his local community.

Tommy: I were frightened when I lost me dad. (Tony: Yeah?) Yeah. Only one in family who were frightened, 'cos we 'ad 'im at 'ome. (Tony: Yeah. Tell me about it). Well he worked all 'is life, me dad . . . 'e was 65 and not even got 'is bus pass. And it *really* 'urt me that. That er, 'e died in pain in 'ospital as well. They fetched 'im 'im home. Fetched 'im over, put 'im at side of wall and they took lid off . . . Me dad were laid there and everybody, when we come down next morning, oh I couldn't go to sleep that night thinking about it. And everybody come down stairs, 'oh God bless', all mourners, everybody came – 'cos 'e were well loved me dad. They loved me dad on estate. And everybody kissed 'im bar me because I were frightened. Eventually we cremated 'im and I went back to work week after and I broke down at work. Because I didn't do what I should have done. I broke down at work, they fetched me 'ome from work and I were off work three week. (Tony: Three weeks?) I broke down, aye. I went to bed one night and I'll never forget it happened . . . summat woke me up. I woke up and I looked at bottom end of bed. Me dad were there. Me dad turned round 'don't worry about it, I still love ya.'

The chain of significances which led Tommy to have a guilty obsession[7] about not kissing his dead father seems to be that people came to kiss the visible body in its coffin because Albert was 'well loved' on the estate; that Tommy was the only one not to kiss him and that this therefore implied that Tommy did not love his father. He broke down 'because I didn't do what I should have done'. Tommy talks in terms of love and kissing, but the conventional phrase is to 'pay one's respects' to the dead. Given his emphasis on the widespread respect for his father, it is ironic that Tommy could not pay his respects in the way that was expected of him, the way that everyone else did. During the subsequent weeks of his breakdown, on medication, he would 'just waking up screaming, why didn't I do it?' He had to convince his father that he loved him despite this failure. His Dad's visitation helped – 'that made me a bit 'appier'- because Tommy was forgiven and still loved, but it remained on his mind long after he went back to work. We find it helpful to interpret Tommy's visitation in terms of unconscious projection into the external world of his 'internal' forgiving father. In this view, a ghost or visitation is an experience produced through unconscious intersubjective fantasy with real – in this case reparative – effects.

According to Klein, love and hate are always co-present in our relationships and the challenge is not to overcome the hate, but rather to acknowledge it as belonging in the same place as love. Alford (1989: 165), following Klein, describes a person's integration of love and hate as 'the common task faced by every human being'. This kind of integration enables ambivalence; that is, the capacity to recognise that good and bad exist in the same object. Tommy, as we have seen, is not always good at ambivalence. The capacity for ambivalence through the integration of splits is achieved through reparation;

that is, through acknowledging the harm that one might have caused some-one, if only in fantasy ('I didn't want 'im to die'), and attempting to repair it (Klein 1940; Alford 1990). Tommy did contrive a way to continue to make reparation: '[It] really 'urt me when 'e'd gone, and when I didn't do that [kiss him]. So I thought there's only one way to do it and that I'd have a tattoo put on. And I 'ate tattoos.'

Tommy treats this tattoo as a symbolic equivalent of his father: 'But I've remembered 'im . . . I've put 'im on me.' It could mean that he compensates for the failed kiss every day of his life: 'I always gi', I always give me . . . arm a little rub and a little kiss. Go in bath and make sure I wash 'im alright.' It is possible that this act is simply one of caring or love, but this would ignore the fact that Tommy hates tattoos. In kissing the tattoo that symbolises the memory of his loved father, and at the same time hating tattoos, he has possibly found a symbolic way of expressing his ambivalence that consciously he could not acknowledge.

Tommy's turmoil and fear at the loss of his father is clear. The literature on death and mourning typically describes a movement from denial of the death to acceptance through grieving (Bowlby 1961; for a summary, see Rycroft 1968: 93–4). That he could not come to terms with his father's death straight away is also indicated when Tommy says that *later* he 'accepted it, that me dad 'ad gone. I couldn't fetch 'im back.' At first, Tommy could not leave the house for fear of meeting someone who would remind him of his father's death. Later he went out but off the estate, where he could avoid these reminders. Now he seeks out older club members who remember his father and enjoys the fact that they speak of him with love and respect. Thus he now takes pleasure in calling his father to mind. Over time, he has retrieved and stabilised these lost internal objects signifying love and respect.

At his father's death, Tommy was faced with the necessity to reorganise aspects of his own identity which he attributed to his father. We have seen how central the notion of respect was in this constellation. How this task was achieved would influence Tommy's current relation to respect. The re-organisation of his self-respect did not happen in a once and for all way. We suggest that it was achieved by engaging in a life-style which reproduced on a daily basis the according of respect to Tommy via similar practices to those which accorded respect to his father. Even though the accessibility of em-ployment was different for Tommy, he did not do all he could to follow in his father's footsteps: when the forge closed down (his father worked in a forge) and he had the choice of being made redundant or being moved to the machine shop, he took redundancy and has not worked since. However, his life is arguably still closely identified with his father despite this difference. He has passed his time very like his father would have done if he had lived to a ripe old age, spending his nights in the local WMC and being a family man. In this way, Tommy lives out those aspects of his father's life that he has constructed as meaning that his father was well respected and well loved. By doing so he secures self-respect and love in his father's image.

Through taking an important event in Tommy's biography, we have tried to show that Tommy's capacity to see himself as well respected depends on living up to those standards he identified, and identified with, in his father. In this way we can add biography to the idea of defensive investments in discursive positioning. Our theoretical point is that this will be accomplished through unconscious dynamic and intersubjective processes in the course of his biography. This is not the same as understanding Tommy positioning both himself and his father in a discourse of respect. What we see in this event (which took place over twenty years before the interview) is that Tommy's internalisation of his father as respected and loved was no easy matter. Tommy's desire to pay his respects was sabotaged by an eruption from his own unconscious which forbade him to kiss his dead father. This left him shamed and guilty and out of touch with reality. Through the visitation and the tattoo, we see Tommy going through processes of facing reality and of reparation. We see him able gradually to hold his father in his mind with pleasure rather than with fear for his own self. In this way, Tommy sustains a local and family identity within a generational tradition of respect; one which is rooted in his own biography of forging a self out of love and loss.

Conclusion

We hope our psychosocial reading of Tommy has demonstrated the importance of defended subjectivity and biography to understanding Tommy's relationship to the discourse of respect. A purely discursive reading could offer a plausible, social understanding of Tommy's positioning. However, with a knowledge of the psychic investments needed to sustain such a positioning, and how these related to Tommy's anxieties and defences, we were able to explain the psychic purpose such a positioning served. We could also explain how such an investment could make sense of otherwise inexplicable parts of Tommy, such as his one-sided account of his childhood or his hatred of Kelly. In other words, once we understood Tommy's story psychosocially we could make better sense of much of what he told us. We also attempted to explore part of the process by which investments become sedimented within biography. By closely analysing Tommy's reaction to the death of his father, both at the time and subsequently, we offered a biographical history of paternal identification: how complex feelings about love and respect for a father became internalised over time and then were lived out as respect. Positioning in discourse may describe the end result of this process but it does not begin to unravel the complexities of this achievement.

Our analysis and interpretation of Tommy's narrative aimed at producing a psychosocial account of Tommy. The dominant constructionist paradigm in narrative research meant that it was inadequate for this purpose and so we developed a method of production and analysis of narrative data consistent with the principle of a dynamic unconscious. Pointers to the relation between narrative claims and real experience (or narrated and lived lives) can be found, we believe, in the traces left unconsciously in the text. At the same time, our concern with the discursive positions in which people become invested constantly implicates the social, thus marking the difference between our interest (as social researchers) in the individual case study and that of clinicians working therapeutically with individual lives.

Notes

1 Freud's method was to encourage his patients to say whatever came into their heads. His idea was that the accounts of his patients, if guided by such free association, would provide the evidence required to interpret the unconscious motivations at work and enable better understanding of the patient's relationship to the events represented in the narrative.
2 See Hollway and Jefferson (2000). Chapter 4 contains a discussion of Tony's reflexivity in relation to Tommy and Chapters 2 and 7 provide other detailed examples.
3 For a discussion of the ethical issues raised by our approach, see Hollway and Jefferson (2000: chapter 5).
4 'Gender difference, anxiety and the fear of crime', ESRC-funded project no. L210252018.
5 We have no space here to explore the relationship between 'respect' and 'respectability' (but see Hollway and Jefferson 2000: chapter 4), so can only note Tommy's clear preference for the term 'respect' in what follows: in discursive terms, his investment in being positioned as 'respected' (not 'respectable').
6 See Hollway and Jefferson (1999) for an analysis of family identifications.
7 Tommy's regret came up numerous times in the two interviews.

References

Alford, F. (1989) *Melanie Klein and Critical Social Theory*, New Haven: Yale University Press.
—— (1990) 'Reparation and civilization: a Kleinian account of the large group', *Free Associations* 19: 7–30.
Aron, L. (1996) *The Meeting of Minds*, Hillsdale, NJ: The Analytic Press.
Bowlby, J. (1961) 'Processes of mourning', *International Journal of Psycho-analysis* 42: 317–40.
Hinshelwood, R. (1991) *A Dictionary of Kleinian Thought*, London: Free Association Books.
Hollway, W. and Jefferson, T. (1997) 'Eliciting narrative through the in-depth interview', *Qualitative Inquiry* 3, 1: 53–70.
—— (1999) 'Gender, generation, anxiety and the reproduction of culture', *The Narrative Study of Lives* 6: 107–39.
—— (2000) *Doing Qualitative Research Differently: Free Association, Narrative and the Interview Method*, London: Sage.
Kersten, J. (1996) 'Culture, masculinities and violence against women', *British Journal of Criminology* 36, 3: 381–95.
Klein, M. (1940) 'Mourning and its relation to manic-depressive states', *International Journal of Psycho-analysis* 21: 125–53.

Mishler, E. G. (1986) *Research Interviewing: Context and Narrative*, Cambridge, MA: Harvard University Press.

Riessman, C. K. (1993) *Narrative Analysis*, University Paper Series on Qualitative Research Methods, Newbury Park: Sage.

Rosenthal, G. (1993) 'Reconstruction of life stories: principles of selection in generating stories for narrative biographical interviews', *The Narrative Study of Lives* 1: 59–91.

Rycroft, C. (1968) *A Critical Dictionary of Psychoanalysis*, London: Penguin.

10 Fictional(ising) ~~identity~~?

Ontological assumptions and methodological productions of ('anorexic') subjectivities

Helen Malson

> I do not refer the various enunciative modalities to the unity of the subject . . . instead of referring back to *the* synthesis or *the* unifying function of *a* subject, the various enunciative modalities manifest his [*sic*] dispersion. To the various statuses, the various sites, the various positions that he can occupy or be given when making a discourse. To the discontinuity of the planes from which he speaks. And if the planes are linked by a system of relations, this system is not established by the synthetic activity of a consciousness identical with itself, dumb and anterior to all speech, but by the specificity of discursive practice . . . discourse is not the majestic unfolding manifestation of a thinking, knowing, speaking subject, but, on the contrary, a totality in which the dispersion of the subject and his discontinuities with himself may be determined.
>
> (Foucault 1972: 54–5)

Introduction: from real to fictional ~~identity~~[1]

The aim of this chapter is to discuss some of the theoretical and methodological issues that emerge from the particular ways in which subjectivities are theorised and researched within discourse-oriented, critical and post-structuralist frameworks. In particular, I am concerned with exploring the status (including the 'truth' status) accorded to subjectivity in critical psychologies and social sciences. Drawing on my previous research on 'anorexic' subjectivities (Malson and Ussher 1996; Malson 1998, 1999), my aim is to explore some of the questions raised by the tensions inherent in such work. On the one hand, the now-familiar post-structuralist notion of subjectivity can be regarded as involving certain ontological assumptions about the nature of personhood. Yet, on the other hand, this particular conceptualisation of subjectivity as an effect of discourse can be viewed as itself a provisional fiction and, more specifically, perhaps as an artefact of discourse-analytic methodologies. To what extent, I would like to ask, are critical knowledges of subjectivity (as discursive constructions and multiple subject positions) produced by the specificities of discourse-analytic research procedures? How do ontological and epistemological questions about subjectivity relate to the ways in which texts are treated (theoretically and methodologically) either as fragmentable *or* as 'whole' narratives?

My concern with these issues around the fictional(ised) or textual(ised) subject follows in the wake of now well-established 'deconstructive' critiques of modernist notions of 'identity'. The conceptualisation of persons as unitary, self-contained, self-knowing and autonomous has long dominated thinking in the social sciences and in modern Western society in general. But as numerous authors (for example, Hall 1996; Jameson 1991; Lyotard 1992) have argued, the last decades of the twentieth century have seen a shift in both academic and societal sensibilities, such that modernist thinking is being displaced by postmodernist thinking. This is a shift which has proved notoriously difficult to define (Rose 1991) but which might be loosely characterised by a deconstruction of modernist meta-narratives of, for example, 'truth', 'progress' and 'identity'. As Hall (1996: 1) argues, certain key concepts of modernity, including the concept of 'the self-sustaining subject at the centre of post-Cartesian western metaphysics' have been reappraised as

> no longer serviceable – 'good to think with' – in their originary and unreconstructed form. But since they have not been superseded dialectically, and there are no other, entirely different concepts with which to replace them, there is nothing to do but to continue to think with them – albeit now in their detotalized or deconstructed forms, and no longer operating within the paradigm in which they were originally generated (cf. Hall, 1985). The line which cancels them, paradoxically, permits them to go on being read.
>
> (Hall 1996: 1)

Thus, while continuing to be profoundly concerned with ~~identity~~ – that is, with subjectivity – critical theorists no longer believe in the Truth of the sovereign individual of modernist thought. They question the very basis of claims made within more traditional paradigms that the 'identity', the essential intrapsychic characteristics of the individual, can be discerned through the empiricist procedures of mainstream psychological research such as personality inventories or cognitive experiments (Stainton-Rogers *et al.* 1995; Stenner and Eccleston 1994). The modernist concept of 'identity' has now been thoroughly reappraised. It appears now, not as a universal 'truth', but as a sociohistorically specific discursive construction that is ethnocentric (Bhabha 1996; Sampson 1993), masculinist (Coward *et al.* 1976; Jordanova 1989; Lacan 1982; Rose 1982) and peculiar to the particular historical period of post-Enlightenment, modern Western society (Foucault 1977).

The modernist notion of 'identity' has then been displaced by '~~identity~~'. It has been put 'under erasure' (Hall 1996) and reconfigured as a plural, uncertain and shifting collectivity (Riley 1988) of discursively constituted subjectivities and positionings. It has become fragmented, multiple, shifting, decentred and fictional (Marshall and Wetherell 1989; Squire 1983;

Wetherell 1986). In the postmodernist paradigm, therefore, social scientists no longer search for universal 'truths' about the 'identities' of individuals. Neither do they seek to reveal particular identifying characteristics thought to be located *within* individuals or groups of individuals precisely because the earlier notions of 'the individual' and her 'identity' have now been retheorised as 'the fictive atom of an "ideological" representation of [a particular] society' (Foucault 1977: 194).

In subjecting 'the individual' and (individual) 'identity' to this deconstructive critique, 'identity' has thus been retheorised *as* fiction, *as* discursive construction, *as* subject position(s) constituted within discourses and discursive practices, and therefore *as* always-already embedded in particular discursive and material contexts. As Hall (1996: 4) has argued, 'precisely because identities are constructed within, not outside, discourse, we need to understand them as produced in specific historical and institutional sites within specific discursive formations and practices, by specific enunciative strategies'. Thus, I would argue, in displacing 'identity' with non-humanist (Mitchell 1982), anti-individualist (Woodiwiss 1990) concepts of 'subjectivity', with retheorisations of subjectivity as fragmented, decentred, multiple, shifting and sociohistorically located, we have not 'just' come up with a new theorisation of the human subject. We have also reconfigured our ontological assumptions about the nature of personhood (however provisional the truth status of those assumptions may be).

Discourse analysis and the methodological production of fictional(ised) subjectivities

This radical critique of individualised and psychologised 'identity', and the concomitant theorisation of subjectivity as 'fictional' has inevitably proceeded hand-in-hand with the development of new methodologies for researching ourselves and others. The 'turn to the text' (Parker 1990) and the development of discourse-analytic research (in all its various guises) is now sufficiently well established as to no longer require the lengthy explanations and justifications that were once almost mandatory. Since the publication of *Changing the Subject* (Henriques *et al.* 1984) and of *Discourse and Social Psychology* (Potter and Wetherell 1987), there has been a proliferation of criticality generally and discourse-analytic research in particular (even as they remain marginalised in mainstream psychology and social science). Indeed, for psychologists of the 'critical' school(s), discourse analysis might be described as *the* paradigmatic methodology, even if it is a term that refers to a variety of, sometimes epistemologically and/or politically incompatible, approaches (see, for example, Antaki 1988; Burman and Parker 1993; Parker 1990; Potter and Wetherell 1987).

Despite this variety, discourse-analytic research can broadly be characterised by its concern with spoken or written language and text in its own right. It takes discourse itself, rather than some putative 'reality' assumed to be anterior to the text, as its object of analysis (Burman and Parker 1993; Potter and Wetherell 1987). Texts are analysed, not as a means of revealing the 'truth' about the speaker or writer (their attitudes, cognitions, traits or whatever), or about the events and experiences that they describe. Rather, texts are analysed in order to explicate the culturally specific discursive resources that have been drawn upon in order to produce a *particular* account of 'reality' (Burman and Parker 1993; Potter and Wetherell 1987). Thus, discourse analysts are concerned with, for example, analysing the particular constructions of an object, event or experience that can be found within a text; with the variations and contradictions between those constructions; and with the functions and effects (of truth and/or power) produced by the deployment of particular discursive resources (Billig 1991; Burman and Parker 1993; Parker 1990; Potter and Wetherell 1987; Walkerdine 1984; see also Abell *et al.*, this volume).

As far as subjectivity is concerned, discourse-analytic research is, then, typically concerned with elucidating the particular subject positions from which a speaker speaks and with the ways in which they and others are positioned within the text; with the various ways in which particular 'identities' are discursively constituted within a text; with the interactions and dilemmas that may be created for the speaker in taking up particular constructions of themselves or others (Abell *et al.*, this volume; Bordo 1990, 1992; Marshall and Wetherell 1989; Swann 1997; Wetherell 1996) or with the functions or effects (whether intended or not) of the particular discursive resources used and the power relations embedded therein (see, for example, Abell *et al.*, this volume; Henriques *et al.* 1984; Walkerdine 1988; Wetherell and Potter 1992).

Fictional(ising) 'anorexic' subjectivities

It is this kind of discourse-analytic approach that I used in my research into 'anorexia nervosa' (Malson and Ussher 1996, 1997; Malson 1998, 1999), and it is, in part, a reflection on the research process, particularly on the process of data analysis, that has led to the ontological, epistemological and methodological concerns I discuss here. The research having been completed, I am concerned here with exploring the extent to which the 'knowledge' of 'anorexic' subjectivities I produced was shaped by the assumptions I made about personhood and by the techniques of investigation and data analysis that I used. Should this 'knowledge' be viewed as a specific elaboration of post-structuralist ontological assumptions about the nature of personhood and/or should it be viewed as an artefact of my research method (see Tseelon 1991)? And, if this knowlege of 'anorexic' subjectivities is an artefact of my discourse-analytic methodology, then what other possibilities exist for theorising and researching fictional(ised) subjectivity?

Like many discourse-analytic studies, my study was interview-based. Having devised a semi-structured interview schedule and contacted my participants, I interviewed twenty-three women (described by themselves and/or others as 'anorexic') about their experiences of and ideas about 'anorexia' and 'femininity'. I audio-tape recorded the interviews, transcribed them verbatim and then discourse-analysed the transcripts.[2] In conducting the analyses, I followed the now familiar 'standard' procedures, such as they exist (see Burman and Parker 1993; Parker 1990; Potter and Wetherell 1987). This involved reading and rereading the transcripts, making copious notes on and about them until various themes, features, commonalities and variations began to 'emerge'. I then reread the transcripts more systematically, searching for as many instances as possible that illustrated these chosen aspects of the texts. In practice, this involved cutting out extracts and sorting them into piles of, for example, talk about fat and thin bodies, talk about control, talk about being a woman, talk about menstruation and amenorrhea, talk about self-starvation, talk about anorexia as an identity, and so on. Focusing on one grouping of extracts at a time, I then sought to interrogate the extracts at the level of text (see Foucault 1977; Henriques *et al.* 1984) to ascertain how, for example, 'woman' was variously constituted within the transcripts? How was eating constructed as a problematic activity? How, despite variations in the meanings attributed to thinness, was a thin body almost invariably constructed as 'a good thing'? Or how was a particular discursive construction of 'control' articulated as a gendered construction? What eventually emerged from this process[3] was a series of analyses of, among other things, contemporary discursive constructions of 'anorexic' and 'feminine' subjectivities.

Analysing the various discourses and discursive resources articulated in the interview transcripts involved, then, an explication of 'anorexic' and 'feminine' subjectivities. For example, within a Cartesian dualist discourse, thinness was construed as proof of the mind's control over the body and thus signified the integrity of a self-controlled, powerful, independent and disembodied subjectivity (Malson and Ussher 1996; see also Bordo 1990, 1992). In contrast, in a romantic discourse (see also Wetherell 1991), the thin female body also signified a quite traditional feminine subjectivity which was heterosexually attractive, requiring of male approval and sometimes fragile, child-like and passive (Malson 1998). However, the extreme thinness of the 'anorexic' body could also signify a rejection of traditional femininity (Malson 1997) and the taking up of a non-feminine, boyish or genderless subjectivity (Malson 1998; see also Bordo 1990). Alternatively the 'anorexic' body could signify a deathly femininity that may be variously construed as liminal, other-worldly and beyond the restraints of mundane femininity; as an ultimate feminine passivity; or as an expression of extreme self-hatred and self-annihilation (Malson and Ussher 1997).

The deployment of a medical discourse in the transcripts produced a range of different subjectivities again. Here 'anorexic' subjectivity was constituted as a psychopathologised identity that was variously constituted as weak, fragile, damaged, sick and deviant. But the interview transcripts also evidenced resistances to this medicalised subject (im)position such that, for example, 'anorexia' was also construed as a personal possession, a form of self-expression and a means of achieving an otherwise lacking identity (Malson 1998). In short, through a discourse-analytic process – which involved fragmenting the interview transcripts and reorganising them into groupings of extracts – I explicated a variety of ways in which 'anorexic' and 'feminine' subjectivities were discursively constituted.

Fictional(ised) subjectivities and some particularities of discourse analysis

By thus mapping out a range of ways in which 'anorexic' and 'feminine' 'identities' (and the bodies and practices by which they are signified) were constituted in everyday talk, the study provided an empirically grounded retheorisation of women's 'anorexic' subjectivities as heterogeneous and plural collectivities (see Riley 1988); subjectivities constituted in and by the sociohistorically specific, and often gender-specific, discourses and discursive practices of late twentieth-century Western culture(s). However, in reflecting on this research process, it occurred to me (as it has undoubtedly occurred to others) that something was being lost in the analysis. In 'chopping up' the interview narratives and focusing instead on extracts (which had thereby been decontextualised from the wider stories in which they had been embedded), the overall coherences and the 'lines of narrative' of each transcript were perhaps being sacrificed in the analytic process of extracting and elucidating the various discursive constructions of 'anorexic' and 'feminine' subjectivities. That is, following through the particular research procedures outlined above involved an *a priori* conceptualisation of 'the text' as an interwoven but fragmentable montage of disparate cultural/discursive resources rather than as, for example, a 'whole' narrative. The knowledge of 'anorexic' subjectivities (as constructions dispersed across a range of discursive sites) that I produced in my research was, therefore, in an important sense, dependent upon the particularities of the discourse-analytic method I used. The particular conceptualisation of the text as fragmentable, implied by that method, foreclosed analytic questions about, for example, how subjectivity might otherwise be evidenced in each text taken as a 'whole' narrative.

My concern with 'whole' texts should, rightly I think, provoke immediate scepticism in so far as it might suggest a distinctly liberal humanist concern with 'the individual' and her definitive story. It might suggest a reinstalment of the self-knowing sovereign individual as originary and unifying author of her own authentic autobiography. For if I am concerned about fragmenting 'whole' narratives – with a violence done *to* the text rather than *by* the text (see Laclau 1990) – might that not be because of a liberal humanist ethical concern that this is equivalent to a violence done to the individual author of that text?

It is of course possible that my concern is produced by an implicit humanistic conceptualisation that runs counter to the explicitly stated critical perspective of my research. Like other feminist researchers, I am concerned to articulate a politically radical perspective on 'anorexia' that challenges inequalities and the hetero-patriarchal *status quo* and that is, in some way, 'empowering' for women. But, equally, I am convinced that liberal humanism is not a useful framework within which to achieve those aims (see Hirst and Woolley 1982; Bhabha 1996). The decision to interview 'anorexic' women was, therefore, politically, ethically and theoretically complicated from the start. Interview-based research has been said to be a means of 'giving a voice' to people who might otherwise go unheard (see, for example, Widdicombe 1993). Nevertheless, it is problematic to regard interview-based, discourse-analytic research as necessarily either emancipatory or empowering on these grounds (to the extent that these grounds are humanistic) because it is discourse, and not the subject who deploys that discourse, that is the object of attention (Burman 1990; Widdicombe 1993). As outlined above, in discourse analysis, texts are not viewed as transparent reflections of some putative reality lying anterior to them. They are not analysed as being true (or untrue) in any empiricist or humanistic sense, but are viewed as creating 'truth effects' (Foucault 1972; Walkerdine 1986). Nor, therefore, are they analysed as 'windows' to the intrapsychic realm of a speaker's 'true' experiences, life, attitudes, perceptions, cognitions or 'identity', precisely because they are theorised as social practices which systematically construct their objects in ways which unavoidably construct, maintain or oppose particular power-relations and 'regimes of truth' (Foucault 1972).

Critical psychological research into subjectivity cannot therefore be concerned with attempting to identify any unifying authorial identity in relation to a given text or with attempting, in any straightforward sense, to make public the voice of that identity. Hence, the potentially radical, empowering or emancipatory effects of interview-based discourse-analytic research lie more, I think, in the elucidation of the cultural and discursive construction and regulation of 'truths', 'identities' and 'experiences' than in giving a public voice to otherwise unheard or unheeded people.

A concern with a 'violence' done *to* the seeming unity of a text may seem therefore to be at odds with discourse-oriented, critical and post-structuralist perspectives. For, in an important sense, it becomes implausible to maintain that there is any unitary and unifying authorial identity lying behind personal narratives, or even to assume that such narratives are the speakers' *own* accounts;[4] first, because the discourses articulated in a personal narrative cannot be said to originate from the individual speaker. Rather, they emerge in particular social, economic, cultural, historical, political and institutional sites (Foucault 1972; Hall 1996; Henriques *et al.* 1984), and are rearticulated in *social* practice in the particular social locations of, for example, the research interview. The discourses deployed in a personal narrative are neither peculiar to the individual who articulates them, nor do they have an origin in that person. Hence, the personal narrative produced in a research interview is not something that can be said to originate in the speaker. It is not simply produced by either interviewee or interviewer, or even by the interaction between them because, from a critical perspective, the discourses and discursive resources that traverse the text have their origin elsewhere; they always-already exist before they can be rearticulated by the speaker in any given social and interactional context.

Second, research interviews constitute a very particular interactional context in which interviewer and interviewee relate to each other at a number of levels, conscious and unconscious (see, for example, Hollway and Jefferson, this volume). The interviewer is concerned to elicit the interviewee's talk about the research topic (in the present case, 'anorexia'), and to provide a facilitating environment for the participant to tell her story. The agenda of the interviewee is less clear, but is likely to include a desire to give a plausible account that '*makes* sense' of herself; that is comprehensible to the listener and that is oriented in some way to the researcher's agenda. Speakers' accounts undoubtedly also have a persuasive quality, and any speaker employs rhetorical devices designed to enhance the convincingness of the particular perspective she offers and to justify her actions and feelings (see, for example, Abell *et al.*, this volume). The resulting text is, then, a product of both speaker and listener, produced in the context of these explicit and implicit local parameters which are themselves conditioned by the wider cultural/discursive context(s) in which the interview takes place.

Moreover, any assumption of a unitary authorial identity lying behind the text is further undermined if the unconscious dimensions of speaker–listener interaction are brought into focus (Day Sclater 1997). Issues of transference and counter-transference, identification and the interactional operation of unconscious defences (see, for example, Hollway and Jefferson, this volume) provide a powerful sub-text for the interview, and link together the lives and subjectivities of interviewers and interviewees in ways that are not easily disentangled. The emotional undercurrents of the interview process thus preclude any straightforward reading of the text as the product of its self-consciously identified author.

Third, the notion of a unifying authorial identity lying behind a personal narrative is problematised further because, as Foucault (1972) has argued, the speaking/writing subject, far from being the origin of her account, is among the objects constituted by its discourse. The speaking subject 'does not await in limbo the order that will free it and enable it to become embodied in a visible and prolix objectivity; it does not pre-exist itself, held back by some obstacle at the first edge of light. It exists under the positive conditions of a complex group of relations' (Foucault 1972: 45). The speaking subject does not exist anterior to discourse waiting to reveal herself but is, rather, constituted and reconstituted in talk and text (Wetherell 1996). She is interpellated (or 'hailed') by a variety of discourses, taking up (or having imposed upon her) a multiplicity of discursively constituted subject positions from which to speak and be spoken to (Davies and Harré 1990; Jardine 1985; Poovey 1988; Wetherell 1986). As Lacan (1977) stated, subjects are themselves 'spoken' by language. From a post-structuralist perspective, then, not only are we not the authors of our 'own' words but, further, we cannot be said to have any (authorial) identity independent of our own, and others' texts. The various discursive constructions of 'anorexic' subjectivities, outlined above, are not, then, artificially fragmented aspects of a unified or unifying 'identity' but are the discursively constituted sites from which the women I interviewed 'fictioned' themselves in a multiplicity of culturally available ways.

My concern that the 'knowledge' of 'anorexic' and 'feminine' subjectivities that I produced through analysing interview transcripts is not, therefore, a concern that I had lost sight of the interviewees' unitary or unifying authorial 'identities'. For the reasons outlined above, I have rejected the modernist notion that the interviewee (or anyone else) could have a unitary authorial identity that could unify the text. Nevertheless, I am concerned that this representation of subjectivity as multiple discursive constructions is one that is produced by the techniques of discourse analysis; that this 'knowledge' of personhood is an artefact of the particular research process I chose to use. As Tseelon (1991: 299) has argued, 'choosing a [research] method is like choosing a language . . . methods, like language, are ideological in that they produce, not just re-produce, meaning'. Just as with the more traditional, empiricist research methods (see Harré 1979; Harré and Secord 1972; Shotter 1984), discourse-analytic methods do not transparently reveal *the* truth about the subject or the object under investigation simply because there is no single 'truth' to be found. Research methods, whatever their ontological and epistemological premises, are, as Tseelon (1991) argues, best viewed as representational systems which construct their objects of knowledge, in particular ways. 'Thus by choosing a certain method we are opting for a particular picture of humans. It is not a question of accuracy but a question of values' (Tseelon 1991: 313).

My reflexive discussion about the way in which my interview transcripts were analysed expresses a concern, not that the discourse-analytic method was 'wrong' or 'distorting' in some way, but that the texts could have been read differently. By this I do not mean only that someone else could have focused on different discursive themes, constructions and dilemmas although, of course, this is certainly the case. Rather, I mean that a critical discourse analysis need not have involved their fragmentation into thematised extracts, decontextualised from the 'whole' narratives in which they appeared. The crucial issue is, I think, about the provisional nature of the choice of how *exactly* a text is to be analysed and about the theoretical and political implications of this choice of analytic procedure in terms of the knowledge of fictional(ised) subjectivity that is thereby produced. How might the analysis have looked if it had not involved the procedural step of fragmenting the transcripts into groupings of extracts and if it had involved, instead, an analysis of 'whole' narratives?

This question about 'whole' narratives does, however, require some clarification of what is meant by the 'wholeness' of a text. As indicated above, the interview transcripts, like any other text, were made up of a variety of different discourses, interwoven to form a provisionally unified account tailored to the interview context. As Foucault (1972: 23) has argued, a text has only 'a weak, accessory unity in relations to the discursive unity it supports . . . the frontiers of a book [or other document] are never clear-cut . . . [because] it is always caught up in a system of references to other books, other texts, other sentences: it is a node within a network'. The fragmentation of my transcripts in the analytic process is, then, only one of many fragmentations that have already occurred in the research process. For example, I made a choice not to include an inevitably endless series of other texts to which the transcripts might be intertextually referenced or related. Similarly, by asking participants to talk as 'anorexic women', other accounts that they might have given of themselves in a different context were thereby excluded. These aspects of the research process themselves problematise the characterisation of the transcripts as theoretically meaningful 'wholes'. Thus, to treat a transcript as a 'whole' narrative is theoretically problematic and might even be seen as consolidating its dislocation from the broader discursive network in which it is produced and has meaning. Yet, at the same time, if 'the method is the message' (Tseelon 1991), then the specific methodological procedure I adopted can be seen as creating only one of several possible critical knowledges of fictional(ised) subjectivities.

Conclusions: losing the plot of fictional(ised) ~~identity~~?

In this chapter I have sought to explore the relationship between 'subjectivity' and 'text' and the dilemmas this raises for the researcher. I have sought to question how the particularities of discourse-analytic procedures (and the conceptualisations of 'text' on which they are premised) mediate that relationship in critical, post-structuralist and discourse-oriented research. More specifically I have been concerned (a) with exploring how the particular procedures of a discourse-analytic research project can be understood as producing (rather than simply revealing) a particular knowledge of 'anorexic' subjectivities as fictional, multiple, shifting and discursively constituted, and (b) with the truth status accorded to such knowledge. If, as argued above, identity has been put 'under erasure' and reconfigured as fictional, decentred, shifting and sociohistorically specific, then new questions arise. In what sense can knowledge of discursively constructed subjects, as fragmented and dispersed across a range of discursive sites, be understood as provisional or fictional, rather than as ontologically 'true'? In what sense might the procedures of discourse analysis be seen as 'fictioning' a particular subject into being?

In exploring the particular ways discourse analysis fragments the texts it analyses, I have not sought to suggest that there is anything 'wrong' with this kind of work, nor that the knowledges it produces are not valuable.

Neither do I want to suggest that it would be 'better' to analyse texts as whole narratives. As indicated above, from a post-structuralist perspective, it is quite problematic to regard a text as 'whole' in any absolute sense or to conceptualise a personal narrative as being unified with reference to an underlying authorial identity. Rather, my aim has been to suggest that treating texts as fragmentable montages produces *particular* critical knowledges of subjectivities and that this, or any other, choice of research method therefore forecloses, at least provisionally, other possible knowledges of subjectivity that might otherwise be produced. What is sidelined by the form of discourse analysis I used are the plots, structures, styles and temporal dimensions of interview transcripts and other narratives (see Gergen and Gergen 1983; White 1973) in which subjectivities are discursively located (Davies and Harré 1990).

As the other chapters in this section of the book amply illustrate, subjectivities are, in important ways, discursively produced, and the discourses we deploy to make sense of our lives, and of ourselves and others, do not stand alone or operate autonomously. On the contrary, they are located within a wider web of intertextual relations across space and time, and discursive positions are occupied, negotiated or resisted by active human subjects, using conscious strategies and making unconscious emotional investments in telling things as they do. People deploy the discursive resources available to them by locating them in broader cultural scripts and narrative structures to construct their personal stories. For while authorial 'identity' has no unity or unifying function and is only manifested in its dispersion across a range of discursive sites (Foucault 1972), the fictional(ised) subject is also made meaningful by the narrative structures and conventions that 'organise episodes, actions and accounts of actions . . . bring[ing] together mundane facts and fantastic creations' (Sarbin 1986: 8–9). In this process, the factual(ised), fantasised, fictional(ised) identity (see Walkerdine, 1986) of the texts' authors and other narrative characters are created.

Acknowledgement

I would like to thank Shelley Day Sclater for her invaluable comments upon and contributions to the writing of this chapter.

Notes

1 The proposition that identity has been put under erasure (see Hall 1996) is central to my argument in this chapter. It is for this reason that I have employed this particular designation of 'identity' in the headings and in places throughout the text.
2 See Malson and Ussher (1996) and Malson (1995) for more detailed discussion of the research procedure.
3 In practice, the process of analysis was a complex one that was never finished, in any absolute sense, because, in the process of analysing any one set of extracts, new possibilities for analysis were continually suggesting themselves.

4 This is not to suggest that participants should not have a right of ownership of their transcripts but to make a theoretical point about the relationship between author and text (see, for example, Barthes 1972).

References

Antaki, C. (ed.) (1988) *Analysing Everyday Explanations: A Casebook of Methods*, London: Sage.

Bhabha, H. K. (1996) 'Culture's in-between', in S. Hall and P. du Guy (eds) *Questions of Cultural Identity*, London: Sage.

Barthes, R. (1972) 'The death of the author', in S. Heath (ed.) *Roland Barthes: Image, Music, Text*, London: Flamingo.

Billig, M. (1991) *Ideologies and Beliefs*, London: Sage.

Bordo, S. (1990) 'Reading the slender body', in M. Jacobus, E. Fox Keller and S. Shuttleworth (eds) *Body/Politics: Women and the Discourses of Science*, London: Routledge.

—— (1992) 'Anorexia nervosa: psychopathology as the crystallization of culture', in H. Crowley and S. Himmelweit (eds) *Knowing Women: Feminism and Knowledge*, Cambridge, Polity Press in association with The Open University Press.

Burman, E. (1990) 'Differing with deconstruction: a feminist critique', in I. Parker and J. Shotter (eds) *Deconstructing Social Psychology*, London: Routledge.

Burman, E. and Parker, I. (eds) (1993) *Discourse Analytic Research: Repertoires and Readings of Texts in Action*, London: Routledge.

Coward, R., Lipshitz, S. and Cowie, E. (1976) 'Psychoanalysis and patriarchal structure', in *Papers on Patriarchy* (Patriarchy Conference, 1976, London), Brighton: Women's Publishing Collective.

Davies, B. and Harré, R. (1990) 'Positioning: the discursive production of selves', *Journal for the Theory of Social Behaviour*, 20: 43–63.

Day Sclater, S. (1997) 'Narrating subjects-in-culture: rethinking reflexivity', paper presented at the Culture in Psychology Symposium, 5th European Congress on Psychology, Dublin.

Foucault, M. (1972) *The Archaeology of Knowledge and the Discourse on Language* (trans. A. Sheridan), New York: Pantheon Books.

—— (1977) *Discipline and Punish: The Birth of the Prison* (1987 edition), Harmondsworth, Penguin.

Gergen, K. J. and Gergen, M. (1983) 'Narratives of the self', in T. R. Sarbin and K. E. Sheibe (eds) *Studies in Social Identity*, New York: Praeger.

Hall, S. (1996) 'Introduction: who needs identity?', in S. Hall and P. du Guy (eds) *Questions of Cultural Identity*, London: Sage.

Harré, R. (1979) *Social Being: A Theory for Social Psychology*, Oxford: Blackwell.

Harré, R. and Secord, P. F. (1972) *The Explanation of Social Behaviour*, Oxford: Basil Blackwell.

Henriques, J., Hollway, W., Urwin, C., Venn, C. and Walkerdine, V. (1984) *Changing the Subject: Psychology, Social Regulation and Subjectivity*, London: Methuen; reprinted 1998, London: Routledge.

Hirst, P. and Woolley, P. (1982) *Social Relations and Human Attributes*, London: Tavistock.

Jameson, F. (1991) *Postmodernism or the Logic of Late Capitalism*, London: Verso.

Jardine, A. (1985) *Gynesis: Configurations of Woman and Modernity*, Ithaca: Cornell University Press.

Jordanova, L. (1989) *Sexual Visions: Images of Gender in Science and Medicine between the Eighteenth and Twentieth Centuries*, Hemel Hempstead: Harvester Wheatsheaf.

Lacan, J. (1977) *Ecrits: A Selection*, London: Tavistock.

—— (1982) 'The meaning of the phallus' (trans. J. Rose), in J. Mitchell and J. Rose (eds) *Feminine Sexuality: Jacques Lacan and the Ecole Freudienne*, Basingstoke, Macmillan.

Laclau, E. (1990) *New Reflections on the Revolution of our Time*, London: Verso.

Lyotard, J. F. (1992) *The Postmodern Condition*, Manchester: Manchester University Press.

Malson, H. (1995) 'Anorexia nervosa: discourses of gender, subjectivity and the body', *Feminism and Psychology* 5, 1: 87–93.

—— (1997) 'Anorexic bodies and the discursive production of feminine excess', in J. M. Ussher (ed.) *Body Talk: The Material and Discursive Regulation of Sexuality, Madness and Reproduction*, London: Routledge.

—— (1998) *The Thin Woman: Feminism, Post-structuralism and the Social Psychology of Anorexia Nervosa*, London: Routledge.

—— (1999) 'Women under erasure: anorexic bodies in postmodern context', *Journal of Community and Applied Psychology* 9: 137–53.

Malson, H. and Ussher, J. M. (1996) 'Body poly-texts: discourses of the anorexic body', *Journal of Community and Applied Social Psychology* 6: 267–80.

—— (1997) 'Beyond this mortal coil: femininity, death and discursive constructions of the anorexic body', *Mortality* 2, 1: 43–61.

Marshall, H. and Wetherell, M. (1989) 'Talking about careers and gender identities: a discourse analysis perspective', in S. Skevington and D. Barker (eds) *The Social Identity of Women*, London: Sage.

Mitchell, J. (1982) 'Introduction I', in J. Mitchell and J. Rose (eds) *Feminine Sexuality: Jacques Lacan and the Ecole Freudienne*, Basingstoke: Macmillan.

Parker, I. (1990) 'Discourse: definitions and contradictions', *Philosophical Psychology* 3, 2: 189–204.

Poovey, M. (1988) 'Feminism and deconstruction', *Feminist Studies* 14, 1: 51–65.

Potter, J. and Wetherell, M. (1987) *Discourse and Social Psychology: Beyond Attitudes and Behaviour*, London: Sage.

Riley, D. (1988) *Am I That Name? Feminism and the Category of 'Women' in History*, Basingstoke: Macmillan.

Rose, J. (1982) 'Introduction II', in J. Mitchell and J. Rose (eds) *Feminine Sexuality: Jacques Lacan and the Ecole Freudienne*, Basingstoke: Macmillan.

Rose, M. (1991) 'Defining the postmodern', in M. Rose *The Postmodern and the Post-industrial*, Cambridge: Cambridge University Press.

Sampson, E. (1993) *Celebrating the Other*, Hemel Hempstead: Harvester.

Sarbin, T. R. (1986) 'The narrative as a root metaphor for psychology', in T. R. Sarbin (ed.) *Narrative Psychology: The Storied Nature of Human Conduct*, New York: Praeger.

Shotter, J. (1984) *Accountability and Selfhood*, Oxford: Blackwell.

Squire, C. (1983) 'The problem of the subject in current psychoanalytic and post-structuralist theory: identity in pieces', unpublished PhD thesis, Exeter University.

Stainton-Rogers, R., Stenner, P., Gleeson, K. and Stainton-Rogers, W. (1995) *Social Psychology: A Critical Agenda*, Cambridge: Polity Press.

Stenner, P. and Eccleston, C. (1994) 'On the textuality of being', *Theory and Psychology* 4, 1: 85–103.

Swann, C. (1997) 'Reading the bleeding body, discourses of premenstrual syndrome', in J. M. Ussher (ed.) *Body Talk: The Material and Discursive Regulation of Sexuality, Madness and Reproduction*, London: Routledge.

Tseelon E. (1991) 'The method is the message: on the meaning of methods as ideologies', *Theory and Psychology* 1, 3: 299–316.

Walkerdine, V. (1984) 'Developmental psychology and the child-centred pedagogy', in J. Henriques, W. Hollway, C. Urwin, C. Venn and V. Walkerdine (1984) *Changing the Subject: Psychology, Social Regulation and Subjectivity*, London: Methuen; reprinted 1998, London: Routledge.

—— (1986) 'Post-structuralist theory and everyday social practice: the family and the school', in S. Wilkinson (ed.) *Feminist Social Psychology*, Milton Keynes: The Open University Press.

—— (1988) *The Mastery of Reason: Cognitive Development and the Production of Rationality*, London: Routledge.

Wetherell, M. (1986) 'Linguistic repertoires and literary criticism: new directions for a social psychology of gender', in S. Wilkinson (ed.) *Feminist Social Psychology: Developing Theory and Practice*, Milton Keynes: The Open University Press.

—— (1991) 'Romantic discourse: analysing investment, power and desire', paper presented at the 4th International Conference on Language and Social Psychology, August 1991, University of California, Santa Barbara.

—— (1996) 'Fear of fat: interpretative repertoires and ideological dilemmas', in J. Maybi and N. Mercer (eds) *Using English: From Conversation to Canon*, London: Routledge.

Wetherell, M. and Potter, I. (1992) *Mapping the Language of Racism*, Hemel Hempstead: Harvester Wheatsheaf.

White, H. (1973) *Metahistory*, Baltimore, MD: Johns Hopkins University Press.

Widdicombe, S. (1993) 'Autobiography and change: rhetoric and authenticity in "Gothic" style', in E. Burman and I. Parker (eds) *Discourse Analytic Research*, London: Routledge.

Woodiwiss, A. (1990) *Social Theory after Postmodernity*, London: Pluto.

11 'Let them rot'

Four boys talk about punishment

Marion V. Smith

Introduction

This chapter is based on the analysis of a 40-minute conversation in which two adult researchers (M.S. and E.G.) talked with four 9-year-old boys about fairness, rules, punishment, right and wrong.[1] The extract I have chosen is lengthy and is reproduced in its entirety, as my analysis focuses upon its structure as a dramatic narrative. I argue that understanding the event in these terms, with discrete but linked 'acts', enables us to achieve insights into aspects of the problem of 'punishment' that would not have been available had the extract been interpreted on the basis of content alone. The narrative was produced when we asked the boys to imagine waking up one morning to find that all adults had disappeared, leaving only children to organise life as they chose.[2] This enabled the boys to discuss what they did and did not like about adult organisation; how things would change and how they would like them to be.

The extract is taken from a point in the conversation where the adults have introduced the idea that some children may want some rules in their adult-free world. The boys do not consider this very likely. After some discussion of rules (using football as an example) fails to impress them, one adult suggests that one of them is mugged in the street, and the mugger is caught by the rule-makers, who then have to decide on a punishment. This seems to make rules more interesting.

During this extract, there are few pauses and a fair degree of overlap.[3] Transcribing it was difficult because the room where the recording was made was acoustically poor, and the boys' voices are similar. Although we worked hard on identifying speakers, the boys' voices rise and fall as they are, by turn, fired or cool, and intermingle to such an extent that we could never feel confident that our allocation of names to the speakers was accurate. So instead, I would like to consider this piece as a jointly constructed story in which the individual identities are secondary to the main thrust of the ideas expressed. The boys were 'in tune' with each other to such an extent, and the tune they produced was so striking, that I believe it is worth focusing on that tune rather than on individual arguments.

Act 1

M.S.: Now the people who are making the rules they've got to sit down and decide on punishments.

Boys: Chop their head off.

Yeah, get a bazooka and shoot, shoot their head off.

Make them eat what they don't want to eat.

M.S.: Make them eat what they don't want to eat.

Boys: Yeah we- we can fly aeroplanes and crash into everyone.

And then jump out with a parachute, (Yeah) and tie them up with it.

Or you could throw somebody out of an aeroplane without a parachute.

Yes.

Act 2

M.S.: If somebody if somebody had taken something from a very small child, about, 3-year-old, and they were 14, and then the same – another boy who's also 14, took something from another 14-year-old and they had a big fight but, that guy won and took it so you've got two 14-year-olds one of them has taken something from another 14-year-old, and one of them has taken something from a 3-year-old, and you've got to decide on the punishments, what would you do?

Boys: The 3-year-old would throw their rattle at 'em

Tie them to a tree

The 3-year-old would throw their rattle at them at their head.

You could have a bowling ball and ??

Tie them to a tree.

Yeah

M.S.: To a train?

Boys: ??

Tie them to a wall

Tie them to a tree and um make an aeroplane crash into the tree.

Make a train go into the tree {laughs}

Or just tie them round the tree, get a bow and arrow. Pchow {shooting arrow noise}

Yeah you could use it as target practice.

No put an apple on his head. And ??

Yes and aim for it

Yeah {laughs}

Act 3

M.S.: Now you're you're saying that these punishments should be, pretty drastic (Yeah Yeah) so that they'd end up dying, (Yeah Yeah) now what if you were caught taking something off somebody.

Boys: Erm

I'd run

I'd just run away.

I'd run.

Yeah

M.S.:   But they caught you. I mean you'd have to have the same punishment wouldn't you?

Boys: No

Beat them up and run away again ?? smack 'em ??

Just kick- kick 'em where it hurts

Run, run away.

I'd go in a secret hiding place

I'd sue

Yeah or lock yourself in somebody's house

I'd sue.

[Who'd] go and get us?

I'd go to the moon {laughter}

How

A rocket, what do you think

Yes, but there is no rockets in Smalltown.

No

Make one!

That would take you seconds yeah *Andy*.

Yeah

Go to erm a car and drive to the nearest rocket place.

You can't drive.

Just learn

So. Still drive!

Just learn to drive {racing car noise}

Get a racing car, the fastest racing car in the world.

Nigel Mansell's {laughter}

Get a racing car with a jet on the back of it.

We don't even know what the punishment is yet.

Act 4

M.S.:   No well you're meant to be deciding on the punishment. It's a serious, serious um task.

Boys: Stick their head down the plughole.

Then they've all got smelly heads

No shove them, shove them down the toilet.

Just erm tie 'em up and leave 'em.

Yeah and let them rot for a bit. Let them rot. Starve.

M.S.:   Leave them for a bit and then let them go again afterwards.

Boys: No, kill 'em after.
        Wo!
        Don't let them eat for about one and a half days and then let them go.
Andy: One and a half, a **week**, a month a year.
        A century.
        No they won't be able to live, they'll just die, *Andy*
Andy: Well okay, about a week then.
        ?? might die
        ?? might die ??
        Not if they ??
        Hey what if they're tied up by the arms and legs they can't [eat]
        They they can chew the ropes
        Noooo?!

Act 5

E.G.:   Why do you think we punish people.
Boys: Because they've done something wrong
        Because they're naughty.
M.S.:   Do you think the punishment stops them doing it again?
Boys: No.
        No
        No
        Sometimes. It depends what the punishment is.
        A different punishment ??
        Get one of them pretend guns, pretend you're going to shoot 'em.
        A potato gun boom.
E.G.:   What kind of punishments do you think are more likely to work.
Boys: Chopping off their head?
        Stretching
M.S.:   That's not going to work, (Why?) because they don't get the chance
        to do it again do they {laughs}
Boys: Yeah almost chop off their heads and that would make them scared
        and ??
        Make a slit in their throats so their food, goes out of the slit.
        Yeah!
        Just erm cut their hands off.
        Just torture them.
        Stretch them. Just stretch them. Stretch them.

Act 6

E.G.:   If you can think of all these punishments, which, are very drastic as
        Marion said, why do you think the adults don't do them?

Boys: Cos they're drastic
E.G.: And if you think they are going to work why do you think the adults don't, have this kind of punishment?
Boys: Cos they're drastic
Because they're round the twist.
They're wrong upstairs.
Because they're goodies.
Yes, they're goodies and we're baddies.
Yeah
Children like nicking.
M.S.: Can baddies grow up to be goodies
Boys: Maybe, maybe not.
Well I'm not
Sometimes.
I'm going to be nasty

Act 7

M.S.: Let's go back to you were saying that you could tie somebody up and not give them any food for a day and a half. How young a child would you do that to for a punishment?
Boys: 1-year-old.
About 14.
About 14-year-old.
They'll live.
They won't.
We want them to live. We don't want them to die.
A 3-year-old won't do anything wrong anyway.
Throw a cake at their face. Make them try to eat one when you throw them.
Yeah they'll eat a cake
You'd have to stretch them out.
They'd have to go like that {miming eating while tied up}
You'd have to tie 'em up
Get get get a tin and make it look like a cake and just **throw** it.
Give it to them. Then their teeth would break.
Nope. Give a tin to them. 'How do you open this thing'.
Hey, you could use them as a tin opener if they've got sharp teeth
Yeah.

This piece is striking; in its violence, in the brashness of the expressions of power and invulnerability; in the boys' complete lack of consideration for the recipients of their punishments; in the casual nature of its delivery. Adult reactions to it vary from horror and perplexity to laughter and complete dismissal as data. The argument for the latter is that the boys weren't taking the exercise seriously: they were simply messing about. Perhaps this is true (although that was not my sense of the encounter at the time); in which case, can we work out *why* they messed about in this way? Did they merely wish to shock us? On the other hand, are there solid grounds for reacting with dismay? How are we to understand these brutalities?

Finally, why analyse this as a story? There are no clear protagonists (we will consider how far the boys identify themselves with the actions they suggest later), no plot and no resolution. No one person has the majority of the floor; and the beginning and end points have been chosen because they enclose all of a stretch of relatively uninterrupted boys' talk stemming from a single issue. I think it is helpful to consider this as a story in the sense that a play tells a story. There is no single narrator, leading us through the action to a final understanding in a purposive sequence; but the boys are creating a drama, improvising a performance in multiple voices albeit within a space devised for them by adults, with those adults (more or less bewildered participants) playing out their roles in a portrayal of the relations of these children to the adult world. Here, to borrow Cortazzi's (1993: 26) phrase, is a 'dynamic production, jointly created by both teller and audience'. We will return to discuss this further in the conclusion: but first, let us enter the drama.

Making sense of the drama

The extract divides readily into seven 'acts', each begun by an adult. These 'acts' have some kinship to Fairclough's cycles (1992: 138) which, in turn, correspond roughly to Sinclair and Coulthard's (1975) exchanges. The differences I wish to draw out are that the initiating sequence of each 'act' elicits no typical structure (for example, Sinclair and Coulthard's 'response' and 'feedback' or Fairclough's 'response' and 'acceptance') but contains developing discussion that may become extended around one topic – sometimes triggered indirectly by the initiation – among a number of participants. 'Act' also, in extending the drama theme, helps to suggest the sense of something happening in each stage. It is significant that the whole encounter took place in school, where children's time and place (that is, where they are meant to be, metaphorically and literally) are firmly controlled by adults. The children did not know exactly what to expect in the encounter, but they are thoroughly used to question-and-answer sequences, initiated and closed by the teacher on a topic of the teacher's choosing (Sinclair and Coulthard 1975). The 'acts' conform to this pattern in so far as they are adult initiated, and the initiations almost always serve also to close the preceding 'act'. The two adults have control of the overall structure of the encounter but, within each 'act', the children control the content with very little adult input, except for the fifth and sixth acts where the adults question the children more closely.

Act 1

M.S. does not ask the boys to generate punishments, but remarks that this has to be done by the rule-makers. This is invitation enough, and there is no hesitation before the first suggestions. These initial responses – beheading and shooting – are simple ones, with a formulaic[4] feel to them. They then start to become more elaborate, involving aeroplanes and parachutes, bringing restraint or death to a subject who is entirely passive. Although it is produced with much overlap, the text is orderly in the sense that the ideas in it are connected rather than generated at random or with no regard to what others are saying. The focus moves rapidly from removing someone's head via a weak army/airforce link (bazookas and aeroplanes) to settle on flying. The exception is 'make them eat what they don't want to eat', a different kind of suggestion, and one that strikes the adult (who repeats it), although it is ignored by the other boys. This is not the comic strip action response of the others containing, as it does, an orientation to distress and prolonged discomfort rather than showy destruction.

The first three suggestions that the boys make are agentless (no 'I' or 'we'), presented as hypotheticals which allow the degree of their personal affinity to the suggestions to be hidden. Their ownership of these punishments is in doubt, perhaps because the whole conversation is premised on a hypothetical situation, perhaps because it isn't serious, or perhaps because they are talking of extreme matters with two strange adults in school time (for a discussion of affinity, see Fairclough 1992). However, one speaker uses 'we', which suggests a greater involvement with what he is saying and also implies group cohesion through its recommendation of joint engagement in the activity. The 'we' is initially accepted without question (note the simple continuation of 'and then' and the endorsement 'yeah'); and then the proposition is again distanced by the use of 'you'. When listening to the tape, the 'you' has the sense of 'one' rather than being directed at anyone in particular. The sense of group cohesion is not lost, because the 'we' is not directly challenged, and the topic remains centred on aeroplanes.

Act 2

M.S. uses the simple agreement 'yes' as a marker of closure to end the sequence. Chipping in immediately after a suggestion would have been more disruptive, and her acceptance or rejection of the boys' talk less ambiguous. She makes no comment at this point, but tries to move the discussion forward by presenting the boys with a specific case to think about. This time, she asks them directly what *they* would do.

Again, the boys do not confront what *they* would do directly, but give agentless answers. Someone makes a suggestion that overtly counters the personal request, but which responds most closely to the scenario presented to them by saying what the 3-year-old would do. He perhaps thinks this answer merits acknowledgement: hence its subsequent repetition with slight elaboration. The other boys, however, are already engaged on a different tack. The talk of tying up follows on from the tying up with the parachute in Act 1, showing that the deep control of the encounter is theirs, and not the adults'. The talk in Act 2 is interconnected in an orderly fashion and tying up is the central idea. The aeroplane reoccurs, and again the suggestions involve violence. The recipients of these punishments, however, are now overtly passive, in that they are bound.

Act 3

Again M.S. uses a moment of agreement to treat Act 2 as closed so that she can introduce a new point of departure. This time, her initiation involves feedback, in the form of a summary of what the boys have been saying. The summary receives immediate agreement that is smoothly inserted into slight pauses in her talk. Note that here death as an outcome is unquestioned. Now the boys are asked to confront a situation in which *they* are due to receive punishment. They respond in the first person: the only 'act' in which they do so. Running away is not contentious in the way that beheading and tying to trees is, but they are primarily concerned to show their invulnerability to the same processes that their offenders encountered so passively. Their role is essentially active, and when M.S. interposes to suggest that they *are* caught (again slotting in after a simple agreement), they fight and run some more. They cannot be caught.

Running away implies the question of 'where to?' and the boys move smoothly on to this over the next few lines. For the two lines about fighting, they have dropped 'I' – because it is a suggestion put forward for group assent, albeit implicit? – but now it is resumed. To this point their talk has been tightly collusive, but now it fragments. The first 'I'd sue' is ignored (to sue someone is an adult recourse, and has not the physicality of everything the boys have said to this point); and talk of hiding places continues. It is interesting that the speaker does not choose his own home in which to hide, but 'somebody's' house. This accords with my sense of impersonality in this encounter. There is no clear sense of identity or of belonging. 'I'd sue' is later repeated, indicating that the speaker wants some response. Again it is ignored, and followed by an unclear question that possibly short-circuits any power the punishers/pursuers have by questioning their identity. Already the talk is losing cohesion, but what really breaks it up is the suggestion made in the first person that one boy would go to the moon. This suggestion is immediately confronted ('how') and serves to break the run-and-hide links that have bound the preceding talk. Technically, going to the moon need not be disruptive in that it is a further suggestion of a hiding place; but it is experienced as impractical in a way that previous suggestions were not. Although the use of 'I', implying personal affinity to this course of action, could invite a challenge which more hypothetically worded suggestions avoid, 'I'd sue', also in the first person, excited no attention at all.

The introduction of the moon effectively stops the generation of escape strategies, and leads into a discussion of the practicalities of getting to the moon. The topic slides from lack of rockets, to travelling to where rockets are, to driving, to racing cars. In the course of this, someone is named as part of a sarcastic comment, showing that the speaker is identifying one of the boys, Andy, with the silliness of his response; and showing how completely the collaborative tune has gone. Someone is again held accountable for the feasibility of what they have said ('You can't drive') and there is a sense of the point of the conversation being lost. This is clearly recognised by one of the boys, who closes the act and reintroduces the topic of punishment. This shows sensitivity to the adult agenda – or perhaps a greater interest in the larger schema of the encounter than in the local potential of fast cars.

Act 4

M.S. takes the opportunity provided by inviting the boys to decide on punishments. The thrust of her statement that this is serious business is not admonitory but recommending consideration. The boys use neither 'I' nor 'you' in Act 4, but return to the generation of connected ideas, all forceful actions visited upon passive recipients. 'Plughole' sets the theme for the following two lines, then a change of direction ('Just erm tie 'em up and leave 'em') simultaneously links Act 4 to Act 2 through the notion of tying up, and introduces the 'leave 'em' which becomes the focus for the rest of Act 4.

It is as though the monarchic aspects of punishment (the power over the subject's body demonstrated by rulers in early modern Europe by committing several acts of violence as a spectacle of punishment, each one of which was sufficient to kill them (Foucault 1979)) give way here to the realisation that power can be more subtly wrought by abnegation; or perhaps the speaker is attempting to be more practical. The passivity of the person to be punished is clear: the 'just' implies at once the simplicity of the action and of its accomplishment; and the victims are then abandoned, discarded, but presumably able to contemplate their predicament. This suggestion is elaborated by the next speaker, who instantly perceives the potential of simple 'leaving', and adds a temporal dimension that is simultaneously a passive process that will take place within the body of the detainee: 'let them rot for a bit'. He immediately further elaborates this to 'let them rot. Starve', which lessens the metaphorical as opposed to the literal force of 'rot' with the explanatory addition of 'starve'. This is a different sense of death, and punishment. It is more akin to the idea of making someone eat what they don't want to eat (Act 1), which also involves food (albeit its enforced presence rather than its enforced absence), than the flying of aeroplanes and tying to trees. These latter punishments have a filmic quality to them: they are the stuff of childhood adventure fictions, full of energy and impossible feats. In the more realisable idea of leaving the prisoner to 'rot', power is being visited upon the prisoner's body by absence of activity. But at the same time, rotting is a directed process rather than an accidental adjunct of abandon-ment because it is delivered as a command: *'Let* them rot.' Although physi-cal aggression would be, one presumes, used to tie 'them' up, the force of the punishment lies in the less apparent power maintained over the victims in the slow advance of starvation.

It is hardly surprising that M.S. intervenes at this point to seek clarifica-tion. The swift response 'No, kill 'em after' receives an acknowledgement ('Wo!') but is not taken up directly. Instead, there is an implicit denial of the desire for death which develops into a brief discussion of how long the prisoner(s) should or could be left without them dying. Then we get the second use of a boy's name, lending weight to the sense that there is a real point of dissent here. Again, the tune the boys are creating is disrupted, over a moral concern with the preservation of life. Paradoxically, this late mani-festation of a sense of accountability, or responsibility, gives the punishment more status as a serious suggestion. Act 4 ends with further unclear discus-sion about death, and a suggestion that the prisoner can chew the restrain-ing ropes, possibly instead of food. They may escape death, but we have no sense that they are entitled to anything more than that.

Act 5

In Act 5, the adults seek to increase their understanding through three question-and-answer mini-cycles. All three questions are personally directed (what do *you* think?), and the third question effectively stops what looks like a return to the generation of yet more punishments. This last question asks the boys to consider an educational or a deterrent aspect to punishment. The immediate suggestion of beheading reintroduces death, and the second, unclear, suggestion seems to be premised upon deterrence. M.S. intervenes with the only example of directive feedback in this long extract, because the initial answer is not appropriate to the question. The boys understand that death is not an option here because the object is to deter reoffending through choice rather than incapacity; they come up with macabre solutions, pre-sumably suggested to them by the starting point of beheading. 'Almost chop off their heads' contains the only reference to how a punishment would make an offender feel: scared. The grisly suggestion of the slit oesophagus again returns us to the theme of food, and the remaining suggestions focus on violent means of physical deformation short of death. It is notable that none of the measures suggested seeks to teach the offender not to do it again; the emphasis is firmly upon physical incapacitation and the fear of brutal repercussions.

Act 6

Act 6 is an interesting digression to what could be viewed as the sub-plot in this jointly created drama. In it, the boys directly confront the difference between themselves and the *status quo* of the adult world. This is not what they are asked to do – rather they are asked to comment on adult practices – but this is the point to which their answers bring them. They create the sense that children live by a different order than adults, with their pleasure in being 'baddies' and in 'nicking'. The boys' responses in the first section of Act 6 are tightly collusive; but later their responses become more individualised. Beside the more equivocal responses, we get highly assertive assurances of their badness (and pride in it) including use of the first person. We will return to this point in the discussion.

Act 7

M.S. attempts to reassert control over the topic by taking the boys back to Act 4, and selects the idea of tying someone up with no food for a day and a half. Her question is directed to the boys personally, and asks how young a child they would be prepared to treat in that way. Two disparate ages are immediately suggested, one and fourteen. The next clear issue seems to concern the 1-year-old's chances of survival. The boys may recall M.S.'s rejection of death in Act 5, but the use of 'we' makes it more likely that the speaker is making an admonitory remark from a sense of responsibility: 'We want them to live. We don't want them to die.' However, it is a responsibility that at least one other boy is wary of shouldering. He replies that a 3-year-old would not do anything wrong anyway, implying that this is something that they don't have to consider. The issue of food now returns in a more extended way. The implicit acknowledgement of the responsibility not to starve people becomes inverted to form new ways of frustrating or torturing the offenders. At first, the boys evoke the difficulty and indignity of eating, bound up, when the food is thrown in the offenders' faces. But the sense of 'throw it' contains a definite desire to give the recipient a shock or worse when what looks like a cake lands on their face. The idea of a tin opens a new dimension on punitive innovation: either the offender will simply break their own teeth on it, believing it to be a cake; or they will experience the frustration of receiving food to which they have no access. This suggests opening tins, and leads to the final bizarre suggestion in the extract: that the offender be used as a tin opener themselves.

Discussion

A dramaturgical summary

In Act 1 the boys start to generate punishments. These first suggestions are totally unrealistic and impractical, but carry a sense of overwhelming force and technical expertise: excesses of the first flush of devolved power. In Act 2, the punishments start to become less improbable. They focus on tying up, and the phrase 'tie them' is repeated at least five times. This 'act' concerns not so much the power for action (as in Act 1), as the creation of the bound subject; power over a completely helpless other.

Act 3 is critical because the boys appear to be talking more with their own voices. They are to consider themselves in the totally vulnerable position they have created for the offender/victims, and it is a role they refuse to accept. This is so important, they respond in the first person, and dissent appears over the unrealistic suggestions of going to the moon and driving a car. Yet nobody pointed out in the preceding two 'acts' that they cannot wield axes effectively, manage bazookas, or drive aeroplanes and trains. Act 4 is also critical. The idea of binding is complemented by the idea of leaving to rot. But the whole process remains in the boys' control, and again leads to dissent over how long someone could be left without dying. A sense of practicality and responsibility arises, giving the onlooker the dismaying notion that the drama has collided with 'reality'.

In Act 5 the boys dismiss, or fail to consider, any civilising or educative processes in punishment. Their suggestions become more bloody and draconian. Fear is the only motivation they acknowledge. Act 6, with truly dramatic plotting, relieves the intensity of Act 5 by introducing a different issue. The boys are asked to comment upon what adults do. However, the relief is temporary. Adults and children are presented as chalk and cheese, two generalised homogeneous cultures with no clear path between them. The puzzle of transition causes some uncertainty, and some reaffirmation of perceived difference. Act 7 returns us to the heart of the story: how old an offender would be bound and left? Again, responsibility arises, but is evaded by an adroit manoeuvre. Instead the feeding of the offender/victims is subverted to new forms of punishment. The 'act' closes with the final dehumanising of the offender: they can be used as a tin opener.

This drama, which gathers savagery as it becomes more real, offers no relief in its disquieting sub-plot, and ends with ingenious indignity, makes depressing reading. But before we rush to take this as an index to the condition of the rising generation (Pearson 1983; King 1999), let us pick out three themes for further consideration: the offender/victim, food, and the relation to the perceived adult world.

Three themes

The offender/victim

At no point in this drama do we have any sense of those to be punished as active perpetrators of wrongdoing. Nobody asks or suggests what the offence might be, except in the largely ignored scenario presented by M.S. in Act 2. All passing references to wrongdoing – 'nicking', being 'baddies' – are non-specific or not especially heinous, yet the punishments suggested are all extreme and grotesque. The offence is not the issue, and the offenders are strangely passive. There are no contingencies for 'then if he tries to escape,

I'll . . .', nor 'if they fight back we'll . . .'. It is the punishments, the realisations of powerful action, that interest the boys: the recipients of these penalties are absent. There are no real victims. When it is the turn of the boys themselves to be punished, the punishers become as powerless as the offenders were before. The boys appear unassailable.

Food

The use of food in the punishments is particularly disconcerting. However, food is a prominent domain of adult power. Adults select and provide food, and children have to eat it. Adults commonly control access to food, and to what children can eat and when. When viewed in this light, the uses of food in the punishments become less extreme. I provide here rough glosses of what may be going on:

Act 1: make them eat what they don't want to eat – like I had to at dinner yesterday.
Act 4: let them starve – like when I was sent to bed without any tea.
Act 5: food comes out of the slit – you can eat, but you're still hungry.
Act 7: throwing cakes – a travesty of mealtime with an incongruous use of cake, usually considered a 'treat' food.

This makes food an issue in the third theme.

Relations to adults

Punishment is a prime metaphor for the adult world of stricture and control. When the adults disappear, the boys are free to behave as they wish; but when invited to punish, their assumption of power and invulnerability, hitherto strictly the domain of adults, is a heady cocktail. In their imaginations, they can do anything. But those over whom they have power have no power themselves, perhaps adopting the erstwhile role of the boys themselves with regard to the adult world. When the power to punish is removed by putting the boys in the position of offenders, although the pursuers appear powerless and the boys appear invulnerable, the boys do not appear to experience themselves as powerful; their recourses are to running and hiding: hardly the actions of the strong. It is possible that the appearance of rockets and fast cars in their talk at this point signifies their need for powerful machines to assist their return to a position of power.

In Act 4 the talk is more of penalties that are within their capacities, and in this context they do recognise that they should not kill the offender. However, in Act 5, they do not entertain any motivation other than fear for avoiding trouble. Act 6 is crucial to our understanding here. When the boys say the adults are 'round the twist' and 'wrong upstairs', there is a suggestion of the inexplicability of the adult world, or of a lack of comprehension of themselves in relation to it. They evince an uncertainty of how 'baddies' (that is, children) might become 'goodies' (that is, adults), and even dispute that this will happen to them. In Act 7, they again show awareness of the responsibility not to kill, but they would rather it did not arise. They are not prepared to deal with such matters. They are on the brink of adult responsibilities (at ten the law will deem them criminally responsible), but these lie within an arena with which they do not engage.

Narrative and dramatic analysis

The encounter that I have analysed here took place 'out of time' in that the boys were given permission to leave a lesson in order to take part, and they were talking with two unfamiliar women researchers whom they would never see again after their school's participation in the research was at an end. Together we created a fiction that I have recreated here, in such a way that the movement and complexity of the event can be appreciated. The two adults accepted the local parameters of the encounter; we never questioned whether the boys were answering 'seriously' or whether they would 'really' carry out their suggestions, and neither did we privilege certain contributions, for instance, by intervening to clear the floor for the boy who said 'we want them to live'.

I have presented this excerpt as a drama because of the story it tells, and because of the means of telling it. The boys make short, punchy contributions. Instead of any one boy having his own story to tell or theme to pursue, they actively work together and it is only by considering the whole that the import is realised. What the boys say is tightly constructed through repeated words and phrases and recurrent themes so that it has a truly dramatic structure and impact. As we circle around the idea of punishment, different aspects are foregrounded and built upon so that the audience's sense of understanding opens out as the dynamic continues. It is an encounter made dramatic by its subject-matter, but also dramatically realised because the story it tells is not related by one voice, but by different voices unfolding over time.

Riessman (1993: 21) reminds us that 'The text is not autonomous of its context.' Whatever we all said arose on that specific occasion and was created for that occasion. It is helpful to think of the 'parts' the boys played in terms of three levels of identity, following Zimmerman (1998: 90). The boys have transportable identities that are relevant to the encounter: they are 9-year-old boys sitting in a school room in school time wearing school uniform. They also have discourse identities through which they manage the moment-by-moment development of the talk, as speakers, listeners and questioners. Finally, they have situated identities, which are roles adopted for the benefit of the current agenda. These are all aspects of what took place that lend themselves to a dramatic analysis.

Of course, in presenting the encounter as a drama I have created a 'false document' (Behar 1993, quoted in Riessman 1993: 13). My analysis has created a 'metastory', selecting and presenting the boys' talk in a particular way. However, as Riessman points out, 'false' here does not mean that it is not necessary and productive. This analysis brings out the coherence in the boys' production and ideas, and above all shows that even if they don't usually share similar outlooks and fascinations, they can all readily adopt and work with the themes and directions introduced.

Finally, were the boys messing around, were they out to shock or were they serious? What is the relation of this episode to their 'real' lives? This question cannot be answered in a literal sense, because the boys' talk has many elements that change over the course of the encounter. What has come out of the 'performance' is a fiction, and whether or not they would do these things to offenders *in real life* misses the point, just as whether it really happened is not the point in *Othello*. As Coffey and Atkinson (1996: 55) write, 'stories our informants tell can be seen, on the one hand, as highly structured (and formal) ways of transmitting information. On the other hand, they can be seen as distinctive, creative, artful genres.' What is at stake here is the social action that took place. These are the elements that the boys were able to assemble on the spot without prior consultation, and use collaboratively. What is revealing is the impression of four boys who do not experience themselves as powerful with regard to the adult world, but who would like to. They are unsure of what their relation to the adult world is, and they are uncertain of the trajectory by which they will reach that state themselves.

If we had read this extract simply for content, we would have achieved uncertain insight into why the boys created this ludicrous or disturbing scenario of violent retribution. By looking in detail at the dramatic structure of this encounter, we are brought to confront aspects of the enigmatic and intractable problem of punishment, including its seductive attractions and their relation to experiences of power and powerlessness.

Notes

1 The project from which this chapter arises is entitled 'Moral education and the cultures of punishment'. It has been carried out jointly with Professor Richard Sparks and Dr Evi Girling, both of the Department of Criminology, Keele University, and is supported by an award from the Economic and Social Research Council (award no. L129251051) as part of its 'Children 5–16 Research Programme'. We gratefully acknowledge this support. The project explores various aspects of children's understandings of justice and punishment and their orientations to adult disciplinary practices. Several papers are in preparation on specific topics, e.g. bullying, uses of historical reference, images of imprisonment, as well as papers on more conceptual issues.

2 It is important that this is not confused with a *Lord of the Flies* scenario: the children are at home in the familiar environment of their school, clearly situated in their own infrastructure. In William Golding's *Lord of the Flies*, a group of boys are stranded on an island.

3 I have left the text as free as possible from the usual transcriber's notations so that it can be read easily and with minimum disruption. Brackets () show a brief interruption which causes virtually no disturbance in the flow of speech; square brackets [] contain unclear speech, and curly brackets {} contain remarks on delivery. Double question marks show missing speech, and bold typeface shows marked emphasis. A single question mark shows a rising inflection, a period shows a stopping fall in tone, a comma indicates a slight pause with a continuing intonation, and an exclamation mark shows an animated tone. I have not shown where talk overlaps. The names of the town and the child have been changed.

4 'Chop their head off' in particular has a unitary quality reminiscent of Sacks' composites (1995: 8), which are idiom-like constructions heard as a unit and having a proper response. The proper response to beheading at this point is probably a smile.

References

Behar, R. (1993) *Translated Woman: Crossing the Border with Esperanza's Story*, Boston: Beacon.

Coffey, A. and Atkinson, P. (1996) *Making Sense of Qualitative Data*, Thousand Oaks, CA: Sage.

Cortazzi, M. (1993) *Narrative Analysis*, London: The Falmer Press.

Fairclough, N. (1992) *Discourse and Social Change*, Cambridge: Polity Press.

Foucault, M. (1979) *Discipline and Punish: The Birth of the Prison*, Harmondsworth: Penguin.

King, M. (ed.) (1999) *Moral Agendas for Children's Welfare*, London: Routledge.

Pearson, G. (1983) *Hooligan: A History of Respectable Fears*, London: Macmillan.

Riessman, C. K. (1993) *Narrative Analysis*, London: Sage.

Sacks, H. (1995) *Lectures on Conversation* (edited by G. Jefferson), Cambridge, MA: Blackwell.

Sinclair, J. and Coulthard, M. (1975) *Towards an Analysis of Discourse: The English Used by Teachers and Pupils*, Oxford: Oxford University Press.

Zimmerman, D. (1998) 'Discourse identities and social identities', in C. Antaki and S. Widdicombe (eds), *Identities in Talk*, London: Sage.

12 Narrative and the discursive (re)construction of events

Jackie Abell, Elizabeth H. Stokoe and Michael Billig

The exchange of narratives or stories infuses social life at every level of interaction, from mundane conversation to mass media communication. In this paper, we explore what Campbell (1998) has termed the most important narrative or social document of its time – the BBC *Panorama* interview between Martin Bashir and the late Princess Diana. We adopt a discursive approach to the study of narrative, in which we treat it as constructive and performative, rather than as a neutral reflection of social life. In particular, we interrogate the use of narratives in the accomplishment of 'facticity', in the interactional distribution of blame and accountability, as a strategy of persuasion and, more generally, in the construction and positioning of self and others. By treating narrative as a discursive phenomenon and a routine accomplishment in everyday talk, we show how accounts are mobilised to perform rhetorical functions in the construction of social life.

Narrative, discursive psychology and conversation analysis

> The essential difference between cognitive and discursive approaches to narrative is that cognitive approaches treat them as expressions of how people understand things, whereas discursive approaches treat them as interaction-oriented productions.
>
> (Edwards 1997: 288)

In psychology, narrative has been theorised from both cognitive and discursive perspectives. These two approaches use narrative for fundamentally different purposes. Within cognitive psychology, narrative has been used as a tool for understanding how individuals structure information about the social world. It is assumed that narratives throw light on internal structures of thinking; the verbal material of narrative is taken as a sign for inner, essentially non-verbal, mental processes (Britton and Pellegrini 1990; Bruner 1990). By contrast, discursive psychology claims that states of mind, traditionally studied by psychologists, are themselves constituted within outer talk. Discursive psychologists, consequently, do not seek the inner processes supposedly lying behind narrative (Edwards 1997; Potter and Wetherell

1987). They concentrate on the ways that narratives relate to interactional business, and examine how speakers constitute themselves within the interaction.

The 'turn to discourse' and 'new paradigm' social science has seen an increased focus on narrative within a more general shift towards textually based research. These new approaches can be divided into three main schools of thought. First, drawing upon literary theory, narratology has emerged as an interdisciplinary project. Here, the focus has been on the structural organisation of narratives, narrative typology and the links between narrative, self and identity (see Murray 1995; Ochs 1997, for overviews of this work). A principal concern has been to develop a unified methodology and analytic framework to deal with narrative analysis (e.g. Lieblich and Josselson 1997). However, this has been criticised for its emphasis on structure at the expense of discursive function. Edwards (1997: 265) argues that the 'analysis of narrative in human and social sciences has mostly ignored the interactional business that people might be doing in telling them'.

Conversation analysts have a longstanding interest in the interactional organisation of storytelling. This second approach is concerned with when and how these typically long stretches of talk are signalled and told in everyday conversation. Hutchby and Wooffitt (1998: 131) argue that 'stories are not produced in a vacuum, but their telling is always situated within an interactional and sequential context'. Sacks (1992) was interested in how stories 'get told' in talk, how recipients respond, and how the prefacing and telling of stories follows particular interactional patterns. While conversation analysis provides a fine-grained study of stories-in-interaction, it ignores the rhetorical dimensions of stories as discursive resources.

In the light of such criticisms, a third strand of narrative research has developed. In 'discursive psychology' (Edwards and Potter 1992), narratives are considered for their rhetorical and constructive functions; the focus is upon the negotiation of narrative detail and the social actions that are accomplished. The influence of conversation analysis is apparent in this approach but the key difference lies in the treatment of rhetorical context. For conversation analysts, this context is built up by interactants such that analysts do not go beyond the data in their analysis of interaction. By contrast, for discursive psychologists, an understanding of the cultural situatedness of discourse is relevant to talk's explication. Narrative is therefore treated as a part of situated, mundane, everyday interaction. Thus the application of discursive analysis to the study of narrative focuses upon 'how specific story content, produced on and for occasions of talk, may perform social actions in-the-telling' (Edwards 1997: 266). In contrast with cognitive approaches, life stories and narratives are treated not as reflections of reality but as actively shaping the social world. Discursive approaches have embraced an analysis of narrative in a number of ways. These include the role of narrative in different interactional contexts, such as managing accountability (Antaki 1994; Buttny 1993) and the conversational construction of authentic 'identities' (Abell and Stokoe 1999), and the deployment of narrative as a 'fact construction' device (Edwards and Potter 1992).

Narrative and accountability

Speakers regularly attend to issues of accountability in talk. Buttny (1993: 18) notes that narrative can 'function as an account by verbally reconstructing a temporal sequence of particular events and the action part in them so as to justify actions'. Narrative enables speakers to connect events over time and make certain incidents relevant to the business in hand (see also Antaki 1994; Ochs 1997). Accountability is managed at two levels of narration (Edwards 1997). Speakers manage accountability not only in the recounting of past events but also in terms of the ongoing interaction. The business of the analyst is to ask why a story has appeared at a particular point in the discourse. Narratives can also be used to make the emotional and mental states of self and others inferentially available. As Antaki (1994) points out, the management of accountability typically occurs when multiple and opposing versions are possible. Speakers produce versions that counter other versions, which might have a critical import. They have a rhetorical stake in such versions (Edwards and Potter 1992). In this way, accountability is related to the argumentative context of criticism and justification (Billig 1996).

Narrative and fact construction

In the discursive reconstruction of events, an overriding concern of participants is that their descriptions are treated as factual, authentic and plausible. Theorists have explored techniques that may be deployed in talk in ways that increase the facticity of an account. Edwards and Potter (1992) (see also Potter 1996) have investigated the role of narrative in fact construction. Two complementary themes appear in their research. First, they suggest that 'the plausibility of a report can be increased by embedding it in a particular narrative sequence in which that event is expected or even necessary' (Edwards and Potter 1992: 161). The focus here is on the overall structure and organisation of narrative. The second aspect concerns the content of narrative in terms of levels of detail. Potter (1996: 117) notes that 'vivid, detailed description can also be used to build up the facticity of an account. They can produce an impression of being there by sketching features which, although not substantial to the claim or argument, would have been apparent to someone who actually witnessed some event.' Narrative, from this perspective, is a warranting device.

Princess Diana's *Panorama* interview

To illustrate these ideas we now consider how narratives may be analysed within the context of a televised interview. We develop Murray's (1997: 10) notion of a storytelling society in which 'there is much interest in what the ordinary person has to say [and for them] to narrate their experiences to an inquisitive public'. This public consumption of narrative extends beyond an interest in 'the ordinary person' to a fascination with 'celebrity interviews'. There is a trend in public interviews for interviewees to distance themselves from presenting a (possibly superficial) 'celebrity' identity and instead claim a 'private', authentic identity. The public fascination with royalty fits this public presentation of simultaneous ordinariness and extraordinariness. In modern constitutional monarchies, royals are portrayed as 'ordinary' people occupying extraordinary positions; in fact, their ordinariness can be depicted as 'superordinary' (Billig 1998; Edley 1993). The dilemma for modern royals is that to fulfil the formal, public role, they must present themselves, in some way or another, as private individuals. Thus the presentation of a private self is part of the public role.

This dilemma is demonstrated in an analysis of the BBC *Panorama* interview between Martin Bashir and the late Princess Diana. The interview was aired on 20 November 1995 and was videotaped and transcribed.[1] The resulting transcript was analysed using a method that draws upon discursive psychology and conversation analysis, an approach that Buttny (1993) has termed 'conversation analytic constructionism'. We were interested in the sequential organisation of talk and how information was presented in interaction. In this ordering of details, it is important to consider what participants *make relevant* to their account. As Buttny (1993: 35) notes, 'in the course of turn-taking, persons participate in a number of conversational practices: . . . telling stories . . . blaming, accounting, and all the various speech activities engaged in through talk.' The focus is upon how Diana constructs a plausible and authentic account, as she presents her own self, discussing the relations between this self and the public role. Her presentation occurs in a rhetorical situation of blame and criticism. Thus, there is a tendentious, or rhetorically argumentative dimension, to the narratives employed in this construction of the self.

The *Panorama* programme is structured as a progressive narrative, starting with Diana's engagement to Prince Charles and ending with her 'new', post-divorce life as a single woman. We analyse two extracts from the interview in which Diana narrates a past event: a public engagement with Prince Charles during a tour of Australia. In the first extract, the analytic focus is upon narrative as a resource for constructing the 'self'. We focus on the detail that is built into the account which, together with other discursive phenomena, adds to the plausibility of the description. In the second extract, we examine narrative as a resource for managing accountability and explore the overall organisation and structure of the account and consider what this sequential design achieves rhetorically for Diana.

Narrative as a resource for constructing identity

The extract below comes from the first few minutes of the interview. We explore the notion of 'identities' and how these can be constructed in conversation. Whereas cognitive psychologists have tended to treat identity as an internalised cognitive structure, discursive psychologists argue that identity is a dynamic and flexible resource. People invoke identities or ascribe them to others in the course of everyday conversation. However, the interview has a particular context that frames Diana's construction of her own identity; she is talking about her self in relation to the dilemmas of the royal role. She is speaking publicly, not privately, about the relations between her public and private selves. She draws upon commonplaces about royal roles, public performances and private selves. Her talk deploys the lay sociology which non-royals typically use to discuss the behaviour of royals (Billig 1998). Diana constructs her identity in terms of a conflict between what we have termed her 'true self' and her 'royal role'. She tells the story of the 'true' or 'person self' initially unable to meet the public and how she accommodates herself to duties of the 'royal role'. The text below follows an earlier claim by Diana that she realised that she could either 'sink or swim' in the management of her new 'royal role':

Extract 1

Bashir: and what did you do?

Diana: I swam (2) we went to erm (.) Alice Springs (.) to Australia (2) and we went and did a walkabout and I said to my husband (.) what do I do now? (.) and he said 'go over to the other side (.) and speak to them' (.) I said I can't (.) I just can't (.) an-he said 'well (.) you've got to do it' (1) and he went off an did his bit (1) an-I went off and did my bit (.) an- it practically finished me off there and then (.) and I suddenly realised I went back to our-my hotel room (.) and realised the impact that (.) you know (.) I had to sort myself out (.) we had a six week tour (1) four weeks in Australia and two weeks in New Zealand and by the end (.) when we flew back from New Zealand I was a different person (.) I realised (.) the sense of duty (.) the level of intensity of interest (.) and (.) the demanding role (.) I now found myself in.

Diana orders the events and introduces the characters of the narrative yet the precise details remain unspecified. She responds to Bashir's question regarding whether she sank or swam, claiming *'I swam'*. While this answer would be sufficient, Diana moves on to describe a past event; it is a key moment in deciding to 'swim'. The pronoun *'we'* suggests that the trip to Australia was a joint undertaking, and draws the listeners' attention to this public engagement as a shared duty, 'we went and did a walkabout'. The term 'walkabout' carries a cultural understanding of the royal family and its activities. It positions both Charles and Diana as belonging to the royal family.

While this appears to be a mutual venture, Diana goes on to construct differences between herself and Charles. The division between the couple is expressed in Diana's question 'what do I do now?' This question positions her as untutored in the art of being royal, with Charles as the expert source of information. The listener is told that 'he said "go over to the other side (.) and speak to them"'. The inclusion of sections of quoted talk has been termed 'active voicing' and this detail adds to facticity of the account (Hutchby and Wooffitt 1998). By quoting her conversation with Charles, Diana signals the beginning of a contrast being developed between the two of them. This is further emphasised in a second reported statement 'well (.) you've got to do it'. We are not informed why Diana has 'got' to speak to people. Instead, the 'royal role' is treated as a sufficient explanation. By making Charles relevant to her account, Diana is able to contrast her husband, as someone familiar with formal royal duties, with herself who is unfamiliar and uneasy.

The precise details of the trip remain vague. Using internal focalisation (Genette 1980), Diana narrates events from her own point of view. She scripts the royal duties as follows: 'he went off an did his bit (1) an-I went off and did my bit'. Edwards (1997) notes how script formulations can be used to render narrative detail as routine or exceptional in some way. In the present example, the use of the term 'bit' suggests that the actions performed were routine for members of the royal family. As Potter (1996) suggests, vivid details given in narrative accounts can easily be undermined, whereas vague descriptions provide just enough material to sustain some action without producing descriptive claims that are open to attack.

Further, the scripting of events can serve to make the dispositional states of the actors involved inferentially available. This can be seen in Diana's claims that doing her 'bit' 'practically finished me off there and then'. This emphasises not only the differences between Charles and Diana but also the profound effect the new role was having on her. This is stressed further with words such as 'suddenly realised' and 'impact' which function as inoculations against a potential accusation of stake; that is, that Diana knew what the royal role would involve before she got married. One of the prominent rhetorical aspects of this interview is Diana's use of passive language in constructing the royal role. For example, she claims that she found herself in a 'demanding role'. This suggests that she is not in control but dependent upon the expectations of others; the use of passive language precludes the possibility of personal agency and choice.

Diana's use of 'stock' expressions such as 'finished me off' and 'sort myself out' are further examples of discursive phenomena that may be built into narrative accounts. Several commentators have noted that idiomatic expressions and metaphor occur in talk at particular junctures and can function to drive narrative from description to explanation (Antaki 1994). This can be seen in Diana's account as she uses the description of past events to warrant the role she now finds herself in. Diana refers three times to the mental state of 'realisation'. Edwards (1997) notes that the use of words such as 'realise' commonly feature in narratives and are used to attend to issues of speaker authenticity; 'realising' is an interactional resource. Diana 'realises' the implications of her new role and emphasises her unreadiness for royal life in contrast with Charles' preparedness. In this talk of royal roles and personal identity, she deploys commonplaces which are used by the general public in their talk of royalty (Billig 1998). Her talk suggests that she is, at that moment, talking as an ordinary person, not as a royal. Hence, she uses 'my husband', indicating an ordinariness and suggesting the sort of rhetorical identification with the imagined audience that Burke (1962) claimed was one of the key features of persuasive discourse.

A sense of time pervades the account as Diana develops the tension between her conflicting identities. Ricoeur (1988) notes that narratives have a chronological dimension and often incorporate a temporal transition from one state of affairs to another. At the beginning of her response, Diana's 'true self' is unable to speak to the public in Australia. However, as the account progresses, the category of 'royal role' is mobilised as Diana obeys Charles' orders, 'well (.) you've got to do it'. The listener is told that this tour lasted for six weeks and, at the end of it, the 'royal role' had been realised and accepted. Diana states: 'I was a different person (.) I realised the sense of duty (.) the level of intensity of interest', thus attending to an issue of stake. It is possible to accuse Diana of being aware of the attention of both public and press and even of actively encouraging it. However, she inoculates against this in her assertion that she suddenly 'realised' the level of interest and, moreover, she became a 'different person'. This final turn in the conversation is structured as a list, exemplifying what Smith (1978) terms 'contrasting discourse'. Diana compares the 'true self' with 'royal role', emphasising the transformation of 'self' by contrasting someone who does not realise the implications of royal life, with someone for whom realisation 'suddenly' dawns. This progression in narrative is further indicated by the use of the temporal adverb 'now'. Schiffrin (1987: 249) suggests that such discourse markers 'point to a prior event in the discourse to establish its temporal relationship with a next event in the discourse'. It is used by Diana to signal a progression from her inability to cope with her new situation to her realisation and acceptance of her new identity.

In this first extract we have demonstrated how the identities of 'true self' and 'royal role' are discursive, commonplace resources that are used dynamically in accounting for past events, self and significant others. In our discursive approach, identity is explored by examining how people talk about themselves – how people claim to have identities – and how people tell stories to substantiate their claims. Such talk necessarily occurs in particular contexts; Diana's talk is situated in the context of a broader dilemma of contemporary monarchy: royals can be criticised for being too formal and role bound, or too informal and insufficiently role bound (Billig 1998), and she deals with this dilemma. Diana presents her private self as dutifully filling the formal role at considerable cost to herself; she neither becomes nor shirks the role. In this way, she becomes the heroine of the story that she tells. In so doing, she tells of the private self behind the role, eliciting sympathy for that private self. We suggest that the descriptions of past events Diana produces are used to warrant the authenticity of her account and to make available the behavioural states of others with whom the self can be compared. In the next extract, we focus on the deployment of narrative detail and structural organisation in locating accountability and blame.

Narrative as a resource for accountability

One of the main features of the interview is Diana's location of accountability and blame for the breakdown of her marriage to Charles. Again there is a rhetorical dilemma. Blame must be managed carefully. Unrestrained blame could be interpreted as vindictive and, moreover, unsuitable for someone who should maintain the dignity of a royal role. Thus, the rhetorical stake of blaming must be presented as if there is no rhetorical stake. The blamer should be seen not to be blaming or to be engaging only in relevant, justified blaming.

Elsewhere we have explored how blame may be located directly and indirectly to significant others (Abell and Stokoe 1999). We argue that Diana's blaming of Charles is carefully managed by her employment of a number of discursive techniques. First, the use of emotion categories in the text is important. Emotion categories such as 'proud' and 'jealous' should not be treated as neutral, objective descriptors of internal emotional states. Rather, as Edwards (1997: 173) suggests, emotion categories 'provide a flexible resource for situated discourse, including the potential for rhetorical opposites and contrasts'. Second, the overall narrative structure is significant. Diana selects particular emotion categories and attributes them to Charles at different stages of the interview. The analytical interest then is in what this achieves for Diana.

Extract 2

Bashir: at this early stage would you say that you were happily married?
Diana: very much so (1) but (.) er the pressure on-on us both as a couple (.) with the media was phenomenal (1) and misunderstood by a great many people (1) we'd be going round Australia for instance .hhh (2) and (.) you-all you could hear was oh (.) she's on the other side (1) now if you're a man (1) like my husband a proud man (.) you mind about that if you hear it every day for four weeks (.) and you feel (.) low about it y-know instead of feeling happy and sharing it
Bashir: when you say she's on the other side what do you mean?
Diana: well they weren't on the right side (.) to wave at me (.) or to touch me (1) ehm

Bashir: so they were expressing a preference even then for you rather than your husband?

Diana: yes (.) which I felt very uncomfortable with and I felt it was unfair (.) because I wanted to (.) share

Bashir: but were you flattered by the media attention particularly?

Diana: no not particularly because with the media attention (.) came a lot of jealousy (1) a great deal (.) of (2) .hhh complicated situations arose because of that

In this extract, which comes near the start of the interview, the rhetorical design of Diana's turns allow her to shift the topic of conversation or reformulate the agenda, a typical move made by politicians in news interviews (Clayman 1993). Bashir asks, 'at this early stage would you say that you were happily married?' In her response, Diana does not simply agree with the question but upgrades the status of the assessment 'happily' to 'very much so'; she appears certain in her evaluation of the initial happiness of the marriage. The information provided by Diana is sufficient in itself in answering the question. However, the next word uttered is 'but', which allows Diana to extend the question towards other rhetorical business. This widens the scope of the question and her answer then deals with the media pressure and its effects on her relationship with Charles.

The 'but' also marks a contrast between Diana's agreement with Bashir, that she was happily married at this early stage, and what comes next. Diana thus prefaces what becomes apparent as a disagreement in the course of the turn with an agreement (Buttny 1993; Pomerantz 1984). She initially agrees that the marriage was happy but, as the turn progresses, we are offered a version of events that suggest that the marriage quickly became unhappy. Again, a temporal transition structures the account as we hear about the 'early stage' contrasted with a later period in which one state of affairs shifts to another.

Having extended the scope of the question, Diana draws the listener's attention to the media as a source of strain: 'the pressure on-on us both as a couple (.) with the media was phenomenal'. This use of the inclusive pronoun 'us' functions to construct the evaluation as applying to both Charles and Diana. Diana describes the media pressure on the couple as 'phenomenal', using an extreme case formulation, which strengthens her claim. A picture of Charles and Diana as a happy couple, placed in a situation beyond their control which adversely affected their marriage, is presented.

Diana narrates an example of this media pressure. By means of active voicing, she draws attention to the media's reaction to the couple as focusing on her: 'oh (.) she's on the other side'. She gives a further explanation in response to the interviewer's request for clarification – the media wanted to touch and wave to her, not Charles. The use of active voicing establishes Diana as the animator of the account, reporting what the media have said. Potter (1996) notes that this strategy allows the speaker to establish objectivity in, and rhetorical distance from, the account; in this case by establishing a group consensus within the media. By providing details of what the media personnel said (although the accuracy cannot be established), Diana remains the reporter of the event: it is not her personal opinion that the media prefer her. As Mandelbaum (1993) notes, events themselves do not lay blame. Rather, the speaker constructs events as negative in order to accomplish certain conversational business.

This 'factual' reporting of an unhappy event is followed by Diana's 'personal' evaluation of it. This shift in footing is signalled by the temporal marker 'now', which indicates 'a speaker's progression through discourse time by displaying attention to an upcoming idea unit' (Schiffrin 1987: 230). Diana provides an assessment of the media's preference for her instead of Charles. It is at this point that emotion categories are mobilised.

First, Diana describes Charles as 'proud'. She moves from the general, 'if you're a man', to the particular, 'like my husband a proud man', placing Charles in the category of 'men-in-general'. In so doing, Diana deploys a general cultural stereotype of gender. Pride is implied to be part of masculinity: Charles is not a proud person but, specifically, a proud man. Implicit blame-at-a-distance is possible. The adjective 'proud' contains a critical element, but Charles is not being personally blamed for it. If there is blame (conveyed by Diana's own implied lack of pride), then it is attributed neither to the individual nor to the royal role: it is attributed to gender. Diana, by her own implied understanding of the failings of masculinity, presents not only her own (praiseworthy) lack of pride but also a public display of non-blaming and understanding.

In this way, blaming is rhetorically accomplished without a display of overt blaming. Diana is able to locate blame and provide her side of a dispute without presenting herself as biased and one-sided. She constructs Charles' emotional reaction to the media's preference for his wife as reasonable and understandable: 'you mind about that if you hear it every day for four weeks (.) and you feel (.) low about it y-know instead of feeling happy and sharing it'. She uses an extended extreme case formulation 'every day for four weeks' to establish the intense nature of the circumstances and discursively positions herself as a wife who can understand her husband's reactions.

Again, Charles' reactions to events are constructed as scripted and normative, providing the listener with a dispositional frame within which Charles is to be understood. Buttny (1993: 88) argues that, during the management of accountability and blame, 'if circumstances do not warrant particular emotions or feelings, then others may question or reproach the actor for such affect displays'. However, Diana constructs Charles' reaction as warrantable. Using the pronoun '*you*' rather than 'he' adds to the generalisable nature of the account – any proud man in this situation would react in the same way. It also adds to the facticity of the account and the constructed ordinariness of Charles. By talking about Charles in terms of his emotional traits, 'the reader is encouraged to feel as if they can actually know him in a very direct and straightforward way' (Edley 1993: 402). This level of narrative detail positions Diana as a knowledgeable witness.

When Bashir says 'so they were expressing a preference even then for you rather than your husband', he provides a formulation of the-story-so-far. The meaning of 'they' can be interpreted from the interactional context as the media, although neither Diana nor Bashir makes this explicit. Hutchby and Wooffitt (1998: 152) argue that when an interviewer formulates the gist of the interviewee's remarks, it is 'usually in pursuit of some controversial or newsworthy aspect'. The media's preference for Diana is controversial. Diana ratifies Bashir's formulation but qualifies her agreement by formulating her own evaluation of the media's attention: 'which I felt very uncomfortable with and I felt it was unfair (.) because I wanted to (.) share'. The media's preference for Diana is constructed, not as her own interpretation of events, but as how things actually were. This asymmetric media attention is presented as not her choice; the listener hears that Diana wanted to share the attention; she 'felt it was unfair'.

Bashir's final question in this extract is an accusation of stake: 'but were you flattered by the media attention particularly?' Diana rebuts this directly by repeating Bashir's words: 'no not particularly' and then qualifies her response: 'because with the media attention (.) came a lot of jealousy (1) a great deal (.) of (2) .hhh complicated situations arose because of that'. This is a key turn in the extract. Diana's previous assessment of the media attention is developed further. In the earlier turns, the media have been mobilised to construct unity between Charles and Diana; they were both under pressure. Later the media are invoked to construct a difference between them; Charles is 'proud', 'feeling low' and, by implication, is not a sharing person. In the final exchange in extract 2, the media are invoked to account for the 'complicated situations' and 'jealousy' that apparently arose.

Ascribing jealousy to Charles implies that he is responsible for their relational problems. Diana is moving from telling problems about the media to telling problems about Charles, and allocating blame to him. She claims that many 'complicated situations' arose as a result of his 'jealousy'. This 'generic vagueness' (Potter 1996), the delay components (long pauses) and affect displays (.hhh), signal the upcoming problematic and the delicate nature of the topic under discussion. Diana has therefore shifted her assessment of Charles from 'proud' to 'jealous'. The order of these attributions is important, as well as the overall organisation of the narrative. By presenting a picture of Charles as a man who reacts emotionally, but understandably, to situations in the early turns of talk, a balanced picture is constructed.

Conclusions

We have presented here only brief aspects of the analysis (for more details, see Abell and Stokoe 1999). The discursive approach adopted does not treat a narrative as a thing-in-itself with an internal structure that may or may not match a presumed structure in the mind of the storyteller. Rather, the narrative is understood in terms of its wider rhetorical context. The argumentative purpose of narratives needs consideration (Leith and Myerson 1989). We have suggested that claims to identity, and thus the management of social identity, are accomplished in narrative.

The context of the narrative possesses immediate or proximal features, as well as more distal ones. The former refer to the interactional business that is being accomplished by the telling of the story. As can be seen, the formulation of the story, especially the terms used to describe the characters and actions of the main participants, are not rhetorically neutral. They belong to a rhetoric of justification and criticism. The wider context indicates that justification and criticism need to be carefully managed because of wider dilemmas of argumentation. Cultural and ideological dilemmas are involved in the deployment of commonplaces, even as immediate, proximal rhetorical business is being accomplished.

The interview situation has a particular rhetorical complexity. Diana can be heard to be speaking to the interviewer: she answers Bashir's questions and he, in turn, picks up her answers. Her answers must be formulated in relation to his questions. Diana thus pays attention to the immediate interactional business. However, it is of the nature of such interviews that the speakers are speaking in order to be overheard. Millions are known to be eaves-dropping. Thus, Diana, in talking to Bashir, is addressing a far wider audience: she is not merely seeking to justify herself in his eyes. Commonplaces are used and the narratives are structured to persuade this wider audience. The presentation of self is a major theme. However, the story is one not simply of self, but of the self in and out of role. While the self is justified, blame has to be carefully managed, negotiating dilemmas of public blaming. If the personal self is presented in these narratives, then this presentation is not entirely personal. The narratives are about the dilemmas of self and role. They reflect the contradictions of the British monarchy in late modernity. An apparently ordinary person occupies an extraordinary (and privileged) role. It is part of the extraordinary role that the ordinariness must be displayed. Even in an interview, in which the royal speaker seems to come out of role, she enacts the extraordinariness, in front of millions, by making rhetorical points with stories about ordinary details of her life.

Notes

1 Transcription conventions: (.) denotes a pause < 1 second, (2) denotes a timed pause in seconds, (.hhh) represents an audible intake of breath.

References

Abell, J. and Stokoe, E. H. (1999) '"I take full responsibility, I take some responsibility, I'll take half of it but no more than that": Princess Diana and the location of blame in the Panorama interview', *Discourse Studies* 1, 3: 297–319.

Antaki, C. (1994) *Explaining and Arguing*, London: Sage.
Billig, M. (1996) *Arguing and Thinking*, Cambridge: Cambridge University Press.
—— (1998) *Talking about the Royal Family*, London: Routledge.
Burke, K. (1962) *A Rhetoric of Motives*, Cleveland: Meriden Books.
Britton, B. K. and Pellegrini, A. D. (eds) (1990) *Narrative Thought and Narrative Language*, Hillsdale, NJ: Lawrence Erlbaum.
Bruner, J. S. (1990) *Acts of Meaning*, Cambridge, MA: Harvard University Press.
Buttny, R. (1993) *Social Accountability in Communication*, London: Sage.
Campbell, B. (1998) *Diana, Princess of Wales: How Sexual Politics Shoot the Monarchy*, London: The Women's Press.
Clayman, S. E. (1993) 'Reformulating the question: a device for answering/not answering questions in news interviews and press conferences', *Text* 13: 159–88.
Edley, N. (1993) 'Prince Charles – our flexible friend: accounting for variation in constructions of identity', *Text* 13: 397–422.
Edwards, D. (1997) *Discourse and Cognition*, London: Sage.
Edwards, D. and Potter, J. (1992) *Discursive Psychology*, London: Sage.
Genette, G. (1980) *Narrative Discourse*, Ithaca, NY: Cornell University Press.
Hutchby, I. and Wooffitt, R. (1998) *Conversation Analysis*, Cambridge: Polity Press.
Leith, D. and Myerson, G. (1989) *The Power of Address*, London: Routledge.
Lieblich, A. and Josselson, R. (eds) (1997) *The Narrative Study of Lives*, London: Sage.
Mandelbaum, J. (1993) 'Assigning responsibility in conversational storytelling: the interactional construction of reality', *Text* 13: 247–66.
Murray, K. D. (1995) 'Narratology', in J. A. Smith, R. Harré and L. van Langenhove (eds) *Rethinking Psychology*, London: Sage.
Murray, M. (1997) 'A narrative approach to health psychology', *Journal of Health Psychology* 2, 1: 9–20.
Ochs, E. (1997) 'Narrative', in T. A. van Dijk (ed.) *Discourse as Structure and Process*, London: Sage.
Pomerantz, A. (1984) 'Agreeing and disagreeing with assessments: some features of preferred/dispreferred turn shapes', in J. M. Atkinson and J. Heritage (eds) *Structures of Social Action: Studies in Conversation Analysis*, Cambridge: Cambridge University Press.
Potter, J. (1996) *Representing Reality*, London: Sage.
Potter, J. and Wetherell, M. (1987) *Discourse and Social Psychology*, London: Sage.
Ricoeur, P. (1988) *Time and Narrative*, Chicago: University of Chicago Press.
Sacks, H. (1992) *Lectures on Conversation*, Oxford: Blackwell.
Schiffrin, D. (1987) *Discourse Markers*, Cambridge: Cambridge University Press.
Smith, D. (1978) 'K is mentally ill: the anatomy of a factual account', *Sociology* 12: 23–53.

Conclusion

Phil Bradbury and Shelley Day Sclater

Readers of this volume will be struck by the diversity of approaches to narrative that appear in its pages. The objects of narrative range here from schoolboys' wild retributive fantasies, to the 'resurrective' potential of death narratives; from contests over 'family' narratives, to the normalising narratives of weapons of mass destruction. A unified theme seems determined to elude us. But one of the principal attractions of narrative work is surely that it can track ways between competing, exclusive perspectives; we might think, for example, of narrative work as having the potential to 'cross-fertilise' across previously discrete disciplines, or to synthesise competing constructions of individual and social worlds. One of the main strengths of narrative work must lie in its capacity to hold together sociological and psychological approaches, without recourse to the 'figure/ground' configuration in which they are usually found.

At one level, these essays bridge so many dualities, integrating theory with method, the modern with the postmodern, science and non-science, the inner self with the outer world of society and culture, that we are often able to catch glimpses of the radical potential that narrative holds. At another level, however, it is clear that aspects of the old dualities will remain; inevitable perhaps, as long as we lack a language in which to articulate, if not the limitations of Cartesian duality, then the means to transcend it. Paradoxically perhaps, narratives remind us of the cultural scripts within which our identities are formed and articulated, at the same time as they indicate the creative possibilities for living beyond, and behind, the stories that cultures provide. Narratives articulate both sameness and difference, and it is in the various methods of living and reading them that their real potential lies.

Agency, subjectivity and narrative analysis

One way of conceptualising differences that narrative, undeniably, points to is through the concept of 'agency'. In the three sections of this book we see narratives as cultural productions, as manifestations of life histories and as articulating discursive strategies, but in each section the concept of human agency looms large. Agency provides, in some ways, a unifying framework that brings together the diverse concerns of the chapters.

In the first part, as Corinne Squire observes, culture provides resources for individual narratives, but those narratives are never either purely individual or cultural. Rather, the chapters in this part show the ways in which culture itself is actively made and remade by human subjects, individually and in communities; there are identifiable parallels between the stories of individuals, cultures and societies, in terms of narrative style and genre, if not content. At the same time, it is possible to recognise the plurality and instability of narrative forms, and individuals and communities can sometimes appropriate what is on offer to their own ends.

In the second part, as Molly Andrews indicates, the concept of human agency is essential to understanding the ways in which individual life histories are formulated in specific social and political contexts. The chapters here show that telling stories does not just help us to make sense of ourselves and the world, or even just give shape to our experiences, but is one of the primary means through which we constitute and reconstitute our very selves. As Andrews puts it, 'our stories are a cornerstone of our identity'. Human agents use narrative not only to describe experience, but to give shape to that experience; narrative creates us at the same time as we create it.

In the third part, the contributors highlight the dynamic relations between discourse and narrative. Without the concept of human agency that runs through these accounts, it would be impossible to make sense of the ways in which people accept, negotiate, challenge, or even actively resist the positionings provided for them by dominant discursive forms, or to consider the costs and benefits of different ways of deploying discourses. The concept of human agency, then, constitutes a broad focus of agreement that unites the diversities of narrative form and content in this book. As the editors argue in the Introduction, it is the concept of 'agency' that precludes a slide back into determinism. The narratives we read in these pages are stories about struggles towards agentic subjectivities.

But, the very concept of human agency begs the more fundamental question of the nature of the subject who inhabits narrative. It is commonplace now, in narrative work, to encounter the claim that the self is constituted in narrative. The chapters in this book all subscribe, in one way or another, to the idea that narrative constitutes the self. Even Craib who, at his most sceptical, fears that narrative can be a tool of betrayal or denial of the real or authentic self, nevertheless presupposes that narrative is constituting some kind of self, albeit in 'bad faith'. Here, the issue of the distinction between the 'life as told' and the 'life as lived' loom large. To make such a distinction, of course, begs the question, as Corinne Squire points out, of what kind of sense it is that narratives make. Is it psychological, social, cultural or merely linguistic sense? As Craib argues in his chapter, surely there are always aspects of self that narrative cannot capture. Craib is pessimistic about narratives' ability to sustain the genuine complexities of both subjectivities and cultures.

On the other hand, the ways in which we discern the vicissitudes of both subjectivities and cultures with reference to narrative, depends heavily upon our own readings of them. Ways of reading are at least as important as ways of speaking and this, surely, is one of the strengths of narrative work, for (as Malson shows) it brings into the foreground the issue of the enigmatic and shifting relations between 'author' and 'reader', and points to the significance of context in the interpretation of any social-scientific data. In contrast to Craib, Seale takes the view that, far from distorting or concealing the excess of emotion or culture, narratives reveal those aspects of humanity as we read their gaps, failures and inconsistencies. The ways in which narratives may uncover previously hidden aspects of both selves and culture depend upon our readings of those narratives. This may well be a point of discomfort for those intent upon pursuing agendas where objectivity reigns supreme, and where data are assumed to bear some direct relation with the 'real' world. But, as we have said, narrative research has radical potential and is better suited to challenging old positivist agendas than it is to collecting data and providing interpretations that suit the premises of objectivist modes of understanding the 'reality' in which we live. As the editors point out in the Introduction to this book, the new emphasis on narrative work emerges out of a cross-fertilisation of the concerns and methods of science and those of the humanities, after a long period in which they were sharply counterposed. But this reintegration is neither stable nor complete, for it is possible also to identify countervailing trends, as social science takes up new formalisms while the humanities turn their back on them.

The functions of narrative accounting

What we may call 'functionality' is a further common theme that emerges within the diversity of narratives in this volume. Most of the authors take what can be seen as a functional view of narrative. Narratives may be said to be functional to the extent that they achieve some desired effects for the speaker, whether in the public or private domain. The narratives that these chapters discuss address the complex relations between 'the public' and 'the private' and illustrate the shortcomings of making the distinction in the first place. In the section on 'culture', Jacobs' exploration of 'civil society' and Walters' excoriation of traditional notions of family life rely on 'public' narratives produced in the media. Craib and Seale, by contrast, use material from 'private' accounts, in one case from interviews and in the other from clinical work. In the 'life history' section, both Wengraf and Freeman draw the material from interviews and literature, while Konopasek and Wolkowitz both rely on autobiographical accounts that go beyond 'the private'. In the discourse section, Hollway and Jefferson, Malson and Smith all base their analysis on private exchanges. Abell, Stokoe and Billig's analysis uses the late Princess Diana's *Panorama* interview, taken directly from the public domain.

'Private' of course, must not be confused with 'personal'. Princess Diana's interview is both highly personal and very public. In recognising a distinction between the private and the public narrative, we must take into account the different reasons behind their production. Perhaps all narratives are, to some degree, performative, but the public narrative is much more explicitly so. The public narrative can shape and change the cultural backdrop, as well as locating individuals and groups against it. While the cultural backdrop may be, to some extent, common, individuals who talk about their lives more 'privately' are less likely to have a public agenda.

Narrators, especially those in the public domain, deploy discourses and construct stories in a way that may be regarded as rhetorical; they establish, challenge, consolidate or otherwise give weight to the sense of identity and the social relations they wish to claim or promote. Stories in the private domain tend to be more concerned with description, explanation and understanding, justification, or perhaps, rationalisation. Different varieties of functionality are apparent in all three sections of the book. Walters, for example, illustrates the rhetorical importance of lesbian and gay narratives of families to challenge prevailing orthodoxies of 'family life'; Konopasek shows how autobiographical accounts can counterpose 'official' scripts of sweeping political and social change; the chapter by Abell *et al.* highlights narrative's rhetorical functions for Diana as speaker, seeking to justify herself against the background of royal protocol and power. Smith's dramaturgical analysis highlights the complex issue of how adults and children variously position themselves and each other in relation to 'punishment' and other concerns of the adult world.

Among the 'private' examples, narratives of bereavement are, in Seale's account, less about 'repositioning' than 'reorientating'. Death narratives are functional personally; they are part of coming to terms with the loss of 'loved ones' but, crucially, they also maintain social bonds; they enable social 'resurrection'. Craib's critique of narrative reminds us, however, that such functionality is not ordained. People's stories can carry a lie; for example, people are sometimes unable easily to come to terms with the death of a loved one. Within apparently 'healthy' narratives of acceptance, loss can be denied; sometimes, too, narratives of despair, not acceptance, become dominant.

This functional ambivalence, between reconstruction and denial, is evident in some of the other material in this book. Wengraf's two miners, for example, with comparable experiences, told stories whose 'plots', as Andrews notes, were quite different; one is a narrative of 'redemption', the other of 'betrayal'. Wengraf stops short of claiming that the different plots are actually played out in the men's material lives, but their circumstances as described point clearly in this direction. Similarly, Hollway and Jefferson's psychosocial analysis of Tommy's life history is predicated upon 'the difference between honesty and fabrication, between reality and phantasy and between ambivalence and splitting'.

Narratives, power and resistance

Significantly, many of the chapters concern narratives about the 'big' social issues that confront us at the beginning of the twenty-first century, as taken-for-granted aspects of the modern world are inexorably displaced. The narratives the authors present speak of racial crisis, death, gay and lesbian rights, unemployment, ageing, political transformation, the British royal family, 'anorexic' bodies, fear of crime, and violent retribution. These are narratives that afford opportunities for new voices to speak their realities, and those realities are often ones of oppression.

Some of the current popularity of narrative work undoubtedly derives from its potential to give voice to previously marginalised or silenced people. Yet, problematically for any concept of narrative as *a priori* liberating, some of the chapters in this book show that narrative encodes the voices of the powerful as well as those of the oppressed. Narrative *can* be a form of resistance to dominant frameworks of understanding, but is not necessarily so. This point emerges strongly in the chapter by Wolkowitz; these wives' narratives were strongly coloured by dominant discourses, and the atomic bomb was, in an important sense, absent in their stories, while maintaining its paradoxical presence in the mind of the reader. Similarly, Walters' piece shows how narratives, far from challenging power relations, can obscure them in subtle ways. The question of the extent to which narratives may help to articulate a sense of ourselves in relation to dominant power structures is one that is not easily answered.

Yet, many recognise that narrative can have transformatory potential for both individuals and cultures. The use of narrative in post-1968 feminist 'consciousness raising', the recent arrival on the therapeutic scene of narrative therapies, and the growing popularity of autobiographical work, all bear testimony to that potential. But the question of whether narratives can meaningfully transform lives, selves and cultures requires some attention to political and material realities; the import of Craib's work is that telling a good story does not, in fact, make everything OK. The material world acts as both facilitator and constraint on the lives that we live and the stories that we tell.

Facts and fictions, narrative and the real

The issue of the relations between narrative and 'the real' is touched on in most of the chapters, but it is perhaps indicative of the great diversity of narrative approaches that no consensus exists about the kinds of truth claims that narrative work may legitimately make. Scholarship carried out in the traditional paradigms of sociology and psychology necessarily demands that criteria for the validity of 'objective' knowledge be established and maintained. Narrative scholars may reject logical positivism as an epistemological framework, and may argue that objectivity itself is a rhetorical achievement, but they are then faced with the new problem of defining what kinds of claims they wish to make about their work. As the editors point out in the Introduction, models of narrative that are influenced by perspectives from the humanities or psychoanalysis lead to the conclusion that stories 'mean' more than they say; interpretation is required, but does this necessarily take us away from 'truth' and into the realms of 'fiction'?

It is integral to modernist visions of the world that 'truth' and 'fiction' are mutually exclusive categories. The chapters in this book make it clear that narratives do not simply 'reflect' truth or experience in any unproblematic way, but it does not follow that they are 'merely' fictions. Narratives are perhaps best seen as 'reflections on' lives, events and selves, rather then straightforwardly 'reflections of' these phenomena. But the kinds of 'truths' that narratives uncover are not only subjective or personal ones, since, as the chapters amply illustrate, it is possible to reach new understandings of social and cultural phenomena through narrative work. Narratives reveal 'truths' that are both personal and social but, crucially, these 'truths' are seen as necessarily partial, contingent, situated and, like other 'truths', subject to contestation and change.

One of the great strengths of narrative work lies in its potential to forge a new paradigm for social-scientific work that explicitly addresses itself to transcending the habitual dualisms of Western thought. Narrative work therefore presents both challenges and promises for the future. The main challenge lies in the need to develop new languages of theory and method, including ways of talking about reflexivity that can address the ethical issues that arise in narrative research. Foremost among these new languages will be that of the 'psychosocial', in which 'individual' and 'society' are no longer pitted against each other, and where subjectivities and cultures are seen as mutually constitutive aspects of the human experience. The promise of narrative lies in its potential to be the means whereby we articulate who we are, in all our complexity. Narratives have the potential to expose the great diversity of human experiences, the multiple dimensions of lives, and the contingent and transient nature of meaning-making processes.

Index